About the aut

Andrew Fagan is a prominent New Zealand writer, singer and songwriter who gained fame in New Zealand in the 1980s as the lead singer of pop group The Mockers. He is also the author of a sailing autobiography, *Swirly World: The solo voyages*, which captured his epic solo journey across the Tasman. He currently co-hosts a talkback show on Radio Live with his partner, Karyn Hay.

By the same author:

Take the Chocolates and Run (poems)
Salt Rhythms (poems)
Serious Latitudes (poems)
Swirly World: The solo voyages (sailing narrative)
Overnight Downpour (poems)
On Plastic Bag Patrol (children)

SWIRLY WORLD SAILS SOUTH

ANDREW FAGAN

For
Dr JCC !

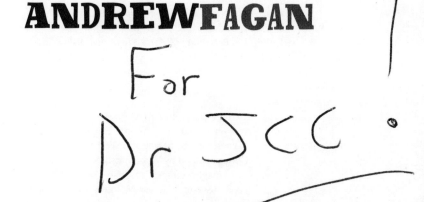

HarperCollins*Publishers* April 18

HarperCollins*Publishers*

First published in 2012
by HarperCollins*Publishers (New Zealand) Limited*
PO Box 1, Shortland Street, Auckland 1140

HarperCollins*Publishers*
31 View Road, Glenfield, Auckland 0627, New Zealand
Level 13, 201 Elizabeth Street, Sydney NSW 2000, Australia
A 53, Sector 57, Noida, UP, India
77–85 Fulham Palace Road, London W6 8JB, United Kingdom
2 Bloor Street East, 20th floor, Toronto, Ontario M4W 1A8, Canada
10 East 53rd Street, New York, NY 10022, USA

National Library of New Zealand Cataloguing-in-Publication Data

Fagan, Andrew, 1962-
Swirly World sails south / Andrew Fagan.
ISBN 978-1-86950-982-8
1. Fagan, Andrew, 1962- —Travel—South Pacific Ocean.
2. Fagan, Andrew, 1962- —Travel—Tasman Sea.
3. Swirly World in Perpetuity (Ship) 4. Single-handed sailing—
South Pacific Ocean. 5. Single-handed sailing—Tasman Sea. I. Title.
910.91648—dc 22

ISBN: 978 1 86950 982 8

Cover design by Cheryl Rowe
Cover images courtesy Andrew Fagan
Typesetting by Springfield West
Commissioned by Vicki Marsdon
Managing editor: Eva Chan
Freelance editor: Teresa McIntyre

Printed by Griffin Press, Australia
The papers used by HarperCollins in the manufacture of this book are a
natural, recyclable product made from wood grown in sustainable plantation
forests. The fibre source and manufacturing processes meet recognised
international environmental standards, and carry certification.

Contents

Map NZ 14600 showing Andrew's route around New Zealand and to the Auckland Islands. (Sourced from Land Information New Zealand data. Crown copyright reserved.)

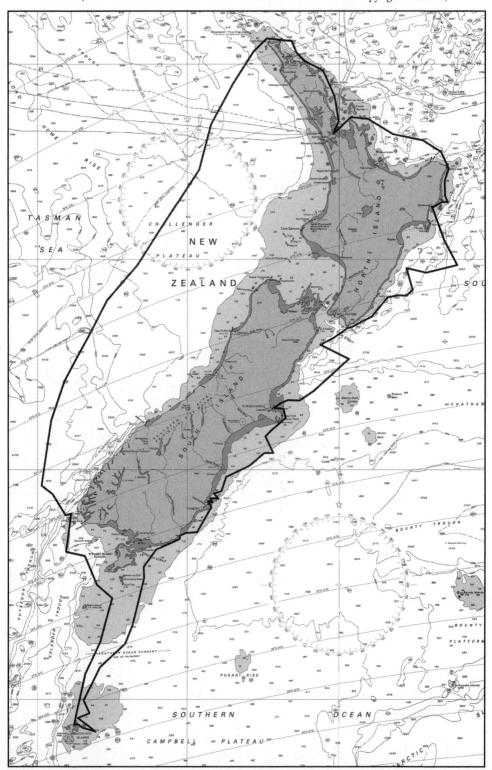

Map NZ 286 showing the top of the Auckland Islands. (Sourced from Land Information New Zealand data. Crown copyright reserved.)

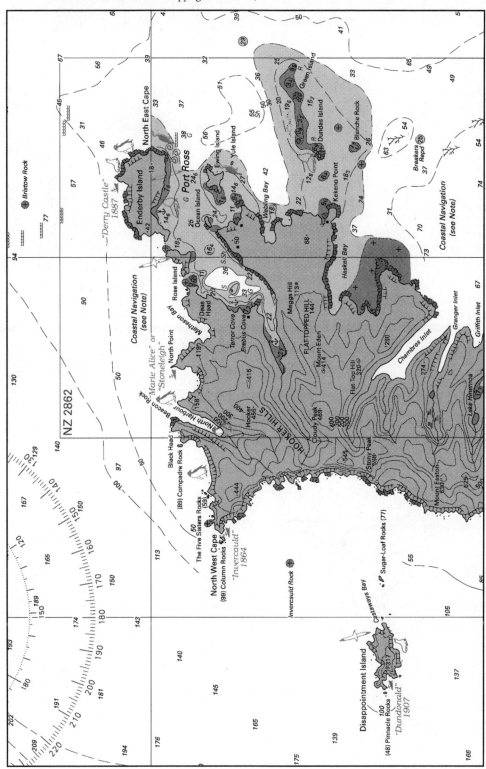

Thirteen years

Boxing Day, 12.30 p.m., 26 December 2006. All the jobs were done. All the vital life-perpetuating objects were on board, myself included.

Swirly World had been rafted up alongside *Ethel* (an 1896 Logan ketch) in the Auckland Viaduct for a week while I slowly filled her up with food and water and other important things. It was finally time to go. A private departure free from the expectations of others had been planned in advance. We were off. Me and the boat, the boat and I. Karyn, Seth and Fabian waved goodbye. So did I.

A big push backwards (no reverse gear) got *SW* out enough from the wharf, then I rushed below and started the engine and we motored slowly out past the moored multi-million-dollar yachts and motorboats lining our pathway to the Viaduct exit. No point complicating things at this stage with sailing in such confined quarters; I'd leave that for later.

Once outside the Viaduct and with more sailing elbow-room, a light westerly wind and well-timed outgoing tide were waiting for us. Boxing Day had brought out many other sailing boats, all departing Auckland harbour and heading for the Hauraki Gulf bays of recreation. We joined the procession.

Thirteen years had elapsed since I'd last sailed *SW* offshore out of sight of land. Life had led me elsewhere, and years of neglect had been bestowed on the boat as it floated like a marine farm in Little Shoal Bay waiting patiently to, hopefully, be reactivated … one day. Two young children, another boat, and a full-time job in another hemisphere had led to the long wait for reactivation.

However, that day finally came and turned into two years of methodical though sporadic work. *SW* — all 17 feet 9 inches (5.4 metres) of her — sat up the driveway at home on a cradle, well away from the water. She was high and drying out, and there was a lot to do. The term 'refit' was well used in many conversations and I became skilled at explaining what I was generally taking too long to do.

The skeg which supported the long, narrow rudder had always tormented me, and for 20 years I had never been able to eradicate the movement and crack line that lived where the skeg met the hull. In 1987 I added another bolt — and sheared off the heads of two others from over-keen tightening — then filled and glassed the crack, but all to no avail. I had finally settled on defeat and the sight of water seeping from the crack whenever we took to the piles for a quick scrub-down.

To start with, a good drying-out was required all round. The old skeg was hack-sawed off, leaving three gaping bolt-holes in the bottom of the boat. It didn't look seaworthy nor feel right, but I knew it was inevitable: I had become committed to making a new one. All other unscrewables were unscrewed and many little holes left everywhere. Bigger, gaping orifices appeared when I took out the old crazed Lexan windows and the Perspex dodger.

One year had passed, and all I had done was to turn *SW* into the bare shell of the boat she used to be. It was a bad look. At this stage I was only a quick chainsaw-cut away from turning *SW* into an adventure playground for the children. A small-person-sized incision with a slide coming out of the side … But somehow the resolve to sail again another day was found, and another year that felt and looked more productive went by as *SW* slowly improved in appearance.

Frank, the live-in temporary childminder (and family friend), was holding the fort while Karyn and I talked to each other in public doing the Kiwi FM radio breakfast show each weekday morning. Frank showed me how to laminate plywood, with grave attention to epoxy 'brews' and clamping. He was working as often as possible on his own 12-metre William Atkin yacht *Alana B* at Span Farm down the road each day, and his expertise and determination to get his boat out of the mud and back to sea was inspirational.

A new skeg with carefully buried new bolts and gudgeons was laminated up, then bolted on with plenty of glue and sheathed in fibreglass, most wonderfully. It felt that the skeg/crack equation might finally be solved.

The other big one was the bottom of the keel. Over the years on the mooring, growing mussels and long tentacles of kelp, *SW*'s keel had suffered. The fibreglass cloth that sheathed the steel and internal lead had peeled away and flapped like wings in the sea. The bottom of the steel keel that encased the lead had slightly opened up and the base plate had rusted away in places.

I made up a cardboard template of the shape of the lower part of the keel, and local steel fabricators Fagan and Hannay made me up a new keel-shoe with a 12-mm base plate and 3-mm rolled aerofoil sides, at no considerable expense to myself. I'd foolishly thought there could have been some fiscal favouritism, given our shared surnames, but I was wrong.

I'd also met Zein, through a friend Gawaine. Zein is mechanical and practical and can weld as well. After continuous pestering he agreed to do the job, and welded the new keel additions on to where they needed to be. He did a grand job underneath the hull, with sparks and his hot jet of burning danger making the welding process look like a glue gun in a kindergarten (apart from the necessity for a mask and his insistence not to stare at the flame). Zein assigned me the role of sitting inside the cabin with a fire extinguisher, waiting for the potential flames to spurt up from the over-heated keel and attached wooden hull. After a late night the night before, I fell asleep inside and fortunately was not consumed by fire.

The self-steering trim tab attached to the aft edge of the rudder had long since disappeared through electrolysis of its pintles and the relentless encouragement of wind and waves wobbling it about in Little Shoal Bay. A new one, made of hardwood sheathed in cloth and resin, and a little larger in blade surface area, was eventually fashioned and fitted with new pintles. The need for continuous, accurate steering when sailing solo can easily be overlooked. The trim tab is a vital piece of the self-steering wind-vane, and without it long-distance solo sailing in *SW* would be more difficult than worth doing.

In the engine room, the situation had deteriorated over the years and now appeared fairly dismal. I'd done a lot of miles with the original old 7-hp Honda air-cooled petrol inboard. The engine plus its water-cooled exhaust pipe and associated water pump had got to know the impatient side of me.

I'd had them both out of the boat before, entailing a minor but annoying odyssey of blind unbolting in a very inaccessible space. This time I gave it to Zein at Gawaine's workshop to assess. He undid a few bits, and laughed in a way that I had not witnessed him do before. I knew immediately that prospects for engine rejuvenation were not looking good. Prior to taking *SW* out of the water for a while, the engine had seized — and I found out that I'd forgotten where the oil was supposed to go. I had mistaken the gearbox oil hole for the important one.

The alternative of buying a new engine and all the work of creating new engine beds and a new exhaust system to fit it were beyond my limit of further application.

I was by then sick of having a non-active boat that required so much activity up the driveway, and fed up with such tediously slow progress to show for my sporadic endeavours. I started looking on TradeMe at other small yachts, and saw all sorts of interesting cheap backyard projects. They were all for sale because their owners had unanimously lost interest in the enormity of their undertakings. The hours and money allocated to getting the DIY project back in the water can easily be underestimated. Even with the best of intentions, the consistent application required, combined with the outgoing trickle of cash, can easily get the better of you. The realization that I was teetering on the cusp of falling into that category didn't feel good.

After a few months, I picked my moment to discreetly go back and gather up the slightly dismembered engine off the floor of Zein's workspace and take it back home. It still had value to me. Optimistically I rubbed the rust off and bolted the head back on, daubed primer paint about and got it looking better on the outside.

A lot of my past bad engine memories had been to do with associated electrics and the mysteries they represented. Michael Brien, the creator of *SW*, had wired in a mind-boggling amount of wire, much of which now seemed redundant 30 years on — or was it? Over the years I'd snipped off this and that. No more rev counter, depth sounder, alternator indicator, compass light. All gone with a little snip of the wire-cutters in the name of simplicity after the unit stopped functioning. Sometimes the whole show had stopped, usually at a most inconvenient moment; no electrics working at all. A little wiggle of a bunch of wires often did the trick, although on the way to Australia in 1994, a day or two went by without any power, no matter how often I wiggled things — and in desperation I wiggled them a lot.

Zein explained how to set up new electrical systems, even going to the extreme of pencil-drawn diagrams, which worked a treat for me. A new water pump, alternator and bus bar, complete with my amateur wiring, joined the old repainted engine in that cramped little compartment called an engine room.

Outside paint was also required. *SW*'s usual bright green

colour was no longer available, so I opted for a garish bright orange: 'Rescue Orange'. The come-and-get-me colour seemed appropriate and one day, but hopefully not, it might come in handy.

The rig (mast, boom and ropes) was another collection of issues. Running rigging (ropes) from the 1970s, and still going strong, had become harsh on the hands from all those sun-bleached years, and I knew I had to treat my paws by getting some new ones. More importantly, the stays that keep the mast standing and which had been replaced for the 1994 Solo Tasman Race seemed OK; but the caps (side-stays that go to the top of the mast) would need renewing. They take a lot of load (and so do the other stays, as I later discovered).

While the mast was down, a new tri-colour LED navigation light that draws negligible wattage was added. In the past, if you left the navigation lights on all night, burning 18 watts all the time, the battery would be almost flat by morning. This light, a single stalk with a cluster of light-emitting diodes on it, drew only a fraction of the wattage and was a space-age opportunity not to be missed.

Folding mast-steps to get to the top when required was another indulgence I couldn't resist. I'd not forgotten an episode back in 1994, mid-Tasman, which had me clinging to the mast halfway up trying to fix a broken spreader. Something to stand on would have been nice.

For a small boat there seemed to be a disproportionate amount of things to do. Several times I lost interest in the whole project, and only the enormity of an ambition to complete the 'refit' drew me back to toil again. Epoxy in hand and rapidly going off, or paint and roller without enough cleaning fluid …

Headsails from the 1970s had slowly become the equivalent of sailcloth tissue paper. I'd made the most of them over the years and miles, but my policy of frugal favouritism could not compensate for their deterioration. Some nice new ones were made by Neil at Quantum in Wellington. A genoa, a number two, and an impressive black gennaker. The smell of new sailcloth is always a pleasure.

Down the driveway

Finally, after a bit more than two years, *Swirly World* looked all shiny and new and a return to her natural element was no longer a preposterous ambition. Every hole that had represented absent screws or bolts was eventually filled with the old ones I'd saved, or sometimes new recruits; all gunked back in in the customary way (except for the windows, but more on that later).

Friends and hired professionals got *SW* floating again, and a second go at putting up the mast rectified the first time's wire-shorting-out problem. That first time, under the pressure of quickly trying to get the mast to stand upright, we pinched the wire under the mast.

Two years up the driveway; what two years? There was definitely now something to show for it.

Over the other years of living a normal life on land, I have become well acquainted with the pleasure of uninterrupted sleep. It's not something I associate with *SW*. But with time, the memories of the arduous, uncomfortable and vulnerable reality of solo sailing get erased, and the ambition to sail to certain places, and to again experience aquatic adventures you'll never forget, becomes something to look forward to.

I'd always wanted to sail around New Zealand. This was a mental badge of sailing honour to be bestowed on anyone who sailed through all the sea areas surrounding New Zealand. All those sea areas announced on the marine weather forecasts always held a solemn appeal for me. Especially the further south they sounded. The likes of Castlepoint, Conway, Rangitata, Chalmers, Foveaux, Puysegur, Milford and Grey sounded like places that needed to be sailed through. Not easy sailing, judging by the wind those areas have to deal with on a regular basis, but compelling nevertheless. Had my adult life so far turned out to be more prosperous, then a voyage in good company on a larger vessel might have sufficed. Instead it appeared that the most practical solution was the one floatable resource available to me: *Swirly World*.

Somehow my sailing ambition became more than just an impulse. It would be good to go for a sail by myself again, out of sight of land, if only to see if I still enjoyed it as much as I remembered I used to. But was the potential ambition to sail to the Auckland Islands, then possibly take the Tasman Sea route back and circumnavigate New Zealand in *SW* a sound plan? It had been 13 years since I'd last sailed beyond the sight of land.

For a while, I had completely lost interest in the sea. I was working with others, and living with others (including toddlers) on another boat in London, on still and murky water, almost not noticing I was afloat. But canal boat living has its charms. Seven years went by living a working-class life in London. The boat made the living more endurable than it would have been, to my mind, in one of those Coronation Street-type brick boxes up the nearby rows of streets.

Beating the blood clots

It really would be good to go for a sail out of sight of land again; or would it?

The future possibility and the planning to do so had nourished my sense of optimism in mundane circumstances off and on for years in the UK. While *SW* floated forlornly and covered in weeds in the Auckland harbour on the other side of the world, I sometimes worked through the lists of things that needed to be done to attempt a visit to the Auckland Islands, and possibly circumnavigate New Zealand.

A kidney stone in my bladder that took me to hospital also nourished my desire to sail away as soon as possible. A prolonged series of unpleasant medical encounters had ensued once the pain had become more than uncomfortable. I'd paid the specialists to look at my insides, then been put on a waiting list that got lost between hospitals. Six months went by, and I made do with plenty of painkillers — until one morning, with no ability to urinate when it felt quite imperative, I drove myself to Accident and Emergency. The experts with the bigger machines saw what my problem was, and in I went into the New Zealand hospital system in a backless gown, being paraded around, down corridors and up lifts, a true victim of my own body.

Never having been knocked out legally by drugs before, the victim role-play of lying on a mobile bed and relinquishing the control of one's immediate destiny took me by surprise in a slightly unpleasant way. So, too, did the realization that the South African female doctor currently talking to me would shortly be forcing a long tube with a light and camera and little hammer on the end of it up my penis. It was enough to knock me out without drugs.

But she did it, and her little hammer broke up my kidney stone into tiny fragments, hopefully small enough to travel out of my bladder and down into the urinal waiting in the outside world.

The first thing I noticed when regaining consciousness was an elderly gentleman partially glaring at me from a bed opposite in the urology ward. All I had to do was urinate, and then they'd let me go home so I could pretend nothing had happened. After their fiddling about down below, however, urinating was the last thing I wanted to do. But I eventually did it, although it looked more like blood than urine.

When the nurse gave me the all-clear to leave, with the proviso to keep drinking fluids and to urinate as often as possible, the elderly gentleman in the opposite bed almost glowered his frustration at having to remain there while I was being set free.

In the few hours I'd been lying there on the hard bed, partially upright and waiting to urinate, I'd looked across at him lying alone all wired up with whatever, undoubtedly incapacitated. I couldn't help but feel sorry for him. The rest of the old men surrounding me weren't much better off, by the look and occasional sounds from them. This was almost *it* for some of them; recovery was not a foregone conclusion. The blatant contrast of their situation with those outside the hospital, free to engage in doing whatever, and taking their mobility and activities for granted, was almost too obvious. The sooner I got sailing, the better.

Within 48 hours, I was back in A&E explaining my previous operation to a person slightly overwhelmed by their workload in the early hours of an Auckland Sunday morning. Drunken brawlers coming down from boozing and looking slightly damaged took up most of the seats. Once they ushered me backstage, a lack of beds became apparent.

I had a full bladder, and despite many attempts to empty it my body failed to oblige. Things down below were becoming very uncomfortable indeed, and often it was that I made an ill-fated voyage to the urinal only to provide a trickle, or to drip like a leak from a tightly closed tap. Listening to other slightly distressed, hospitalized humans hidden behind the thin curtains enclosing me provided a minor distraction, but I couldn't help being self-centred, fully focused on my filled-to-bursting bladder. It was a truly bad feeling, and the nurse who attended me with a little hand-held machine confirmed the reason for my lack of comfort. She measured the volume of liquid trapped inside and casually informed me that it was reaching a dangerous level; within hours she expected it to back-fill up to my kidneys and infect them. The bladder had to be drained ASAP.

It was seven on a Sunday morning now, and not much had happened for a while apart from the odd distressed noise from beyond the curtains. An attractive young female doctor eventually pulled the curtains briskly apart then came and stood close to me, pulling the curtains equally briskly closed. She made it clear, in no uncertain terms, that I needed a catheter inserted in my penis and pushed up into my bladder through what had become a blood clot.

I totally empathized with her plan, and tried not to pass out at the thought of it. Determined not to appear too undignified, I casually pleaded with her to knock me out like the last time. No anaesthetist was available at that early hour that morning, and she was emphatic that the catheter must be inserted *now*. The insertion was not regarded as a knock-you-out job, especially if the intravenous morphine provider was not yet at work.

She whisked the curtains closed, then soon whisked them open again, this time accompanied by a male orderly who looked more like a bodyguard. They put me on a trolley, then rolled me away from the overnight throng to a more private place where, presumably, my previous fellow inmates would not hear my screams of agony.

Lying down, with the long, firm arm of the man I had just met waiting to hold me in place if I flinched, the whole exercise felt like a life-defining moment. The doctor took my penis in hand and, after daubing the end with a jelly local anaesthetic, took advantage of my situation and firmly pushed a tube up and inside me. It didn't feel appropriate, but who was I to complain when they were doing it for my own benefit? Intrusive was the word that immediately came to mind. A plastic bag at the end of the tube began filling, and my life was saved.

Wheeled back to the thin-curtained cubicle, nothing much had changed in there. Most of them were still quietly waiting for attention. Another brisk flurry of the curtain and the morphine provider gave me some, but not nearly enough. An hour later the female South African doctor who had done the damage the day before arrived. She was the one who had directed the little hammer to pulverize my kidney stone inside me. She virtually said sorry for what she alluded to having been 'perhaps quite a rough job'. It seemed that her little hammer might have missed its target a few times and had a go at other bits of me.

After her veiled apology and expression of genuine concern, I was told to get my clothes on and leave. The quiet Sunday morning street where I'd desperately parked the car the night before now seemed a supremely relaxed and inviting place of freedom and opportunity.

For the next week I drank more water than ever before and stayed mostly awake, only allowing myself brief cat-naps between compulsory pissing episodes. I did not dare let a clot develop, and lived in fear of another catheter insertion. Finally the colour came right and it appeared I'd beaten the blood clots. The threat of terminal incapacitation had been firmly brought to my attention, however, and I realized I owed it to myself to get more active, and on to it, and do something before I could only look back on what I had done.

But other, more immediate, responsibilities of living kept suspending the sailing schedule, and seemingly pushing it into some future distant and unobtainable moment.

From Auckland to the Auckland Islands

B ut now that future distant, unobtainable moment seemed to have been obtained, and *SW* sailed, full of food and water, and me, out past Rangitoto Island and into the Hauraki Gulf.

There are two options for sailing from Auckland to the Auckland Islands. Left or right out of the Hauraki Gulf. It took me a while to decide on which way up to the high latitudes I should go.

Gerry Clark, a small-sailing-boat expert, had hammered his way south from the Bay of Islands by going around the top and down the Tasman, beating through a succession of contrary gales and current for 23 days until he got there. His was a 21-foot twin-keeler, *Ketiga*. Gerry set a great precedent that had not gone unnoticed by me.

But why not try to sneak south in the lee of the North and South Islands and stay sheltered from the prevailing winds? Inshore currents would often be contrary, but that would be compensated for by more opportunities to break up the voyage with potential ports of refuge.

I settled on the east coast option; then got some last-minute news, only months before leaving, that no one really expected. Ice. Lots of ice in sight of New Zealand — a place not traditionally associated with the floating frozen stuff, unless it was lamb on a ship.

It was not something I had expected to be thinking about. Fifty degrees south was a long way up (in latitude speak) into the danger zone as far as wind strength and wave height goes, but ice was never anticipated. Certainly not massive islands of ice floating within eyesight of the Otago coast. One iceberg was big enough and near enough to have people hiring a helicopter to go out and get married on it. Shrek the Sheep was flown out to make a guest appearance as well. It was all a bit irregular.

I paid grave attention to what was going on out there: it looked like the ice was following north along the 200-metre line, and slowly drifting up the eastern side of the South Island. If we stayed close to the land, inshore of their course, we should not bump into them nor be bumped into by them.

Another factor most relevant to the success of the expedition was the obtaining of a DOC permit to land on the Auckland Islands. Emails resulted in forms to be filled in; then, to clinch the deal, a proper inspection of the underside of *SW* needed to be undertaken at Otago or Bluff Harbour. Invasive seaweeds are not to be encouraged in preserved places, and I too needed to understand the responsibilities bestowed upon me as captain/

skipper/master of my vessel, navigating in such auspicious waters.

As emphasized before, I had become well acquainted with the pleasure of uninterrupted sleep. Worse than the prospect of constant fatigue was that I'd forgotten how slow and uncomfortable small-boat sailing could be. 'Unpleasant' was the word that would often come to mind over the next two months.

But all that went before, leading up to our departure, and all that was to come was eclipsed by that beautiful Boxing Day that sent *SW* out into a very benign and inviting Hauraki Gulf. Flat off (running before the wind) on a relatively smooth surface, and feeling cautiously nervous but reasonably prepared.

I aimed us towards the end of the Coromandel Peninsula and engaged the self-steering wind vane. The new, larger trim tab felt like it made the tracking more consistent, keeping *SW* on course, so I took up various positions of leisurely intent whilst revelling in the pleasure of simply, at long last, being under way. It was a new beginning for *SW*, and I was pleased I had persevered to finally get to this point. Of the years that had gone before, the most tedious detail is hard to recall; perhaps, like gestation and childbirth, the uncomfortable aspects get biologically erased from immediate, vivid memory in order to leave the thrill of future adventure intact.

Part of the motivation for not trumpeting our departure was my uncertainty about my commitment to sail south and keep on going. The ambition was to get as far south as 50 degrees latitude and visit the Auckland Islands, weather permitting.

I *had* to go to the Auckland Islands. I'd read all the books about the shipwrecks and human suffering that had gone on there. For almost 30 years I'd been absolutely captivated by that remote, inhospitable sub-Antarctic group of islands. There was nowhere I wanted to sail to more so than there. The fact that it remains uninhabited (except for seasonal DOC activity) and looks the same as it did to the desperate survivors of those many shipwrecks, over a hundred years ago, made it even more appealing.

By normal boat-size standards, *Swirly World* is a bit small to attempt a voyage into the Southern Ocean. Two crew would have been a crowd, and extra water and food for two would have been too much weight.

It had been a long time since I'd been out of sight of land alone, and it had become once again a disturbing proposition. That feeling of vulnerability in never knowing what the wind will bring to the party once you're too far away from land to retreat to a safe bay or port. It was all a bit disconcerting, but I knew I'd thought and said that before.

I hadn't been sleeping well for months before departure day. Was I biting off more than I could sail? It felt like it — the uncertainty of what was to come. When do you let caution get the better of you?

Into the unknown, and hundreds of miles away from home ...

Perhaps I could peel off, late at night, while sailing away and go and hide up some mangrove estuary, pull a cover over, and pretend to be out there. Pop back out in a couple of months and sail back up the harbour pretending we'd done it?

Bay of Plenty of wind

The moderate westerly wind whisked Auckland away over the horizon behind us, and the end of the Coromandel Peninsula slowly grew larger. The high sky held large streamers of far-above wind-driven cloud foretelling of more velocity to come, and the long-range evening marine forecast confirmed this. But it would come from behind, a fresh northwesterly to run us free across the Bay of Plenty.

With enough wind for the moment and the promise of more, it couldn't be better, apart from the fact that I was starting to feel a bit queasy and apprehensive, and it was getting dark. Hours went by while I intermittently lay down to cat-nap — or pretend to for 20 minutes before I was seized with the desire to jump up to look out for shipping traffic around Cape Colville.

Nothing much was happening on Boxing Day night out there, except for *SW* running downwind well, with poled-out jib and restrained main, wing and wing, under self-steering. A few course corrections every few hours (spanner on the self-steering adjustment bolt) gave Channel Island, then the southern tip of Great Barrier Island, plenty of space.

Then it starting getting light, and Cuvier Island appeared there in the water just beside us. I'd been aiming for the loom of its light for hours, but had almost forgotten there was land attached to it.

From here on out life would revolve around a compass course. One-ten, one-twenty magnetic was the general direction, allowing for all sorts of slewing and sliding down the small waves and into the back of the next small wave …

As the day began, the promised wind started freshening and we waved goodbye to Cuvier, and to the reassurance that the proximity of land (any land) psychologically provides.

All day we ran fast (for *SW*) at 5 to 6 knots in the right direction, a direction that looked like no direction at all. It was just a nondescript piece of empty horizon that the compass and chart told me was where I wanted to go, the East Cape of the North Island of New Zealand, over 120 nautical miles (220 km) away.

SW rolled about, doing a lot of pseudo-surfing down the little, building waves and general swishy non-productive slewing, this way and that, providing too much movement for an unadjusted occupant to enjoy. This was tough on unconditioned me, and I didn't like it. It was fatiguing holding on tighter than usual to avoid being thrown about inside, and bracing myself via an outstretched leg or wedged-in shoulder required more effort than I wanted to make.

That night I pulled down the mainsail and lashed it onto the boom and the spray dodger that acts as a gallows for the boom; and let *SW* run with just the number one headsail pulling us along at 4 to 5 knots with the self-steering doing all the work.

Inside with the hatch-boards closed up, I was in my little aquatic tomb, all strapped up by the lee cloth, in my sleeping bag, rushing along on top of the sea with no one responsible but me. But was I? During the day I'd seen a couple of ships come up and go past on the rhumb line for East Cape, and had been steering a few miles north of their route to keep out of their way.

All night I kept clambering up from inside, peering out all around every half hour to see if any lights were about that might possibly interfere with us. But most of the time I lay there trying to avoid feeling too ill, bracing myself against the violent, incessant rolling and slewing-about motion and listening to the rush of *SW* sliding fast over the wind-agitated sea.

That first night was very uncomfortable, but not as bad as going to windward, the pleasure of which I would become once again well acquainted with later on.

As the miles rolled and surged by, my sense of acute vulnerability increased. Once again, as so often done and forgotten before, I seriously questioned my own resolve to continue: feeling like this wasn't much fun at all. Wearing a sea-sick face and often throwing up, or more accurately dry-retching, I did the simple things required to keep *SW* rushing fast in the right direction.

One-ten to one-twenty magnetic was the general course, and whenever inside, I kept an eye on my hand-held bearing-compass to make sure the wind didn't shift without me noticing it. It was to become a way of life. Navigation was easy, as all it required was sticking my arm up in the air outdoors while tightly clutching a little AA-battery-powered GPS unit, kindly donated to my expedition by Advance Trident. Once it locked on to a few satellites, it came alive with vital information like exact latitude and longitude. Speed and direction over the ground came in handy, too.

I had a huge pile of relevant paper charts, most of which were out-of-date ex-fishing-boat ones provided by a next-door neighbour, Neville, a few years before. The shape of the land and associated rocks were all still in the same places on the paper and in the sea, so I was prepared to make do with them. A quick ruler along the latitude and longitude lines to define where we were was all it took to feel reassured.

Logbook entries were minimal for the next two days: only latitude and longitude, compass course, estimated boat speed and wind speed and direction being written up every few hours. Ninety miles in 24 hours dispensed with 27 December, and the next day also rushed by in a welter of foam from *SW*'s bow wave until the distant outline of high land inland, the Raukumara Range, came into sight.

Cape Runaway took a lot longer to see, as I'd opted for staying some 15 miles further north than was required, to keep away from coastal shipping motoring on their precise corner-to-corner straight-line courses.

By 4 p.m. we'd closed in on that corner of the North Island known as East Cape, and the wind velocity increased as we aimed in closer to the point of 'no land left', with good visibility and looking keenly for any signs of life. The wind came round more on the back starboard quarter the closer we got, and it was good, fast sailing.

With such a strong, favourable wind direction there was no complaining, and a close-up view of the coast was a bonus. We were too far out to get a good look at Hicks Bay, but with a wide view, what a remote, underpopulated bit of dry land the whole area looked to be.

From Horoera Point on, I steered *SW* as close to the land as I dared to go, in relatively flat water with plenty of wind, moving along at 6 knots on a broad reach. No sign of human life ashore, even though I spent some time carefully looking for it.

A simple matter of necessity

On board were two old charts relevant for this corner of the land. Each one was covered in carefully drawn pencil-line fixes from past commercial fishing-boat trips, none of which were mine.

Out-of-date charts are a no-no in commercial fishing, and regardless of multiple corrections to bring them up to date, the ones I'd inherited had been discarded; Neville had a huge pile of them to give away. A form of maritime gold (each new one being worth 20-something New Zealand dollars), it felt like Christmas or some other festival of getting had come early as I staggered down his driveway and up mine, with virtually a paper version of all of the New Zealand coastline and harbours on one shoulder.

I'd read plenty of tales of difficult times on sailing boats trying to get around East Cape, so the closer we got the more serious I became. The more serious had also come from a degree of fatigue that had crept up on me from my reacquaintance with continuously interrupted sleep, continuous motion and the energy expended just in clinging on and bracing oneself continuously, as a simple matter of tiresome necessity ... did I mention it was continuous?

Approaching Whangaokeno Island, otherwise known as East Island, I faced my first important navigational test. There's a fair bit of space between East Island and East Cape, maybe a mile and a bit? My chart was 1 : 200,000 scale and covered the sea area from Cape Runaway to Table Cape on the Mahia Peninsula. It looked like a tiny gap on the chart, but from what I could see there were no little crosses denoting sunken rocks ready to rip off the keel. Apart from a 2.7-metre patch, it didn't look too shallow on paper either. Outside the island a couple of crosses and lots of squiggles on the chart denoted isolated sunken rocks, tidal activity, and potentially horrible messy associated waves.

With the wind as it was, I opted for the inside passage and aimed accordingly. We hurtled along (by *Swirly World* standards) at 6 knots and I looked about for any signs of shallow water and/or dark patches of rock and weed. To starboard, a bit of long straggly stuff started to show up under the surface. I was cutting the corner fine, but the further we sailed the flatter the water became, and then a new view emerged of more far-distant headlands and a long lot of high, hazy land further down to the south. We were round.

Slightly hardening up onto a beam reach, the sailing felt

good. The wind was coming off the land at around 15 knots but peppered with the constant arrival of stronger, less welcome gusts. Perfect conditions for the self-steering, and seeing that *SW*'s main berth inside was to starboard (the same side the wind was coming from), I felt obliged to immediately go to bed and leave the steering to my Faithful Mechanical Friend (FMF).

I'd done a lot of miles with the FMF keeping us going in the desired direction, and had put a bit of time in, during the refit, to make sure it would remain worthy of my confidence. The tangle of alloy pipes that I'd had welded together and powder-coated back in 1985 had survived well for 25 years, but the lead weight attached to the arm to keep it balanced had electrolysed out the alloy and another bit needed welding on. I got the jobs done, and now the enlarged new trim tab on the aft edge of the rudder and new stainless pintles to keep it wiggling away seemed to be doing their job admirably.

With clear sea to the south, self-steering engaged, sleeping bag engaged and lee cloth engaged (to stop me falling out of bed when the boat heeled over), *SW* was all set to sail on indefinitely until the wind stopped.

Sailing in daylight, from headland to headland, I often find myself over-optimistic in picking which piece of jutting-out land is the next target to aim for. Even if it's blatantly obvious from the compass course that the one we have to go round is well over the horizon and further offshore, I still find myself with the overwhelming desire to consider the next headland I can visibly see as the one I'm after.

A lethargic me managed to emerge just before it got dark, and a GPS fix confirmed what I could see. We were 4 miles off the land, and just north of Waipiro Bay.

Sleeping during the day while sailing near the coast always feels more responsible, if only for the chance it provides for other vessels to get a good view of you if you're not up to looking out for them. That was my theory; but then again, in the dark, with your navigation lights on and away from the distraction of city or rural shore lights, in good conditions, anyone else out there usually gets noticed sooner rather than later.

By 2 a.m. the distant friendly cluster of Tokomaru Bay night lights had slowly come and gone, and been left behind, while the real reason I had got up and paid attention — the Tokamapuphia Reef — was reassuringly 3 miles abeam, according to the GPS. Fixing your position via a few satellites racing around the earth is a pleasure to behold, yet it's quickly become something we take for granted. On a night lacking moonlight it's difficult to judge one's distance off the land, and often an exact-fix paranoia grips me only to be erased by the GPS.

Margins of navigational safety are difficult to judge in the dark without light-houses or anything else to visually point out the important bits. The distant sound of an ocean swell exploding on rocks or dumping in on a surf beach out of eyesight is an unnerving thing at night, but it's easy to overestimate one's proximity to danger.

Three miles off the rocks was good enough for me, and with no sea-traffic lights anywhere to be seen, it was back to bed. The wind was still strong enough to keep the FMF operating, and *SW* sailed on in an easing westerly with me not really asleep but trying to be, lying as still and relaxed as possible and waiting patiently for it to get light.

Through the past few isolated days and nights of sailing I'd twiddled about with my AM/FM radio set, constantly craving distraction or company, or a mixture of both. This part of the coast brought me company in the form of Radio Rhema, the Christian station, and local Maori iwi radio. That was it. The Maori station was mostly talk-back and talking in Maori, and it was like listening to people from another land. Although I didn't understand most words, I did understand the compelling laughter that punctuated the appealing tones of their casual conversation. I've never bothered learning the language but I do like the sound of it being spoken.

Three miles had become 9 miles offshore when it did get light, and Gable End Foreland was abeam. As the coast tracks more southwesterly from there to Gisborne, the next 17 miles became on-the-wind sailing. The westerly wind had a bit too much south in it for my liking, but I had no option but to persevere.

One long board (as sailors sometimes say when sailing against the wind) up to the Ariel Rocks 10 miles east of Gisborne, then another few back. That killed most of the day, and finally at 5 p.m. we arrived at the concrete breakwater at the mouth to the Turanganui River and the Gisborne boat basin.

The last time I'd been into Gisborne on a boat was in 1993 on *Rock Steady*, Steve Raea's ferro-cement Hartley RORC 39. Steve was coming down from the Islands after six months' cruising. They'd saved the crew of a sunken freighter in the middle of the night and Steve was looking for someone to help him sail back down to Wellington.

Rock Steady had been front-page news and for Steve the nine-day sail down was like a lap of honour. In party mode, I don't remember much apart from capsizing the dinghy just outside the breakwater in Gisborne when three of us were motoring round to the river mouth. The sea suddenly became very shallow, and out of nowhere a following short and threatening wave reared up and caught us unawares. Cart-wheeled forward, bow going down and under and us out into the water, with the outboard gurgling defiance and then drowning.

The relief that we were able to stand up, thigh deep, and sort things out was almost all I can remember. That and the way we had to tie up to the smelly tidal seawall next to equally pongy fishing boats and monitor mooring lines 24/7.

Fourteen years had changed Gisborne, but expecting nothing special I started up the engine and puttered up the very still flat channel to the basin.

Every sailing-boat arrival after a few non-stop days and nights at sea feels special. The relative sanctuary from the unpredictability of the wind and the sea, and what they might throw at you. Slowing *SW* up to a virtual drift, I was more than pleasantly surprised to be confronted by a marina with floating pontoons in front of a big social fishing club full of cooking food smells. We were in.

Jobs

Buy reading glasses
Buy shackles
Buy spare $^{5}/_{16}$ spanner for self-steering
Buy reefing and sail tie lines
Tighten aft, caps, inner stays

Buy plastic sporks

Reseal leaking starboard window nuts and bolts

Seal and tape anchor locker inspection ports

Remove and restow in priority all gear!

Make inventory of where things are

Put pulley on boom outhaul

Restow dinghy with carpet under

Put all knick-knack type things securely away

Put flares in grab bag

Buy pencils

The informalities of marina greetings quickly sorted out where *SW* could stay for a couple of days. In a spare berth, mooring lines were attached in the right places, and then the list of jobs was addressed.

Four days and three nights of continuous sailing had focused the project for me. The biggest priority was keeping the water outside and not letting it in. One of the windows had been dribbling on me all across the Bay of Plenty. It was annoying, and then infuriating for no apparent reason other than fatigue. Certain nuts and bolts looked to be the likely culprits, and their removing, re-gunking and replacing took priority.

A dribbling window was certainly intolerable. But it was a bigger issue than just water dripping on me in my sleeping bag when I least wanted to feel it. It meant that I hadn't put the windows back in properly after I took them out up the driveway. I'd done something wrong. I had smothered the cavities in gunk, tightened machine-head screws and washers and nuts as best I could by myself with gunk oozing everywhere. They had felt tight enough. The windows *looked* impervious to salt water ... but alas no.

Doing a mental debrief on the miles just covered, I decided to cut the boat up into little pieces and then eat it. Once digested, I'd catch the bus back to Auckland. It all made so much unstressful sense. Why put yourself through such a potentially harrowing experience by wanting to sail south into serious latitudes in *SW*?

Everyone in the fishing club with well-used boats in the marina was having a brilliant New Zealand Crimbo/New Year time. This was the Kiwi lifestyle personified. It was the holiday period, and it was pumping. Rhythm & Vines Festival, 15,000 out-of-towners besieging the burger bars and bottle stores. A good active vibe everywhere, and that included the gated marina pontoons. I quickly met fellow boating enthusiasts and was invited to New Year's Eve and the end of 2006 just a few boats down from me.

With only a day to go before the shops would probably be shut, I wandered about the Gisborne streets foraging, primarily for good rope. Short lengths of lashing were of special interest to me, but I could find nothing appropriate anywhere. A long walk down the main street got me to a busy New Year's Eve's motor-parts omni-shop, and I acquired a terrible bundle of poly-something poor-substitute 'rope'. I would have to make do.

Gisborne was truly teeming with humanity, wearing all sorts of scanty summery costumes. Some good-hearted marine-oriented people like Peter Millar paid attention to *SW*. He was preoccupied with newborn twins, but still found time to be in his salt-water element as often as possible. It didn't take me long to recognize him. Back at the P Class nationals in 1978, he was sailing fast and from somewhere I wasn't sure where. PB on his P Class mainsail I found out meant Poverty Bay, which meant Gisborne. Aged 15 like me then, now 40-something and evidently still sailing fast in a Young 88.

Peter gave me some good local knowledge of Mahia Peninsula anchorages if we needed them and, more importantly, held the screwdriver when the re-gunked bolts through the windows needed tightening properly.

A German man, Trevor, on a huge white live-aboard yacht was very interested in *SW*'s voyage and invited me aboard his round-the-world project. He and his partner had been many years building it in Gisborne, and now it floated in the marina and they were working towards setting a leaving date. The boat was superbly buoyant and strong. Their voyaging prospects looked excellent.

He scared me with a piece of unsolicited advice regarding body cramps caused by a lack of salt. He recommended sprinkling salt in all fizzy drinks in order to avoid agonizing limb cramps that someone sailing and sweating like me might be in for if I didn't follow his advice. Freaked out and late in the day, the last one of 2006, after saying goodbye on the pontoon I quickly went foraging earnestly down the main street for the salt I knew I didn't have on board. I couldn't find any salt anywhere. I certainly tried, but returned to *SW* empty-handed. Disconcertingly, it proved to be a provision that would not be on board prior to departure. It never dawned on me to borrow some from Peter.

7

To wait or not to wait —
that is the question

This next leg was going to be a very serious piece of sailing. Gisborne to Lyttelton, or, if the wind was nice to us, possibly Gisborne to Dunedin non-stop. At least 400 miles (644 km) through sea areas Portland, Castlepoint and Conway.

Castlepoint has a reputation for being a potentially lethal sailing area. My shake-down cruise had been just that. I'd learnt that I didn't hate sailing alone out of sight of land, despite the discomfort. I also knew that where I intended to sail *SW* from now on would be some of the most challenging areas we'd ever sailed in together.

The wind was worrying me. I could get busy and do the jobs, but regardless of on-shore distractions, the wind was everything in dictating what sort of sailing I was going to have to do. And I was about to do lots of it.

Easy sailing with the wind blowing just enough, not too much, and anywhere from behind, straight-lining it to where you wanted to go would be great. For this leg a 20-knot northerly would be ideal all the way.

A low-pressure system had been slowly tracking across the bottom of the South Island, and its momentum had stalled off the Otago coast. A decent southerly gale was building big swells for the marine weather forecaster to read out. All the way from Dunedin to East Cape the sea could be expected to be building, with a southerly swell and a gale-force wind that would eventually ease but would remain from the south for some time.

It was going to be on-the-nose beating against the wind, the most unrewarding sailing possible, but it shouldn't last too long as the system moved east. The long-term wind forecast was for southerlies of varying strengths for at least four more days, so it wasn't very promising.

Zigzagging to Lyttelton would take weeks in *SW*. Roughly 400 miles in a straight line, but who knew how many more miles would have to be sailed to get there against the wind? To wait or not to wait, that was the question. I had a long way to sail and only a short ration of spare time away from my normal life to do it in. A week waiting around for a favourable shift in the wind seemed like a long time on the calendar.

I kept telling everyone I was on a holiday cruise to the South Island, and stunned by my intention to sail such a small boat that far they usually stopped asking more questions. That was good, as my secret expedition to the Auckland Islands far beyond the South Island had me sailing on a schedule that meant we needed to get there by the first day of February at the latest. We had 30 days to sail 1000 miles south. Mucking around in Poverty Bay wasn't going to be very productive.

Even if I tortured myself going out into it, on the wind, beating against the wind for a few days, surely we'd still gain a few more miles south before it all became better. *SW* seemed OK, but could I find it in myself to make the effort?

Come New Year's Eve, I'd gathered as much as I could, like a scavenger, knowing I had to stock up for an unknown amount of feral survival time to come. Refilling used-up water bottles, finding more citrus fruit and some kerosene for the pump-up stove and petrol for the engine. I'd drawn satisfied lines through the words that meant jobs to do, and was ready to party. Bring on 2007.

Almost asleep, as it was getting dark in the *SW* space-capsule with the hatch open, I heard the call and physical shake of tugged mooring lines, so I instantly rose to the occasion. Alf Turner let me know the show was on down the end of the pontoon on the motor boat *Sports Girl*, and I was welcome to join them.

I was leaving in the morning, but there was nothing left to be done except prepare myself. A good night's sleep just wasn't written in the stars.

It wasn't often that a sailing boat the size of *Swirly World* was due to depart in the morning for Lyttelton 400 miles south. In conversations I found myself conspicuous for my sailing ambition. One man seemed vaguely familiar, and disturbingly I recognized him from another New Year's Eve party in Gisborne I'd attended in 1994. Myself and 'Swirly World' (the band) had thrashed out a big one with 'Dead Flowers' at the Albion hotel on New Year's Eve.

Afterwards I'd been invited to a party by Moana Maniapoto, who was evidently connected with landed gentry in the area. By request I was asked to sing a song, which I did. Just a guitar-and-voice job, but I remembered the words and Moana sang along as well.

After this a tall man whom I perceived to be the owner took pleasure in calling me a wanker. And here he was again. I recognized him instantly. On the boat *Sports Girl* down the pontoon, New Year's Eve again 13 years later.

He was a local organic farmer and, according to a newly made acquaintance, also a stuntman when drunk. He didn't remember that, or me, and I didn't antagonize him. It was like meeting some bully from the playground later in life that had (hopefully) mellowed into a simmering pit of self-loathing.

But he was still tall and seemed quite happy in himself.

One hundred horrible miles and more

Dawn the next day, and it seemed like only I was paying attention. The marina and streets were understandably deserted. Somewhere a few miles away, 15,000 Rhythm & Vines punters were asleep in tents or puddles of self-indulgence, or just about ready to crash.

My immediate priority was to see what the wind was up to out in Poverty Bay. It wasn't as bad as I expected. Fifteen knots out of the south-southwest, with a bit more south in it than necessary. The forecast was for it to slowly build as the low-pressure system responsible for it tracked east-northeast across towards the Chatham Islands. The sailing looked to be pretty much in the lee of Young Nick's Head to start with, and that was good enough to encourage me to set off.

One lone vehicle with a man watching intently was the only company I could find to wave goodbye to. He was the local MAF (Ministry of Agriculture & Fisheries) man, determined to keep a solitary eye on fishing traffic and suspect catches. I don't know what he made of *SW*, or whether he had seen in the New Year and was determined to keep awake for the rest of it. He had sunglasses on even though it wasn't sunny.

I started feeling sea-sick straight away — hung-over from the party only a few hours before, knowing it hadn't been the right way to start. I knew the FMF (Faithful Mechanical Friend, a.k.a. self-steering wind vane) would reliably take over when I couldn't stay focused enough to steer any more.

Good moderate-air sailing got us up close to Young Nick's Head and the big white cliffs towering over the low curve of Poverty Bay behind us. The sky was overcast with drizzle coming off the shore, and large clouds blotted out the view of the land behind them. Not the kind of morning to be inspired to go boating. Only *SW* and myself were out there waving goodbye to Poverty Bay.

All day the wind became more determined to make the sea state unpleasantly lumpy and our progress slower. Any substantial activity was accompanied by a convincing display of throwing-up by me. It was nothing too windy, just a good solid 20–25 knots on the nose and building, but with short 2-metre swells with equally short waves, just the wrong size for *SW*'s boat length.

Towards the end of the day the prospect of a dismally uncomfortable night to come had become inevitable. A 7 p.m. GPS fix attested to 25 miles having been sailed to windward since our day began. The land had slowly got lost in low grey cloud, and the rain had enveloped everything to the west.

As the wind got stronger the sail plan got smaller, until two reefs in the mainsail plus the new number two jib had *SW* snugly sailing well, all by herself, under the control of the FMF. By 5.30 the next morning we were 40 miles southeast of Portland Island and I was slowly adjusting to enduring the constant unpleasant motion as we smacked into the growing offshore seas, now beyond the shelter of the Mahia Peninsula. It was still raining and blowing 40 knots as the heavier squalls came through.

I lay inside, strapped up to windward in the lee cloth, and stayed there for the day, listening to the water noises outside and resting as best one can in such uncomfortable conditions. In the evening I turned on and tuned up the SSB radio, and after the evening weather forecast called up Taupo Maritime Radio who are, not surprisingly, in Taupo. A strange place, so far inland, to site a radio station concerned with the sea. But it has very good coverage and signal strength all around the country. I let someone know of my ambition to reach Lyttelton or go direct to Dunedin if the wind was favourable. From then on, each evening in the hour following seven o'clock I promised to report *SW*'s position and wellbeing.

It was dull sailing, that was for sure. I wanted out but knew that was a pointless thing to think. All night we had beaten, hard on the wind, on starboard, smacking into building seas.

From Poverty Bay it was only 20 miles out to beyond the 100-metre line. The deep ocean water where depths of 1200, 1900 and 3000 metres could be found was not far away. Big waves are generally further apart out there, and *SW* sails better in the longer intervals generated by deeper water rather than the often short, closer together, inshore seas.

We'd covered just over 60 miles to windward in 24 hours, which wasn't too bad. It was good efficient sailing: hand-steering by day in full wet-weather gear, wedged comfortably in the cockpit, sitting on my blow-up plastic cushion and making the most of the wind under double reefed mainsail and number two jib. An easily balanced and efficient sail plan for any wind strength between 20 and 35 knots.

When it started getting light again the next day, we were 80 miles east of Napier, heading southeast towards the Chatham Islands. There wasn't much to see outside, all wet and windy, noisy and grey, and totally uninviting.

I'd spent the night strapped up to windward inside, hanging in the lee-cloth hammock, being held comfortably above the rest of the heeled-over boat down below. While this might sound like some S & M dungeon fetish, there was too much fatigue involved and too much incessant motion to make it pleasurable. But it was good sailing progress considering the bad wind direction.

SW was also just a few miles northeast of the Ritchie Banks, a place of shallow sea I had been thinking about for some time. These are a couple of underwater sea mountains that spike up from the 900-metre seabed to 250 metres. Bad steep and breaking waves are associated with the banks, and fortunately we didn't have to sail to windward of them or bear away to miss them.

Slowly *SW* just slammed on past them to the northeast, a few miles to leeward and heading happily offshore. But I wasn't happy. The day and night had been a series of dry-retching and 'quick spit sick' episodes after or during most activities. I felt weak and lethargic and mentally disinterested, verging on disillusioned.

Apart from that, somewhere in me I knew it was good to be there.

All day it was more of the same, except that the wind increased and blew a minor gale from the south-southwest with bad visibility and frequent rain squalls. We were sailing slowly away from that area and into even deeper water.

John Mansell in *Innovator of Mana*, a 28-foot Nova yacht, had once been knocked down and required assistance near the Ritchie Banks. He cited the freak waves as possibly being caused by the proximity of the banks. I didn't want to hang around with a building southerly gale and associated sea state to accidentally follow his example. This bad weather was anticipated, and I only had myself to blame for being there.

There was no intent to visit Napier in Hawke Bay. Any approach in a southerly would sail us over the Lachlan Banks and then into the gradually shallowing bay which could get nasty, and a stop would be just that. Instead we stayed on starboard, heading out offshore.

At five that night we were 80 miles east of Blackhead Point on the Wairarapa coast, although it was nowhere to be seen. The sailing was truly slow and tedious, smacking away, up and down, at 3 to 4 knots tops; the sound of cold salt water swilling everywhere, up on deck and in the cockpit. Unfortunately some of it was finding its way inside as well. My attempts to seal what I thought had been a few leaking bolt holes in Gisborne had failed dismally.

Every time a broken, crumbling wave crest slapped along the

side of *SW*, the window willingly dribbled water down inside, onto me and my sleeping bag. The steep angle of heel gave each drip the perfect target of my face and hair, and I was not amused. Salt-water dampness was everywhere. I rigged up an elaborate false ceiling of black rubbish bags just above my face, gaffer-taped in place and angled to let the constant dribble run off down to the bilge.

The water was coming in around the frame of the window, from what I could make out, and the whole window would need to be removed and refitted properly at the next stop. In the meantime it was guide the drips down, sponge the bilges regularly, and don't forget to have a 'quick spit sick' while you're doing it.

The air vents on deck were also leaking. Stuffed-in tea towels and other fabrics soon became saturated and dripping. I should have gaffered plastic bags over the outside of them on deck before leaving. But ventilation is nice, especially when you feel like you're suffocating; very necessary.

I was getting my air, but with a dose of unwelcome and unnecessary salt water.

We had sailed through sea area Colville (leaving Auckland) and then Plenty, and were now labouring on the southern outskirts of sea area Portland. Next would be Castlepoint and the serious weather forecasts and wind speeds often associated with it. I had almost started dreading it. Too many horror stories for sailing boats on the Wairarapa coast; I didn't want to be involved in one. *SW* was just passing through, *all good, see you soon, bye* … hopefully.

It was by then a 35 to 40 knot south-southwest gale with three- to four-metre seas. But there was nothing scary or threatening going on, just a lot of wetness and, at times, with the reduced ventilation inside from having the weather-boards in and hatch closed up; a lack of air.

One afternoon I thought I was suffocating. It had happened before on *SW* — waking up from another exhausted cat-nap and feeling like I needed to concentrate on my breathing. Either there was not enough fresh air inside, or I'd unwittingly attained some yogic meditative state that had rendered breathing normally redundant. Feeling like breathing normally would be a refreshing exercise, I rushed the hatch open and sat in the companionway gulping in the oxygen.

Going about onto port tack after 100 miles on starboard made for another welcome change. There was 80 miles of sea room between us and the North Island, and it was time to head back inshore and get ready for the inevitable northwest or westerly wind that would come to get us in the very near future.

While *Swirly World* was up the driveway, I'd made the bold decision to cut out some of the original internal woodwork that cluttered up the port side inside. Michael Brien had originally built a navigation table with chart stowage under it, and a sink and a bench stuck next to it attached also to a gimballed kerosene pressure stove. That pressure stove was gold on board — no matter how rough the sea state, I always managed to boil water on it.

The sink was a waste of space for me, however. A portable plastic bucket positioned in the most convenient place at the right angle, relevant to how the boat is sailing, is far better. I'd plugged up the outlet fitting in the skin 20 years ago. The chart table was used like a shelf, but chart-work on a piece of plywood on my lap worked better.

The last factor in my judgement upon the woodwork was the very important concept of movable ballast and the part it plays in *SW*. I could never get to lie down inside, when sailing to windward on the port (left) tack. Starboard was fine — I could hang in the lee cloth either smacking to windward or reaching along, with my weight in the right place, up to windward, and making the sailing far more efficient. But sailing on the port tack under self-steering, while being inside, was often nothing short of atrocious. There was no way to get my weight to windward, resulting in an ineffective trim and less efficient sailing.

Leaving the gimballed stove where it was, a lot of plywood was cut away and a new space was made to squeeze myself into on the port side, just aft of the stove and down low, almost touching the bottom of the hull, and sharing leg room with the engine's exhaust pipe.

After 100 horrible miles to windward we went about and I had my first chance to sample the new port quarter-berth. It was certainly a secure spot, if a little too much so — not quite enough shoulder room, and a few jagged corners became noticeable when *SW* heeled over hard, slamming and shuffling slowly to windward, into the fresh southerly and big uncomfortable sea outside.

I positioned my thin squab more on the lee side of where I was lying, which was what would be the upright side-wall bit if *SW* was upright. It was tight and uncomfortable, but my weight was in the right windward place and it made for hugely more efficient sailing.

A tiny theatre of vital importance

The four-metre seas, and solid southerly wind that didn't feel like it was leaving in a hurry, saw in the dark.

Squashed into a very small space, bouncing together with *SW* all over the place, I just lay there listening to the loud, repetitive noise of slabs of water slamming on board and draining away back where they came from. *SW* shunted through, and over, and up and down, lots of waves and swells. When it got dark, nothing changed in that noisy place.

I rested there, occasionally drifting off into a shallow imitation of sleep. All night the motion and momentum felt the same. Now and then I covered myself up in waterproof clobber and, earnestly clutching the end of my lead (safety harness lanyard), went out and clipped on, then crouched defiantly on deck, or just peered from the cockpit scanning with survivalist intent to make sure no one was about to run *SW* over.

It was a productive night's sailing: almost 40 miles made good on the wind. The southerly was easing and we were heading towards Castlepoint according to the chart and compass course. Unfortunately, the third day of 2007 found me at my most dissolute so far. A big sloppy sea really was bad for our sailing momentum, and as the wind eased I found it difficult to motivate myself to get out there and pull up more sail area. I just couldn't be bothered; I was sick of it. The leaking windows had remained just that — the sea endlessly trying to dribble down onto me.

The wind had eased and I needed to stack up more sail, get a bit of heel on, adjust the FMF and keep sailing efficiently. Lack of application based on lethargy meant more of a tight reach than hard on the wind, but seeing that a northwesterly was bound to come I didn't really care, and preferred a more comfortable tight reach so I could catch up on sleep.

The North Island appeared some tired moment later that afternoon. It was the high land behind Blackhead Point, 20 miles to the west. It was nice to see it but with no safe place to anchor anywhere near, there was no real point. No need to stop.

We went about again and started listening to the slapping and pouring and draining-away water sounds once more. Back towards the southeast, more sail up in a big leftover and unproductive (in sailing terms) sea.

Twenty miles in 11 hours was all I should have expected that night. Who knows what the current was doing, as I was once again beyond caring. A dying southerly on top of that large, dissolving sea was a foregone recipe for a bad night's sailing and sleep. The only consolation prize was knowing that we'd crossed officially into the sea area known as Castlepoint during the night.

That was cancelled out by the 5.30 a.m. weather forecast for Castlepoint. A northwesterly gale warning had been issued.

On the fourth day out from Gisborne, there was the first glimpse of the sun, and my appetite also returned. Peanut butter on crackers, handfuls of scroggin, three lemons and a drink of water. The southerly had almost blown itself out, although not quite. A large, sloppy sea heading in the opposite direction from where I wanted to go remained. The sea felt like it had it in for *SW*. The wind agreed, and eased, to make going to windward very difficult sailing indeed. Those 20 miles made good in 11 hours are best not remembered.

Just before it got dark I put us about, and *SW* headed back west towards Castlepoint to wait for the new wind shift. The prospect of a freshening northwesterly offshore wind to sail us south stirred a bit of optimism in me, and I went to bed and slept off and on through a long night of little sailing progress.

SW had taken on the southerly, and now it was spent. For all the discomfort and lack of straight-line progress, it was obvious that we'd made good some distance: 150 miles in three days and nights on the wind. We were that much further on, and now becalmed 40 miles off Castlepoint. The physical unpleasantness had been worth it — more than a third of the way there.

Daylight brought the wind back, this time from the promised new direction. A northwesterly. *SW* was away again, and for the first time so far aiming directly for Lyttelton. Fifteen knots of wind and 5 to 6 knots of good sailing over flat water used up another day, and much eating was done by the passenger inside. Thrice the pressure stove was pumped and it roared with fire to heat boiling water for two-minute noodles, then boiling water for potatoes that ended up hot and smothered in cold oily tuna from a can, and sprinkled with pieces of raw garlic. Eating had once again become attractive, and a bowel movement finished the day off nicely (the first for 2007).

The wind again left us to be becalmed 8 miles off Honeycomb Point, rolling about. I sat on the dinghy on deck, looking at the high land of Mount Adams up above a hard and dry Wairarapa coastline that stretched away, both north and south, into long-distance hazy oblivion.

There's nowhere to stop on this coast. It was the Port of Lyttelton or nothing as far as I was concerned. If the wind became extremely favourable and the possibility of carrying on for Port Chalmers opened up, then great. But for now, there'd be no anchoring in the lee of Castlepoint to wait for nice weather. No wasting time trying to get to Wellington with all that Cook Strait wind-funnel amplification to worry about. No seeking shelter in Port Underwood or Cloudy Bay near Cape Campbell. No respite from the wind by getting in close amongst the rocks on the Kaikoura Peninsula.

No way. Better to not even see those temptations. Better to stay a good way out and take whatever was written in the Book of Wind for January and hopefully make the most of it.

As the fifth became the sixth of January, the promised gale-force gusts arrived. Closing in on a compass course towards the Cape Palliser corner brought the unseen high land to the west closer, and that helped to accelerate the strength of the nasty night-veiled squalls.

Reduced once more to double-reefed main and number two jib, the FMF did its best to hold to our beam-reach course with me hiding inside. Repetitively flattened and forced to let the mainsail flog, I started feeling slightly overwhelmed by the wind. By 2 a.m. *SW* was reduced to the number two jib alone, and was efficiently beam-reaching south without the FMF being over-powered.

It would have been nice to see the wind, or at least get a look at the dark patches of fury rushing across the sea from the land. It always makes it easier being able to read the wind on the water. But this was a black night with no visibility, and every squall would arrive unannounced and unwelcome.

The wind lived up to its gale-force reputation. Out there alone in the dark, torch in mouth and spanner in hand, leaning over the stern weather-cloth to adjust the bolt on the self-steering to get the best advantage out of the angle of wind on vane; it was a tiny theatre of vital importance that I often visited.

Once tightened with the spanner, a little favouritism to one side or the other, in relation to the pressure of the wind on the vane, always paid compass-course dividends. Too much pressure favouring one side or the other, and once you'd clambered back into bed you'd find *SW* running downwind off course or rounding up off course. The trick was gauging the physical feel of the pressure of the wind on the vane, feeling its velocity through the resistance of the wind-vane stock that you're holding, and choosing the right pressure moment to tighten the bolt that engages the whole thing. Then *SW* would self-steer for hours on end with no need for anyone to hold the tiller.

All night the wind alternated between savage squalls and periods of light to moderate nothingness (considering our lack of sail area). By 5 a.m. we were close in to Cape Palliser and becalmed in its wind-shadow.

Some current convergence at the bottom of the North Island was most evident. A horrendously short and steep, confused sea was bouncing about all over the place making little pyramids of going-nowhere waves; with no encouragement from the wind. It was most peculiar, and like being on a mechanical bucking bronco with some manic stage manager trying to turn up the speed and sadistically flick you off. I clung on. How many styles of tedium should one expect to encounter on this sort of expedition?

We had four hours in the washing machine, sails strapped down, *SW* rolling and rocking in a thoroughly unacceptable way; with me wedged inside and once again fatigued and humourless. The close-up view of Cape Palliser was at least a welcome distraction and I knew that in this sea area the wind would not be leaving *SW* alone for long. They were forecasting a normal northwesterly gale for Cook Strait, and once we drifted away sufficiently from the lee of the Cape a building northwesterly filled in and came as absolute relief from the bucking bronco going nowhere scene of the last few hours.

10

In the darkness on the seabed

A local Wellington radio station was already reporting 40 knots of northwesterly that morning and it was interfering with their beach volleyball at Oriental Bay. It was inevitable we'd get more wind soon.

An hour or two later it did come, freshening slowly and from the expected direction. Optimistic and steering two-twenty magnetic on a beam reach with the FMF in control, double-reefed main and number two jib doing all the work, I went back to bed. I lay suspended above the clattering pot on the gimballed stove below (that wouldn't stop swinging around), strapped up in the lee cloth, well heeled-over and rushing along with the wind side-on.

The wind was warming up for a Cook Strait gale, and while I was fast becoming a bedroom sailor, the progress away from the south end of the North Island was discernible. Mentally I waved the North Island goodbye, lying inside in my warm but slightly damp sleeping bag.

Late that afternoon it really started blowing hard, and *SW* could not be expected to stagger on much longer with so much sail up. The violent shaking of the rig when well over-powered and leaning too far over to call it sailing eventually became too much for me to put up with. I found the sacred storm jib and sat inside with it on my lap, bracing myself and locked in to the profound movement of *SW*.

This was the original storm jib from 1970-something. I'd had the sail hanks replaced and the sailcloth reinforced back in 1994 for the solo Tasman race, but other than that had not paid any attention to it at all. The cloth felt very thin and the hanks took a bit of work to free up, but it didn't complain and was soon crackling in the wind outside, then hastily sheeted in and doing the pulling expected of it. But how long it would last I wasn't sure.

Storm jib only up and the FMF adjusted to pull *SW* more away onto a broad reach, away we went. A consistent 42 knots from the repeater station on The Brothers islands sounded ominous but confirmed the whole reason for the overt windiness we were feeling.

The Cook Strait currents write their own rules, and combined with the wind a nasty rushing, overbearing and forceful sea was running. I tried to ignore it most the time, lying once again strapped up in the lee cloth on the windward side, with *SW* often sailing on her ear, heeled over and surging along, being jostled roughly about by the waves and occasional breaking tops. It was very uncomfortable sailing, but easier to bear than going to windward, if only because the progress south we were making at 4 to 5 knots was excellent.

There was good visibility, one of those clear and sunny but windy Wellington days that I had witnessed and experienced on land so many times before. The Inland Kaikoura range made a high visual landmark to steer for, and skirting the southern entrance to Cook Strait it was obvious we might escape the worst of it.

And so another noisy afternoon of mad motion started becoming evening, with a portent of a rough night to come written in the clouds racing above. I'd spent most of the afternoon listening to *SW* quickly sailing south while I lay inside fending off periodic cascades of accumulated salt water that relentlessly pooled on my elaborate plastic rubbish bag drip-defence system hanging above me.

A longer, steeper and more exciting sea was running as it got dark. It was now coming more on the back starboard quarter and pushing us on our sailing sleigh-ride south towards Kaikoura itself. In the twilight I got my wet-weather gear on and safety harness attached outside, and on the right slope of the right wave, I carefully climbed out into the cockpit and inserted the hatch-boards back in and closed up the hatch.

To keep the inside dry if we got smacked by a breaking wave was the first priority. To stay on board if I got smacked was the second, but equally important, priority.

Outside and clinging on for a very good reason, I had a good look around. *SW* was travelling a long way up the front of the waves as they marched on through and underneath us. The speed that the slope of oncoming water was travelling was hard to tell, but it was obvious the waves were not waiting for us.

The evening forecast was for an expected southerly change. Nothing epic to endure, just another well-precedented contrary set of sailing circumstances. Later that night it only took an hour for the day's northwesterly to quickly fall away and be replaced by a hard southerly wind, right on the nose. The leftover sea still travelling south took a while to flatten out through the rest of the night, but again I wasn't paying much attention, and was by then almost pretending not to be there.

SW slowly beat southeast away from the land, once more on the wind in an annoying way. Outdoors the FMF and double-reefed mainsail with new number two jib were doing all the work.

All the next day the wind softened, and once again a sloppy sea got the better of *SW*. Despite shaking out the reefs (untying the ropes that hold the slabs of mainsail shortened down onto the boom), as sailors say, and putting up larger headsails, we slowly sailed to a halt 50 miles true west of Kaikoura and 120 miles away from Lyttelton. There was neither wind nor land to be seen.

The next morning, a charming northeasterly agreeably filled in right from behind and off *SW* went again. Flat off and sailing faster as the wind increased, you could hear the miles gurgling and sloshing past outside.

Wing and wing, with the mainsail restrained to one side and the jib poled out to the other, progress was great — but with it came a constant roll from side to side. Something up front in the anchor locker under the dinghy on the deck was starting to slide from one side to the other. It was a monotonous, regular *thud* that didn't sound good. It sounded like the anchor was angry and trying to smash its way out into the sea.

New noises on board a boat should always be addressed promptly, but I couldn't be bothered untying the dinghy that was well lashed down on deck to get to the anchor locker. I had packed it full of plastic fenders in Auckland to stop the anchor thumping around, but something must have shifted. I told myself it would be alright and pretended it was only an annoying noise and nothing more. But there was that substantial thud each time it moved, and over a 12-hour period I told myself, on many occasions, to put up with it but do a better packing job next time we stopped.

SW kept rolling vigorously from side to side in what started feeling like an almost hazardous way. I decided to err on the side of avoiding breakages, rather than focusing on speed, and pulled down the mainsail.

While gybing the number one jib, I put the spinnaker pole down on the dodger for an instant to change hands or something, and in an instant it was gone. Just out of reach, I watched it take a slide off the side and overboard, down into 1372 metres of steely blue, uninviting sea.

There was something horrific in that moment of realization that *SW*'s long-serving vintage 1972 spinnaker pole was irretrievably gone. A disturbing sense of real loss engulfed me. The depth of the water below us made it even more apparent. All that way down, by itself it was going, going, gone to live in the darkness on the seabed floor.

After a little sit-down on the upturned dinghy on the foredeck, contemplating the fragility of our mutual existence (both mine and the spinnaker pole's), I gathered myself together and drilled holes in the ends of one of the dinghy oars, lashing that in place to pole out the jib instead. It held the sail poked out and stopped it flogging about.

Then I went back to bed to listen to the anchor sliding and thumping to the rhythmic and aggravating roll of *SW*.

After another night's appalling sleep punctuated by frequent scanning for lights and the constant solid banging by the aberrant anchor, it was time to make an important navigational decision. The possibility of pressing on for Port Chalmers had always been just that.

If this northeasterly wanted to stay, it was most welcome. I had enough food and water and enthusiasm (just) left on board to carry on past Banks Peninsula. It wasn't that much further — another 180 miles if you straight-lined it to Otago, but only 60 miles to Lyttelton if you wanted out.

Torchlight at 2 a.m.

Since we'd left Gisborne, the SSB marine forecasts had been prefixed with a navigational warning that had gradually been creating a heightened sense of apprehension in the crew. The gigantic floating icebergs that had been serving as platforms for sheep getting sheared and couples being married on had made their way up the east coast of the South Island, and the leader of the pack was now 30 miles east of Banks Peninsula.

Only 30 miles away, and floating our way. They were doing their inanimate business drifting northeast outside the 200-metre line. I really didn't want to bang into one.

The northeasterly was forecast to disappear within 12 hours and apart from that, I'd almost had enough. The windows had maintained their treachery and remained non-watertight. Let's go in to Lyttelton and sort things out.

After a morning sleep, at midday on 8 January I saw Banks Peninsula there on the horizon, and more low land was noticeable up almost behind us, stretching away to the north, just where it was supposed to be.

A group of Maui dolphins hung around for a look and did a swim-by before losing interest in us. I gave them as much eye contact as I got back, videoing them from the bow, and instigated a fair bit of inter-species banter that went unreciprocated.

The wind left us completely with the last of the light, 15 miles off Godley Head. For an hour I waited patiently and looked intently for any sign of a new land breeze springing up with the incoming darkness. It didn't look good. It looked like it was going to be a long windless night out there, tantalizingly close to all those Christchurch lights that were starting to appear and twinkle and taunt at me from afar.

I was not content to drift about any more; it was time to give the engine a chance to prove its worth. I'd bought a big truck battery and relied on that to power the SSB radio transmissions down the coast from Gisborne, and the engine had gone mostly unused. I expected to recharge the batteries at every stop. The engine delightfully started, and with all the hatches open, *SW* puttered along over a lethargic swell, heading for the bright light of Godley Head.

The exhaust pipe was leaking badly inside (difficult connection access was my excuse), and when the engine was running the whole of the inside of *SW* became the exhaust pipe. Or at least a part of the system. Before leaving Auckland, I'd also found another hot jet of exhaust-type fumes blasting out from somewhere equally inaccessible, behind the engine, when it was running.

On a trip to Waiheke I'd left a child I'm related to steering in the cockpit while I peered into *SW*'s constricted engine room and felt around the hot running engine and exhaust pipe system. The hot blast from near the bad exhaust pipe connection baffled me.

I remembered back to 1985 when first aboard *SW*, and how fast the engine made her go at full throttle. Almost a bow wave and planing, with quite a wake streaming out from behind. Tonight, after all those years, with the engine revving quite hard and the cabin full of fumes, the wake was almost negligible. Something wasn't right, but having no alternative I was prepared to make do.

The lights seemed to take far too long to get closer, but they eventually did. Six hours later, 15 miles; work it out for yourself. Just another minor test of emotional resolve or resignation; I couldn't work out which.

Another 4 miles pushing the tide; that was my excuse for such a bad performance. *Swirly World* tediously motored, as lifeless as a sailing boat can be, in the still darkness slowly up the harbour. Paranoid about bumping into any unseen thing, I was on maximum red alert after the last few days and nights in relatively sleepless circumstances.

It was certainly enjoyable looking at the slowly passing dark outlines of ridges on the exceedingly flat, calm water. Distant flashing lights were seemingly everywhere, and grave attention had once again to be paid to where I was steering *SW* and what obstacles might appear where, according to the chart on my lap, in the cockpit, by torchlight at 2 a.m.

Two forty-five and the flashing lights on the promised marina breakwaters looked close enough together to justify what was on the chart. I slowed the engine revs to an almost stalling putter, and carefully steered *SW* down a lane between pontoons, shut off the engine, and drifted in to bump up against a vacant pontoon by a wall.

I could see a Portaloo just up a walk-bridge, and I was ready to use it.

Not anything other than tired

Log: 3 a.m. 9th Jan 2007:

All motionless. Immensely still and tied up to the pontoon.
What a great feeling of absolute disengagement from the
usual overbearing focus of being on constant survival duty.
Looking at clouds around the moon, they seem to be jerking
and jumping unevenly, even though they should be just
floating there and slightly moving across the night sky
gradually.

This was perception distorted by being tuned into constant
motion. I was not out of it, not drunk; not anything other than
tired. But still the dark clouds crossing the bright, reliable stars
in my small view through the hatchway above me jumped

about without any apparent reason other than my own physical maladjustment to the immediate stationary circumstances.

Lying in the bunk, feet up, looking up, no motion whatsoever; unnaturally still. The clouds were doing things that clouds can't do unless they're UFOs. The perceived motion they were exhibiting was beyond reality. Something had happened to me. It was fun to watch until I fell asleep.

When I tried to walk up to the Portaloo, my imitation of how to do it was pathetic. A good bit of staggering, accompanied by the odd leg buckle, and a tight grip on the hand rail, got me there with little grace. Temporary sensory distortion stuff. Good, honest, out-of-it-for-free sensory maladjustment.

Three hours later, when it got light, I couldn't resist having a look around. This is always the best bit: the arrival after a sensory-adjusting trip, and absorbing all the new stuff you find yourself immersed in. *SW* looked genuinely and deservedly at ease, tucked in on the finger pontoon, secure and at rest. Just as if all that recent sailing had never been done.

Jobs

Remove and reseal windows
Buy more Sikaflex
New spinnaker pole
New storm jib
Get weather cloths reinforced
Charge batteries
Tighten port cap shroud
Tighten inner forestay
Get number one jib leech repaired
Buy decent rope and spare shackles

New bung to replace lost main-hatch drainage one

Dry everything inside

Buy salt, oranges, lemons, potatoes, petrol

Phone card top-up

Repair damaged anchor locker

Repack anchor locker

Sort charts

More water

13

A summer cruise to the South Island

Eight days and nights had got us to Lyttelton. All the non-stop sailing had instilled in me the ways of doing jobs carefully and effectively while expending the least amount of energy. I'd re-learnt how to do it, remembering all the other times I'd done it before.

I was tired, but elated by getting this far south. A few things needed to be done ASAP. The dripping windows were first, and a new storm jib next. The original storm jib was feeling too thin and ready to blow out along its seams if another gale was to provide encouragement. Also, being tied down to the stanchions and safety rail waiting for action and being slapped and taunted by the waves hadn't been doing it much good. And where I wanted to go we would probably need to use it.

Phil Fraser from *Emma, Lady Hamilton*, a large live-aboard ketch, pointed me towards a local Lyttelton sailmaker, also called Phil.

Phil Fraser was part of the Canterbury Cruising Club, and got *SW*'s permission to park sorted. I pulled her around inside the floating pontoon into the small space next to the boulders of the reclaimed car park.

Aft windows removed, *SW* didn't look right with two vulnerable rectangular holes in her. Ray from *Bandwagon* very kindly obliged me by holding the screwdriver on the pontoon while I tightened up the nuts on the inside. A consortium of sailing enthusiasts all agreed on what I had done wrong when putting the windows back in during the refit up the driveway in Titirangi. I'd liberally applied the gunk, then immediately fixed the frames in by tightening the nuts and bolts. Heaps of gunk had oozed out from around the edges of everywhere, and I'd been satisfied that was a good sign.

According to the amateur experts gathered around me on the pontoon, it was apparent I'd made a big mistake. The trick was to gunk it up, then wait patiently for half an hour for the gunk to go semi-hard, forming a bead that's not so easily squeezed out. Then you go for it. Following instructions, partly through a desire to please, *SW* got her windows back in and looked better for it, just before it started to rain.

Acutely aware of so much sailing ahead of us, I didn't want to hang around Lyttelton too long. While it was officially summer we had to push south as quickly as possible. The expedition demanded a sense of swiftness that was never far from my thoughts.

Stark's, an engineering firm that does the business at an industrial-strength level on huge boats, next to the massive dry dock for ships, looked like the place to procure a new spinnaker/headsail pole. Chris Cameron identified with *SW*'s progress made so far on our 'summer cruise to the South Island'. The right piece of round, hollow stainless extrusion, with holes for attachments on each end, was sourced and went to live on *SW*.

Scott of Antarctic fame had stopped in Lyttelton in 1910 aboard the *Terra Nova*. They'd been having a few underwater issues on the way to the ice on their voyage from Cardiff. The ship was dry-docked and worked on prior to heading off to the southern ice, and of course Scott never came back.

I took heart from the thought of all their activity back then in 1910 when they'd been just across the water from *SW*, like us in the sanctuary of Lyttelton. In that placid, safe corner it seemed as if only the ambition of mortals could jeopardize the integrity of any boat. My ambition was inconsequential in the scheme of things, but naturally a very big deal to me. It wasn't as big as going to the ice and the South Pole, but it was an ambition that would lead *SW* further south than she'd ever been before.

To get to a mere sub-Antarctic island would definitely do. It felt like we were, historically, at least, in good company.

I walked around in the rain, past the large petrol and diesel storage tanks, to see how Phil the sailmaker was getting on with the new storm jib. He wasn't there, so I carried on out to the end of the road and Magazine Bay, where I knew the Naval

Point Yacht Club and marina were situated.

Being technically on holiday, and away from home, the focus of only having to replenish *SW*'s stores and do maintenance for the next leg of the trip was pleasantly uplifting. One's whole sense of purpose was bound up for the moment in such a simple objective. To sail *SW* to 50 degrees south, where I was reliably informed we would find the Auckland Islands, was the objective. Being almost at latitude 44 degrees, we still had a lot of sailing miles to cover, all in the direction of more probable danger, but somehow it still felt like an exciting grand plan that was worth having a go at.

The Magazine Bay marina had taken a serious bashing back in 2001. The fetch (distance) across the bay at its greatest is no more than 4 miles. Nevertheless, a southerly storm of unexpected (or un-engineered-for) ferocity had arrived back then, and the reasonably new marina got a thorough seeing-to. It was tested and found wanting.

Who would have thought that such destructive, savage little seas could have manifested there at the bottom of Lyttelton harbour, almost on the mudflats of Governors Bay? But they did, and the wind was the only element responsible. A big state-of-the-then-art marina breakwater made of something floatable was pummelled to death by the waves. Broken loose and on the move, the breakwater created its own involuntary havoc and many clients called yachts were annihilated. Lines of unsuspecting, sedate and tidy, well-cared-for vessels tethered lovingly to piles and pontoons had no idea what they had done to deserve this. When it was over, masts were left poking up out of the sea, and whole sections of wooden walkways were submerged or missing.

Looking through the rain, six years on from that storm, it all looked fairly dismal still. Some veterans from that time were still floating neglected, growing their own private mussel farms and still wearing their untended battle scars. Large mooring-rope abrasions had cut through toe-rails and topsides; their badges of storm-damage honour most obvious. Absolutely tethered, they looked like they were not going anywhere soon.

It might have been because of the rain, but a shudder of something — a realization, or a reminder of potential danger — entered me. It took a lot of wind to do that kind of damage, and the question I was thinking about was 'Are we [*SW* and me] up for meeting that kind of malevolent wind velocity if it wants to come a-hunting for us?'

I wasn't convinced that we were. One can only do so much when it comes to preparation. Tramping back through the puddles to *SW*, with the new bright-orange storm jib over my shoulder, I tried to convince myself I was.

In three days I got plenty done, with the help of fellow sailing enthusiasts.

Ray drove me to the local chandlery on the other side of the Port Hills. A short-cut through the tunnel took us to a well-stocked little boat shop. I needed some decent rope instead of the polypropylene imitation that had been the only rope available from the auto shop on New Year's Eve back in Gisborne.

I found the quality stuff at the expected expensive price, and a replacement plastic screw-in bung. The missing one usually lived in the sliding hatch recess that was crucial for drainage to stop overhead water accumulating in the closed-up recess, and cascading merrily down on me, inside, in rough conditions. Mentally I was storm-proofing *SW* as best I could.

Phil Fraser also took me through the tunnel, and kindly waited while I ferried a shopping trolley's worth of food into the back of his van and onto the boat.

A well-appointed large blue yacht called *Haku* arrived one afternoon, direct from a long voyage to the Pacific Islands and back. Tied up next to us on the other side of the pontoon, they executed a highly efficient de-pack and quickly had *Haku* back and secure in her marina berth.

Sue Stubenvoll, a Nordic-looking blonde, was very interested in *SW* and an invitation to dinner was kindly extended. Not being able to carry *SW* up the hill to her place, I decided to go alone. It seemed to be one of the steepest streets in Lyttelton, and my walking legs were surprisingly inadequate.

Almost up in the clouds, Sue and Ken's place was a rural sanctuary complete with sheep in view on the hill outside the window. I took advantage of their hot running water and cleaned myself for the first time since Auckland. Hygienic and well fed, I found myself bad company as I fought to stay awake through conversations. I still had a bit of sleep to catch up on from the last leg, and boozing in the afternoon with songwriter and show-off Lindon Puffin hadn't helped my social endurance capacity.

Lyttelton is my kind of compact town. A history of numerous sailing-ship arrivals and departures back in the nineteenth century imbue its buildings (or what's left of them after the 2011 earthquake) and streets with a genuine sense of tangible nautical history. Even the rusting, disused railway lines that led from the town to the boat harbour reeked of memories unavailable to me.

Graham Perrem was preparing his yacht for the solo Tasman Race. He had a bakery over the hill, and glorious fresh bread appeared in *SW*'s cockpit without my having to ask. He'd sailed down south to Stewart Island before, and knew the places to stop or not. He also had a copy of the Mana Cruising Club guide which explains where to go down there, which he lent to me, again without having to be asked.

Three and a half days was what it took to be ready to go again. The final job was filling the hole in the anchor locker that had been punched straight through the plywood side of *SW*. All that sliding and banging about by the Danforth anchor had not been good. A slab of epoxy filler roughly applied did the job, and I managed to find some chunks of polystyrene to wedge into the cavity to prevent a repeat performance.

A good roast chicken dinner and too many offers of rum aboard *Emma, Lady Hamilton* the night before leaving had me fortified and ready to embark on the next leg. A forecast for little or nothing, and if anything from ahead, was not promising wind-direction news. But on the positive side, we were beset by a non-threatening weather system that looked set for some days to come.

On Friday 12 January 2007, a light northeasterly breeze filled in at midday, blowing gently down the harbour. It was the wrong direction for us, but a very nice day regardless. There was no point waiting for a brisk northwesterly to blow us south on a reach, although that would have been welcomed. We just had to get on with it, and carefully sail as many miles south as possible before the weather changed; and who knew what that might bring in these serious latitudes?

But now the sun was shining, and it was a perfect beat to windward, slowly out of the harbour. It was a chance to see the shore up close, sailing as near as I dared to go; going about just before we ran into the kelp-coated rocks.

Pushing out from the pontoon after another quick rush downstairs to start the forward-or-nothing engine, I got *SW* moving through the calm water without bumping anything in the inner boat harbour, and out we went through the breakwaters.

Enough breeze for efficient sailing, full main and genoa, hard on the wind. Wonderful scenic sailing in such a steep and relatively narrow harbour. It was, naturally, far more dramatic and endearing when viewed in daylight, unlike it had been on our arrival.

A little island on the other side of the harbour was in our way as we beat out on port tack. I went as close as possible and shouted threats, but still it wouldn't move.

Ripapa Island was a penal detention camp during World War I. In 1918 Count Felix von Luckner, a German naval officer, had been imprisoned there for 109 days. Having been previously confined as a German naval prisoner of war on Motuihe Island in the Hauraki Gulf, he had escaped, commandeered a scow, and sailed it (with captured New Zealanders on board) hundreds of miles northeast to Curtis Island in the Kermadecs group.

Shortly afterwards he was recaptured and returned to New Zealand, then sent south to a more secure island exile. Von Luckner would have been watching from behind the barbed wire as *SW* sailed up, tantalizingly close, before going about.

Von Luckner complained about the cold and boredom on tiny

Ripapa Island. Having had more walking room on Motuihe, and with the lights of Lyttelton civilization twinkling at him from across the bay, his confined and womanless, cold Canterbury winter nights would have felt as punitive as his captors intended them to be. Here the island now was, metres away; I could almost see him waving: 'Come over here, I'm ready to escape.'

We had to go about or hit the rocks, and looking back I could see him again, with his frustrated German mate Kircheiss, wishing they were sailing with us.

By midnight we were drifting in a sea mist with no visibility in a very light northeasterly, 7 miles northeast of Pigeon Bay. The wind had stayed light but reliable. As it got dark I preferred to get some sea room — perhaps too much so, but the wind had been blowing onshore all afternoon.

Running out of decent wind in the dark, the instinct was to pull up to windward away from the land until it got light, but going very slowly there was no real hurry or ability to do so. All night becalmed, we drifted the wrong way but didn't really notice, surrounded by a fine mist and seemingly suspended in a world of our own. Frequent bleary looks from the cockpit, out and around at the dark nothingness that surrounded us, always confirmed my confidence that no one else was anywhere nearby that night.

Daylight brought a freshening northeasterly wind to help *SW* get back on course, and by midday we were 3 miles east of Steep Head and running on a broad reach, looking at the grey cloud hanging low over Banks Peninsula. The compass course came right, 190 or 200 magnetic — suitably south — and *SW* was away again, freely sailing with the FMF steering us south.

A New Zealand navy ship, HMNZS *Kahu,* came up close in the afternoon to have a look at *SW*. It rolled horrendously, the superstructure looking a bit tall for its own good. I spoke to them on the VHF, explaining the circumstances regarding my solo cruise to the South Island. They too were cruising down there, and around the bottom bit of Fiordland on fisheries patrol, and we agreed we might meet again.

A good day's sailing was had by all: 20 knots from the northeast and no possibility of wasting progress by peeling off into Akaroa Harbour for a look, even though I wanted to. The peninsula became consumed in low mist, then was gone, and by the time it got dark *SW* was out of wind, and out of sight of land.

After another broken night of something that can't be called sleep, we were, according to the GPS, 35 miles south of Akaroa, 25 miles southeast of Lake Ellesmere, and 65 miles short of Timaru. We were also becalmed, with no visibility in sea mist but far enough offshore to feel safe from the threat of breakers and rocks.

The ice bulletins were still coming through on the SSB radio warnings. *SW* was now as close to them as I felt we needed to be. The navigational plan was to stay inshore well enough away from them, out there drifting northeast on the edge of the 200-metre line. They were 20 miles southeast of us at the time. That's what they said, in serious tones, too often each day on the radio.

With a very dull and settled weather forecast that promised light southerlies on the nose, or nothing much, accompanied by afternoon sea breezes, curiosity got the better of me. The bad visibility (some said it was from the proximity of cold ice) seemed to lift a bit with the mid-morning sun, and with a contrary south-southwesterly breeze over a flat sea, it seemed only right to head southeast on starboard tack, offshore, for a look.

In settled conditions a big iceberg would be quite a find.

By 5.30 that night there was nothing to be found, just the usual seascape of grey surface, grey sky, nothing different or compelling to greet the eye. We went about for another night becalmed, listening to the slap of wires inside the mast and refusing to let them drive me crazy.

Without labouring the detail, although I had to at the time, a good trustworthy northeasterly returned with the morning sun and *SW* started surging productively along again, aiming on course for the Otago Peninsula 100 miles away. One hundred miles away sounds like a reasonably short non-stop sailing distance to me. You can usually stay awake for that many miles if you have to. *SW* has often done 100 miles in 24 hours.

Another night of no wind became emotionally taxing, however. It was written on my paper chart that an adverse current was making more than the most of any moment we spent becalmed. This current was sucking northeast up the coast, and it didn't care about where *SW* was attempting to go. The forecast started promising wind from the west, so drawing in closer to the South Island felt like the right sailing thing to do.

In the 1980s I'd spent a few years sporadically frequenting Timaru, Oamaru and Balclutha on tour with a band, playing music in pubs and meeting temporary new friends quite often. Most tours provided the opportunity to commandeer the band van and get to the town breakwater, or isthmus, where the local sea was to be found. I visually imprinted the approaches to Timaru Harbour, Oamaru, Port Molyneux (Kaka Point) and Otago Heads in my brain. At the time I hoped that one day I might get to be there again, but this time by boat.

Now it was happening. The next day, once the wind kicked in after another night tediously rocking with all sails strapped down, I could see that *SW* was 15 miles off the high headland of Oamaru. The distant view of that headland almost completed my circuit in time, 22 years later. Fulfilling that earlier person's ambition to be sailing out there, in that view. It felt so long ago that it had, perhaps, become a memory that belonged to someone else.

14

Conspicuous

The wind was as predicted, and came occasionally from all over the place. I diligently sailed whenever it would let me, acutely aware that a current, up to 1½ knots in places, was flowing against us.

No-wind nights drifting backwards were to be expected, and out of sight of land, the benefits from turning the inside of *SW* into an exhaust pipe and getting a couple of fuel-burning knots out of her became more attractive. But it wasn't really worth doing; not enough fuel and not enough thrust.

The next day the wind came back, pushing *SW* from behind, and all on board became happy with only 30-odd miles to the Otago Peninsula left to run. In the afternoon the weather forecast started getting serious, with talk of a southerly front moving our way quite quickly. Easily convinced by previous delusions of a sense of 'almost being there but not', I happily convinced myself that being just off Moeraki Point, only 25 miles from the Otago Peninsula, we were certainly almost there. No nasty southerly front was going to beat us to Dunners …

A large pod, or school, or whatever, of dolphins joined us for an hour and made the most of showing off, leaping and falling most impressively all around us. I filmed them up close from the pulpit at the bow, and from the stern, and there was more two-way major eye contact for no apparent reason on their part, other than their own self-amusement.

The co-operative northeasterly had gone more east and then started faltering, which could only be expected given the forecast. I wasn't comfortable with the prospect of an adverse wind change and paid intense attention to the southern horizon, where we wanted to go. Sure enough, there it was. Low clouds and some surface rain connection, just within sight and coming our way.

The full mainsail and genoa that had been so relevant in making good light-wind progress seemed inappropriate for what was now visibly rushing at us across the sea. Getting up out of the cockpit after steering lethargically for hours, I managed to remove the genoa and clip on the number one jib, and make a start on reefing the main. As I was doing so the southerly gale arrived in a huff with plenty of puff. It was moving faster than I expected, and stronger. A classic Wellington southerly change (the kind I grew up with) that had no intention of mucking around.

It was instant wind evilness as far as I was concerned. Gale force and laced with rain and lifting salt-water spray, the wind was in a hurry and once again we were in its way. *SW* staggered, over-canvassed, while I slowly executed a second reef in the mainsail and then withdrew to the cockpit to brace myself and do some serious hand-steering on the wind.

What had been a nice day with the prospect of arriving at the Otago Harbour some time later that night was instantly blown away. A short, steep sea quickly built up, and it became obvious, by the angle of heel and the staggering sideways motion, that I still had too much sail up. Easing the mainsheet a bit to take the pressure off the mainsail wasn't really helping, so with the safety harness clipped onto the wire that runs the length of *SW*'s heavily tilted deck, I climbed up and along the windward side to drop the jib and pull up the smaller number two.

Those few moments with the sail pulled up but not sheeted in allowed the sail to thrash about in a noisy, disturbing way that never looked, nor sounded, good. The dash back to the little winch to pull the leeward rope tight and sheet the sail in was more of a jungle-gym climb, holding on to the solid bits of the boat for security.

I loathe being over-canvassed and not sailing as efficiently as possible to windward. Letting the mainsail out a bit to shake itself through sporadic squalls is OK, but being over-powered on a constant basis is unacceptable. With everything sheeted in, *SW* now felt well balanced and totally in control, regardless of the turmoil of steep waves and rushing wind that seemed intent on sending us off to the north, from where we'd just come. It was time to fully apply myself to the art of heavy-weather windward sailing. This was a fight to get there now. The waves were coming surprisingly steeply and close together, making it rough, slow progress. A note on the chart said that a current was running south inshore, where we were, against the gale, and that perhaps explained the sea state.

As it was getting dark we went about again, 5 miles off Katiki Point, and started heading painstakingly offshore for the night. The high land of Mt Pleasant and Puketapu showed up to the west in the gaps between the rain, and it was mildly comforting knowing it was that close — but without a sheltered anchorage available, it was no good to us. There was a slight temptation to give up and run downwind to shelter at Moeraki, but having no appropriate large-scale chart and remembering the kelp-strewn rocks I'd mentally recorded some years ago from the shore, on another tour, it would have been asking for trouble. Especially in the dark.

A few times I'd driven along State Highway 1, by the stretch of Katiki Beach where the road follows the coast. It was always refreshing to see the sea there, and now we were on it, in between waves, looking back at the land.

As I sat there in *SW*'s tiny, secure cockpit, slowly slogging to windward and the southeast, the Katiki Point light started blinking its reassuring existence every 12 seconds, and I resigned myself to a long, relatively non-productive sailing night to come. Four hours later we'd sailed 10 very uncomfortable miles, and I had been forced, out of a lack of physical endurance, to put myself to bed. The FMF was doing a grand job outside, steering. I expected no valuable distance to be made good, and by two in the morning my expectation was still being fulfilled.

It was dismal sailing that would probably put a lot of people off — but it was self-inflicted, and I was on holiday so I really had nothing to complain about. Trying to rest as *SW* smacked away, jerking and shuffling up and down, too often to count, was monotonous to the max. This was endurance sailing, and in a way what I'd come for.

A loud, heavy *bang* and *thud* followed by more substantial, repetitive knocks up on deck sent me into a clumsy fumbling frenzy to get up and outside as soon as possible.

It didn't take long to realize that another living creature had joined us on deck, and was very unhappy about it. Constant banging, accompanied by the odd squawk, continued while I got up and out through the companionway into the wet, turbulent darkness on deck. In the time it took to get there, and shine the torch through the flying spray, our visitor had gone.

I'd seen a lot of inanimate albatrosses, young and old, floating on the sea earlier in the day. They just sat there on the surface, staring at *SW* as we slowly sailed by. I had no idea that some of them enjoyed night flying. The bird obviously hadn't paid attention to *SW*'s masthead tri-colour LED navigation light beaming out at the top of the mast. A low flyer, just skimming the steep waves, it must have found it a shock to glide smack into *SW*'s mast, stays and sails.

I expected to find a torn sail or a dangling, broken stay, or even a big bird blood-bath on the deck, but thankfully nothing was different. I'm not sure the albatross, or whatever it was, came off entirely unscathed.

Going about again at 1 a.m., I got the FMF locked in with just the right amount of tension from the wind on the blade and the spanner on the locking bolt. In a disturbed sea state, positioning the wind-vane blade to make it steer *SW*, balanced and sailing as efficiently as possible with me hiding inside, was most important.

Five a.m., and we were close enough to Danger Reef (3 miles away) to go about again and keep sticking at it. It seemed we'd had a couple of big knocks sailing-wise in the night. When you are sailing to windward, one tack is often more favourable than the other — it will let you point closer to where you want to go (a lift) compared with the other tack (a knock). When racing, picking the lifts and knocks, essentially the slight shifting of the wind in gusts or local trends, is one of the fun parts of it all and often provides the most opportunity to gain distance on your opposition. You need to be good at reading them.

The big knocks along with the current had meant we'd sailed only 10 miles to windward during the whole night. But at dawn, the wind seemed to be veering more to the south-southwest and it felt like we might be on a lift at last. The worst of the weak southerly front had hammered on through the night, and left 30 knots and a steep, inappropriate-sized sea for *SW* and me to cope with.

I'd picked up phone coverage the day before and now had people expecting me. Karyn's parents were living in Dunedin at the time, and my father-in-law, Keith, had been following our tediously slow progress with great interest. He wanted an ETA. I had given one, but then involuntarily kept having to extend it.

Dunedin had become a compulsory stop destination on our expedition. Not just anyone can go to the Auckland Islands. They are now regarded as special environmentally preserved pieces of land, and to be allowed to go there and touch them, you have to be special as well. That was what DOC told me in no uncertain terms. I had to apply for a permit and be perceived as a fit and proper person to be allowed to step on the islands. Not only me, but the boat as well.

The Auckland Islands are a marine reserve, and the DOC people are understandably concerned about pests (smaller than myself) again being liberated in areas where hard work has been done to eradicate them previously. Invasive seaweeds are high on their list of priorities, and I had been directed to Bluff or Dunedin (the choice was mine) in order to have the bottom of *SW* inspected by divers to ensure no nasty invasive seaweeds like *Undaria* were hitching a ride south to set up an environmentally unwanted colony, like the humans had done in 1850.

The DOC guy organizing his calendar, and that of the divers, preferred some certainty, but fully understood when I rang him that morning to let him know we couldn't make the appointment because we'd been detained by a southerly gale that was now subsiding but was still being difficult. He laughed down the phone at me, talking of how his house had been shaking last night when the front came through.

We made another date, but Keith just had to keep waiting, as although I could finally see Taiaroa Point at the mouth of the Otago Harbour, it was obvious that while it was becoming a sunny day, the wind was still fresh from the wrong direction. Covering that distance on a time-consuming zigzag course, beating to windward and not pointing where you want to go, made predicting an ETA out of my realm of bothering.

Just keep sailing without the expectations of others, and it all feels far more endurable — tiredness was obviously getting the better of me. The wind eased, but stayed coming at us from the wrong way, so *SW* slugged on, all wet with passing spray and waves.

Mid-morning, I saw a smallish fishing boat running downwind, upwind from us and obviously dragging some fishing gear. I put *SW* about to save him freaking out about possibly scooping us up in the net he was dragging behind. We headed back in towards Blueskin Bay and the South Island. He might not have seen us anyway.

By 2.30 in the afternoon we were there — almost. Keith had been expecting us for far too long, and had given up waiting out on the breakwater. Despite the previous horrendous night, it had turned into a perfect-looking Otago afternoon.

I tacked us in as close as I dared, to take us west of Heyward Point and into a sheltered bay to the west. A few more long tacks out and about, and there it was — the breakwater at the entrance to Otago Harbour, tucked just inside Taiaroa Head. The closer we got, the flatter the water became and the easier the sailing. I'd almost had enough of beating to windward, but the view and incoming tide were more than enough to keep me totally enthralled.

Sailing in, by wind alone, is always the most gratifying way to arrive somewhere new. This looked like an ideal opportunity and the narrowing gap up ahead to windward, just to the left of the settlement of Aramoana, required my full attention. With the help of the last of the incoming tide some enjoyable accurate sailing was had, tacking carefully up past the old battered concrete breakwater and the weedy sunken rocks on one side; the steep port-side cliffs of the albatross colony and the ancient concrete gun emplacements on the other.

Once we were inside the narrow mouth of the Otago Harbour, a new set of minor navigational challenges revealed themselves. Up the little channel we went, keeping to where the buoys denoted we should be. You could see by the colour of the water where you should *not* be. It was extremely gratifying and easy sailing on a beam reach, all the way over the very flat sea.

Port Chalmers up ahead and nestled beneath the hills looked safe and charming. Tucked into a bend in the channel it also looked like a place worth stopping at, especially seeing that the tide had turned and there was no point in trying to get to the Otago Yacht Club where the DOC divers expected us in the morning. Better to wait till the tide started coming back in, as it always conveniently does.

Carey's Bay looked like the place to be. Tied up with very long lines to the fishing-boat wharf, *SW* had arrived and was ready to wait for the turn of the tide, and so was I. Karyn's parents, Keith and Shirley, found us there, and back in Ravensborne for a shower, I felt as if I'd just flown down from Auckland, apart from being more fatigued than usual. The view from their window across the bay was exactly the same as it had been back when I last looked out of it, Boxing Day 2004, when the Indonesian tsunami had punctuated the serenity of that Christmas period with its overwhelming contrast.

Barely awake but in good spirits, I was back at 9.45, just after dark, to join the tide journeying up the harbour. The cabin was full of exhaust fumes, and there was just enough steerage. All the many red- and green-lit channel markers snaking up-harbour did their best to confuse me as they moved by; and then, somehow, we were almost there.

The mouth of the man-made harbour at Otago Yacht Club is quite narrow and, I found out, shallow as well. I had no idea that having arrived early, before dead-high tide, we would be denied access.

By then I was selfishly ready to tie up, lie down inside *SW* and lose consciousness as soon as possible. But it wasn't to be just then. The engine kept ticking away, prop going around, but normal progress dissolved. *SW* came to a sluggish halt right in the middle of the narrow entrance. We were stuck in the mud, and motoring was only digging the keel in deeper.

A sense of nautical duty beset me and I was tempted to put out a VHF message registering *SW* as a navigational hazard, hard aground in the mouth of a potentially busy waterway. But there was no movement from any other boats in the basin and, all things considered, it looked like a very quiet night on the water.

I tried to rock *SW* from side to side, then lean over one side to get the keel out of the mud, but it didn't work. I ended up opting for a quick lie-down inside, once again almost beyond the realm of caring. That strange relentless capacity for subconscious self-preservation kicked in at midnight, and jumping up out of my coma of non-involvement I found *SW* floating free again, the keel nudging the side of the mud lane. We were now allowed to move into the sanctuary of the Otago Yacht Club basin.

Five days and nights had elapsed since von Luckner had enviously watched us sail out of Lyttelton. It had been a slow passage, but we had avoided the ice and sailed through our third southerly front so far. All dark and suitably devoid of humans, this was *SW*'s moment again — on time, and ready for the DOC divers who were scheduled to turn up in the morning.

A few hours after it got light they did arrive: three people, one more attractive than the others. An elaborate camera system was set up and the diver went down, sending back video pictures of all he was seeing on the underside of *SW*, with us watching on the pontoon monitor. No bad weed was found, and all was good down below. There was no charge to me for this environmental service, and the whole thing was fascinating. Their real business was dealing to bigger fishing boats that were quite possibly dragging an invasively unpleasant thingy, just waiting to repopulate where they are not welcome. Fair enough.

With the physical all-clear given for *SW*, I was asked to appear in person in Invercargill to meet DOC and get the low-down on how an environmentally friendly boatie should behave at the Auckland Islands. Sensible precautions to stop pests gleefully leaping ashore and chewing on baby special somethings, and serious crewing policy when anchored with crew ashore all had to be addressed.

Again, it is fair enough for someone to be concerned, yet I felt we offered little to be worried about, given the scale of us, and took minor offence at being summonsed south by road to discuss things. Sense prevailed, and a good phone call was had by all. I swore to alleviate all their concerns to the best of my ability, and talked through the practicalities of what I was expected to do when I got to the Auckland Islands. It was exciting stuff. I'd told them I was going there; I'd come clean about my true intentions. It meant a lot to me. I wanted to go there, but wasn't sure I'd make it. As a subject of the wind, there can be no surety about reaching a destination. You never know what you're going to get.

I was still made to go to Dunedin and see DOC. I would have preferred not to. It was unnecessary and, worse than that, conspicuous. So conspicuous that the local paper and TV station were invited by DOC to have a look, and trumpet their activities for the greater public good.

I was happy with having come so far south in *Swirly World*. Showing off with *SW* was fun. But I had no desire to court attention prior to leaving and trying to sail alone all the way to the Auckland Islands. But because I had to get a permit to sail there, the cat was now officially out of the bag.

SW was, conspicuously, tied up in the Otago Yacht Club marina and being carefully inspected by DOC while I was reprovisioning for an expedition to the Auckland Islands. It was official. I read it in the morning paper myself. Now people who had seen *SW* on local TV and read about my Auckland Island ambition in the paper started coming down the pontoon for a look. No more pretending I'd make do with a look at Stewart Island like most of the Dunedin cruising fleet sometimes did.

It was time to find somewhere more discreet to hang out. *SW*'s bottom needed another wipe-down, just to make sure we were going to be sailing as quickly as possible in the coming weeks. The locals let me know about a grid with piles to lean *SW* against, when the tide went out, back up the harbour near Deborah Bay.

Under no pressure, and with formalities concluded, no wind and late in the day on an outgoing tide, we were away again. There was enough water at the yacht club entrance this time to ensure *SW* didn't get tripped up in the mud. That's all I remember, puttering slowly up the winding channel with all the hatches open and exhaust fumes streaming out behind us.

It was Saturday night in Port Chalmers, and by the time we got there the Carey's Bay Hotel was relatively pumping. I drank enough beer to make myself feel momentarily not quite so uneasy about the next leg of our expedition, then some time later lost consciousness in *SW*. The alarm woke me, my mouth dry, before dawn, and I puttered us up against the piles that I'd been reliably informed had a few beams under the water next to them that would take the weight of *SW*.

On the grid with the tide out, I finally had the chance to have a good look at the keel and skeg joints that had been the focus of so much of my attention up the driveway in the past two years. *SW* had taken quite a stressful slamming about on the way from Auckland, and I was eager to see if the new skeg and repaired keel were holding up. Sure were.

Danny was another solo sailor from Dunedin and he was very keen on *SW*, specifically the shape of her. He'd done his solo miles in these latitudes in his own larger yacht and knew the wind around the South Island. But now he was determined to build a tiny, 11-foot (3$\frac{1}{3}$-metre) ocean cruiser out of alloy with hard multiple chines like *SW*'s. He subsequently has, and cruised it to Stewart Island. We can expect more impressive endurance sailing from Danny in the future. He also had some photocopied pages from a guide about anchorages in the Auckland Islands that someone had written and I'd never seen before; I was most grateful.

There was now no excuse to stay any longer in Port Chalmers, so as soon as we started floating, I was keen to get away. Too keen for one awkward moment, when I rushed below to turn on the engine and get a bit of steerage control in the light wind, at the top of the tide. Revving up too soon, I managed to fluff my steering and get one of *SW*'s side safety lines caught under a sticky-out bit on the finger pontoon.

With no reverse, I manhandled *SW* back to untangle things, but the damage to the base of an already weakened stanchion was done. With a little extra wiggling it was ready to break off, and I made a mental note not to put any weight ever again on the safety rails on the port side. I never did anyway, but now it was confirmed that I shouldn't.

I waved a flustered wave to Keith and Willy (his dog), and motored away into the channel to pull up the sails. The minor damage to the stanchion was my fault, and I pondered the solemn realization that *everything* from now on would be up to me, and me alone, for good or bad.

15

A temporary root into the earth

A beautiful Otago afternoon with a light northeasterly wind that the forecasters promised would freshen in the night and blow us south was all we could hope for, and that's what we got on that Sunday evening, 21 January 2007.

They'd been drinking all afternoon at the Carey's Bay Hotel and it looked like a very inviting place to be, tucked in there under the hills, just across the calm water. A good night's sleep would be great, but the wind, once again my master, was dangling a favourable carrot in our direction, and only a landlubber would not make the most of it. By now, the darkest night made little difference to *SW* or me.

Keith and Willy were out on the old concrete breakwater at Aramoana waiting for us when we got there.

Carefully zigzagging to windward, the noise of the engine gone, on the beginning of the outgoing tide, sailing efficiently and bound for the Auckland Islands over 350 miles south-southwest. This was the real start of the trip, and I was acutely aware of it. Getting to Dunedin was like getting to the starting line only. From now on, although the wind would dictate the pleasantness or unpleasantness of our sailing experience, I had to get this part of the expedition right. There was nothing else to do or think — just get on with it. Sail.

After a brief waving session, Keith started walking back down the long breakwater to his car, looking lost in thoughts that I hoped were not full of concern for us. Willy the dog had the right idea, as he was fully distracted by seashore smells and frantically scouting about for some living creature to harass and/or taste.

We sailed clear of Taiaroa Head, then bore away for the open water east of Cape Saunders; watching the sun go down over the nearby Otago Peninsula. I'd been there in various states of elation and/or disrepair over the years, looking longingly offshore, sometimes trying to write a good poem or song. The number of tidal inlets and coastal indentations had impressed me, but tonight there wasn't really time to revisit those memories. I had more important sailing to do.

The first of the rain came splattering down on us from the northeast, not long after it got dark. In totally the right direction, even the rain could exact no complaints from me as we sailed quickly just to the left of the land.

Cape Saunders light flashed goodnight, and with no sign of

ships nearby I took its advice and went inside to roll uncomfortably about for a number of hours, leaving my Faithful Mechanical Friend to steer and the number two jib, all on its own, to sledge us south, down the growing short, steep and occasionally breaking waves.

I popped out for a compulsory look every 20 minutes, given our proximity to the coastal shipping lane; the friendly lights of St Clair and St Kilda made an appearance some time after midnight and shone their emotional reassurance at us between rain squalls. The lights were a welcome change from the previous dark foreboding nothingness of the coast north of Maori Head.

And that was about it. Our course took us well away from Taieri Mouth as we ran almost flat off, surging downhill at 4 to 6 knots, with not many regrets and once again not much interest in the immediate surroundings. Twelve hours had gone by, mostly covered in night and rain and plenty of wind, since we'd left Carey's Bay. Twelve very productive sailing hours had got us 45 miles under the keel, and left us slowly sailing south-southwest of Taiaroa Head.

At 6 a.m. the forecast was for a fresh offshore northwesterly with another southerly front to follow. Determined not to let the wind get the better of me, I set a compass course for Nugget Point, a proper corner of the lower South Island, and started sailing attentively for it. More hours went by as I sat there holding the stainless-steel tiller, making the most of the then faltering breeze. The short-lived northeasterly blow had departed, and a new set of sailing circumstances was emerging.

That's one of the nuances of long-distance sailing: constantly having to adjust to a new wind pattern and trying to resist the natural temptation to anthropomorphize the wind (turn it into a thing with human emotions). I told myself that with our combined experience (*SW*'s and mine), together we knew what to do. (Anthropomorphosis of boats is well precedented and in nautical circles quite normal.)

By midday the barometer was dropping, and the sky was starting to look a strange pale-yellow colour strewn with dark clouds. The short but sharp southerly gale off Moeraki had shaken my confidence slightly, and it seemed another one was on its way. I tried to act normal, and just sat there holding the piece of stainless tiller while often eyeing the growing land of Molyneaux Bay and Mount Misery just north of it.

The northwesterly never properly filled in and let us down completely near Nugget Point, and I resorted to turning *SW*'s interior into an exhaust pipe again to assist our tediously slow sailing. A current of up to 2 knots was listed as being against us, right here, right now, and any chance of accelerating against it became a craving.

And then, as the hours went by — there they were on the starboard bow, slowly growing closer and more visually defined. Nugget Point, Kaka Point and Port Molyneaux. Another magic circle of personal closure for me.

In the 1980-somethings I'd done a lot of Balclutha gigs. The hotel on the corner with accommodation above and a balcony to sunbathe on with a view over the main street had always been a favourite with the band. A select group of insistent groupies had followed us in their car, after explaining the way out to Kaka Point and the lighthouse beyond. The local pronunciation of 'Kaka' was a source of amusement and ridicule in the rental van on the way to the sea. The non-Maori meaning of the word being 'faeces' naturally resulted in humour all round.

I was keen to see the sea, in case one day I could find myself just out there in that view, beyond the top of the cliffs: the seaward approaches to Balclutha and the mouth of the Clutha River. Those in the band who had ulterior carnal motives came as well. It was a pleasure to see the harsh kelp-ridden coastline exposing itself to another inevitable low tide. I'd read a book about it: the French wanting to get ashore here from sailing ships, crossing a bar into the Clutha River that had then shifted and was now somewhere else.

The lighthouse was a long walk for some of the band crew, who remained preoccupied back in the van. There it was, a tough corner of the South Island, where many a compass course had been altered when following the coast north or south by sea. The romance of all that random trying on land and sea had strangely connected with me at Nugget Point. And now here I was again, this time doing what I had then wished to do. It was only 22 years later. Better late than never.

But looking at Port Molyneaux, the expanded Kaka Point settlement and Nugget Point, surmounted by an ominous mustard-yellow sky and low banks of purple clouds, I realized that I had better get a move on. I didn't want to do another night smacking away against a gale-force southerly if there was any way to avoid it. And obviously there was. There was no need to fall away on starboard, like Captain Cook did near here in 17-something, sailing away from the shore hazards and having a totally unpleasant night reaching east in a gale on starboard. Not if I could help it. Again I became acutely aware that only I could help me. I was totally in control of my own destiny and experiencing a strange mixture of dread and elation, both at the same time.

A rugged fishing community had resided and operated just in the northern lee of Nugget Point many years ago. They pulled their fishing boats out of the water as a mark of respect for northerly onshore gales, then presumably pushed them out again afterwards.

Hanging out with those long-gone sea-sailing ancestors was one option, but while the light wind remained from the northwest, I wasn't keen on anchoring on a sort of exposed lee shore, being worried about the anchor and listening to breakers trying to squash the beach all night. The next option was looking fairly compelling on the chart, but as I was motor-sailing against the current with not enough wind and feeling a bit nervous, it took longer than necessary for me to see what, according to the chart, was a promising potential sanctuary, away from the southerly front soon to arrive. Somewhere to anchor, to put down a temporary root into the earth that would keep me and *SW* where we wanted to be — sheltered and relatively secure when the wind decided to turn into Satan for the night.

The Catlins was fast becoming our almost mythical sanctuary as I tediously monitored our dismal progress past Nugget Point. All sorts of sharp, dramatic pinnacles of rockiness like the Triplets snarled in the backwash of their waves at *SW*'s passing. Slowly, at not many knots, we left them behind.

The sky was looking even more serious, and having seen that look before I was more than in a hurry to get an anchor down and let out plenty of chain. Anything to avoid a tired night heading offshore, smacking into waves (and albatrosses), and only gaining a few miles in our chosen direction. A big safe bay opened up to the south of Catlins Head and it looked, from our distance, the ideal sanctuary from any southerly. The only hitch was a sand bar across the entrance to the tidal estuary. There was a line of regular white water closer inshore where my chart showed I should steer if I wanted to find the entrance to the winding channel that led to the placid inner haven that I was by now quite keen on.

SW slowly motored past a small fizz-boat well loaded down with fishing people. They were hanging on right to the last moment before pulling up the anchor and blasting back to the ramp. They eventually did so and roared past with a few waves, then cut their power and circled back for a closer look at *SW*. I asked them about the entrance to the more sheltered upper reaches of the estuary, and enquired as to what the bar was like. The driver wasn't that positive about it, given the state of the tide, and he failed to instil any confidence in me about having a go at getting in.

He offered me a crayfish, almost out of guilt at knowing that his local knowledge had disappointed me, although I tried not to show it. I said no thanks but thanks, and took up his second choice of a stopping place that we agreed should be safe as long as the wind didn't shift: Jack's Bay, just to the south.

The low, malevolent clouds got closer, and then the oily, still surface of the sea became ruffled as the first advance party of the southerly arrived; dead from where we wanted to go. But we were almost there then, and scanning the shoreline for the right place to anchor.

It was low tide and a barrier of giant floating kelp between us and the lethargic waves flopping on the beach looked like a good reason to stop. This kind of seaweed growing up from the seabed floor or submerged rocks had always made me feel unwelcome. Stand-alone bull kelp swaying ominously just under and on the sea's surface is not attractive stuff to someone in a boat.

At 7 p.m. in a light southwesterly just before the rain, the anchor went down and *SW* drifted back, away from the kelp bed, with me feeding out copious metres of chain to give the Danforth anchor the best possible chance to keep her exactly where she needed to stay for what had all the hallmarks of turning into a long and nasty night.

Close enough to the beach to have a good look at what was going on ashore, it was good to see that some people were still enjoying themselves that evening. It looked like a great holidaying time was being had by most. A big white camper-van was parked up with two tourists stoically sitting in their portable folding deck-chairs in the middle of the beach, on the verge of packing up and leaving now that the sun had gone and the clouds, wind and rain were creeping up over the low hill range behind them. Making the most of the last of the daylight, some teenagers were rushing in and out of the small surf waves on the sand, shouting squeals of cold-water bravery.

Down the east end of the beach, a cluster of 'cribs', known as baches in the North Island, all looked occupied, festooned with towels and other debris from a good day at the beach. As the rain started speeding up and coming at us from across the low line of hills to the south and over the beach out to us, it looked like the cribs, tucked down low and facing north, were the place to be tonight.

This was our first anchoring experience on the expedition,

and it was something I knew I would have to get used to. You feel more vulnerable at anchor, no doubt about it. Give me an inspected mooring any day or, if you can afford it, a marina berth inside a stone breakwater on a floating pontoon. None were available that night, and I peered, feeling quite serious, downwind to see where, if we dragged our anchor, we might end up. It was the north arm of Catlin's Bay, a beach with big, breaking ocean surf, 2 miles away. There was plenty of space and, hopefully, time to react if I found *SW* dragging her anchor and heading away from Jack's Bay.

The other issue at anchor is what to do if the wind shifts. The forecast was for a southerly front passing through in the night followed by moderate southeasterlies. Tuhawaiki Island made a bit of a breakwater to the southeast, but a narrow little channel between it and the rest of the South Island worried me. With any extra easterly slant to the wind we could be in for a bit of a sea building up in the anchorage. That was a worst-case scenario, but as the night stretched on my constant preoccupation became listening for unusual sounds related specifically to *SW*'s ground tackle.

On arriving, through the binoculars I had had a good look (as best you can, bobbling about on a ground swell) at the clientele in the cribs. Some of them seemed interested in seeing *SW* in their usually boat-less view of the bay. Or so I thought at the time, alone and enjoying being within sight of human company.

I'd given up the idea of untying the dinghy on the fore-deck and rowing ashore for a chat or to stretch my legs. With the barometer still dropping, the south-southwesterly wind steadily increasing and rain rushing over *SW*, it wasn't worth going ashore. There were no shops I could see, and nothing was needed in the ship's stores. More importantly, an anchor watch needed to be kept in place. No shore-leave tonight.

It blew hard and rained hard in the night, and at 3 a.m. I got my wet-weather gear on and went outside to let out more chain. It was then high tide, and for the last hour or so *SW* had occasionally been jerking horribly at her anchor chain when lifting on the surge of a swell passing under us. Sick of hoping for the best and putting up with it, I was finally out there, peering to windward into virtually zero visibility.

I quickly retreated and put on the spreader lights that bathed the deck in 12-volt light, then was back on deck and into it. I let out as much chain as possible, then retreated back to the cockpit and listened for more jerks. None came, and the increased scope of the chain length seemed to be taking the lift and fall and hard-out pressure of the gale-force wind well.

I'd bought a 20-dollar, 500,000-candlepower cigarette-lighter-powered spotlight from a supermarket years ago with the intention of using it on some future expedition, and now was the time. Shining it out into the black wind and rainy nothingness to windward and the beach, all I saw was wet, white-out rain and not much beyond. With no lights on deck or in hand, the sea ahead and bay and low hill-line behind it was complete blackness. I might as well been out at sea in terms of the view. Then, while I was peering around, hoping to get my eyes more accustomed to the dark, a light came on in a crib.

Someone was up at 3 a.m. with me, and had noticed *SW*'s short light-show there in that horrible night of too much wind and rain. The light was a welcome reference point as to where we were, and whether we were dragging the anchor. To me just then it was a strange moment of human connection in a gale, a connection with someone I wasn't ever likely to meet.

It blew hard for the rest of the night, but fortunately *SW* and the shore light stayed where they were expected by me to be. Mean, invisible gusts flew down over the low ridge above the beach, and *SW*'s chain rumbled and grumbled over the seabed more often than I needed to notice. For a good night's sleep, anchoring in strong winds is not to be recommended.

As the tide slowly went down, the wind also backed to the south, then south-southeast and eased. When it got light, after making sure that no disturbing sea was coming down the gap or round Tuhawaiki Island, I went back to bed, set my alarm for four hours hence, and slept soundly.

By midday, the gale had gone away. There was no excuse not to leave. It was all sunny, slightly colder, but really a very nice day that had simply put a bad night behind it. Where the light in the rough night had been, a window with someone watching from it was there in the eastern corner of the bay.

The wind was from the southeast, and the island had now become our shelter. I pulled in the anchor chain, and once the anchor broke free from the seabed I rushed back to start the engine and veer our momentum away from the kelp bed ahead. Puttering out, I pulled up the full mainsail and genoa, knowing that to make progress in light winds with a sloppy leftover sea it was vital to present as much sail area as possible. In the process of doing so, I moved up onto the fore-deck, grabbing hold of the inner fore-stay as I'd done so many automatic times before. It was a stay to be trusted: on a bucking bronco, in a big sea, or even in flat water, an easy hand-hold that often took my weight when moving about the fore-deck. But this time the stay came away in my hand, and I collapsed uncomfortably all over the dinghy on the fore-deck. Reacting quickly, but with bewilderment that a permanent fixture called the inner fore-stay that I had previously taken for granted had obviously deceived me.

I motored us up close to more kelp beds in the lee of Tuhawaiki Island, threw the anchor over the side, then went below to have a serious think.

16

Retreat?

Thinking about the broken inner fore-stay led to the realization that it was actually the original stay and had been on board since 1972. All the others had been replaced in '94 for the solo Tasman Race, but that one had been regarded as OK back then. Thinking that the loss of an inner fore-stay wouldn't be as horrendous as the loss of one of the others, I'd parsimoniously not bothered to replace it the year before when I'd had the caps (masthead side-stays) done.

But what did it do, anyway? I'd never really paid any attention to its function. It looked like it pulled the mast forward, or at least stopped it inwardly curving aft in the middle. But why would it want to do that?

There was a spinnaker pole topping-lift pulley at the same point on the mast, and it looked like I could jury-rig a very tight line to hopefully do the same job. But it wasn't the same as stainless-steel wire when tensioned up, so would it do? I wasn't sure, but did it anyway, with a tie-down knot as tight as I could get it.

Then I started worrying about what a prudent mariner would do if he was in my sea boots. Retreat to Dunedin to replace with stay? Or push on with a detour into Bluff to sort it? Or accept that it had happened and be confident in my rope substitute? It was turning into a beautiful day out there, and the wind had eased then backed, as prophesied, into the southeast. Turning back just didn't feel right, so I hung a right and pulled up all available sail once well away from the leftover swells slamming onto the rocks on the exposed eastern shoreline of the lower South Island. *SW* tight-reached slowly away from the Catlins in a confused and sloppy short sea.

From over the ridge behind Jack's Bay the short, green grass of sheep farmland seemed to back right down to the cliffs on the other side of the headland. The few sheep knew where not to stand, and weren't paying any attention to *SW*.

Then, surprisingly, two little humans appeared on the ridge and stopped, looking seaward for some time. I sat there hand-steering and making up all sorts of ridiculous reasons why they were there. Surely one of them was the person who had turned their light on when they saw *SW*'s deck-lights go on last night? It didn't really matter, but somehow I convinced myself it did. It seemed we had a far-away audience, and the human company was surprisingly comforting.

They were a pair of tiny humans on a green ridge speckled with white sheep, with a fresh clear blue sky above them. When they'd eventually had enough of looking, they turned and walked slowly up the grass slope and disappeared over the ridge. Whoever they were, I missed their company.

The cliffs around White Head down to Cosgrove Island all looked fairly uninviting, so I kept *SW* well out to sea and admired the view from a relatively safe distance. The visual temptation was to keep following the curve of the coast around to the southwest and slowly sail past each distant headland, as we had done down from East Cape to Gisborne.

I hung in close (but not as close as a fishing boat that passed inshore of us), until Tautuku Peninsula and Chaslands Mistake were the next distant headlands. The southeasterly kept slowly backing to the east, then freshened from the northeast. According to the chart, the south end of Stewart Island was where we needed to go, so a compass course of 200 magnetic was set, and the FMF was engaged to slew us more or less in that direction. We were sailing away from the coast and out to sea, and the wind direction and strength could not have been better. I went to bed, temporarily contented.

By 3 a.m. some 30 miles in benign sailing conditions had been made good, but along with the wind the barometer was dropping and the advice on the radio was that a northwest gale turning to a southwest gale was coming to get us. Doing much 'westing' (getting as far west as possible) became an impulse I couldn't ignore.

When it got light the land was still available to see, way off in the distance to the north, just over 15 miles away. We were now south of the South Island and almost becalmed. The wind mucked us around for most of the day, and the barometer kept dropping while the sky clouded up and started looking full of unpleasant intent.

Another crucial navigational decision now needed to be made. By then becalmed and waiting for bad weather, all sorts of non-productive thoughts entered my mind and became difficult to dislodge. Twenty miles north, I could just make out Waikawa Harbour and Porpoise Bay, and to the west, the surprisingly high land of Stewart Island was there for a while before the clouds got the better of it.

So many places to get away from the wind and feel more secure, rather than being out there in big waves, by myself, in a thin plywood adult-sized egg, bouncing about and not really enjoying myself.

This was for real, and an impending sense of imminent doom beset me. This was the beginning of a voyage properly offshore. No more coasting: it was time to set a compass course 180 degrees south and enter the Southern Ocean, if I dared. The jury-rigged inner fore-stay had stayed where I'd put it since leaving Jack's Bay. But it had not really been tested with a windward bashing like the one that was about to begin in a few hours' time.

Graham Perrem's Mana Cruising Club guide that he'd lent me had all the places around there where I should be, and should not be, and it became compulsory becalmed reading for all those on board. It soon became disturbing reading. SW was almost an equal distance from each of the two islands and Bluff was expected to become a windward beat, putting it out of the question.

I gave a few longing looks north, and west, in no particular order; pensive and full of the honest desire not to suffer the prolonged torture of a night smacking to windward and having to dodge low-flying albatrosses like off Moeraki. If the wind went southwest as expected, Waikawa could be hard to get out of, after waiting out the gale, and would be 20 miles in the wrong direction; a true retreat.

A local sea breeze came back at 15 welcome knots from the northeast, and away we went again for a productive few hours, sailing 210 to 200 degrees magnetic. It was great, convenient sailing, absolutely unexpected and contradicting the forecast. To boot, Port Adventure was only 15 miles west of us, and looked on the chart like not a bad place to retire to to weather a gale. But it might as well have been 50 miles, because *SW* was becalmed again, going nowhere, and it was getting dark.

There are no lights and plenty of reefs on that part of Stewart Island, and given the time that the wind was now expected to arrive, it was the last place any sane person would put oneself or one's boat, in the dark. The Mana Cruising Club guide also confirmed that *SW* should not approach this coast. Outrageous tidal activity and winds almost so savage as to be called feral had to be expected around there, and a powerful and reliable engine is espoused as an essential passenger.

Thankfully there were no pages pertaining to the Auckland Islands to put me off going there as well.

It was too late in the day to seek refuge in a bay on Stewart Island. The radio had given up on a northwesterly gale and was now betting on a *southwesterly* gale, arriving in the night. From what I could see, looking at the southern skyline, they were going to be right.

I got the double-reefed mainsail ready early and swapped to the number two jib just before it got dark. There was no wind on a two-metre swell, and *SW* rolled about looking ridiculous with such a small amount of sail area up. But it was the only sensible option. We needed to head south and get away from the land, out into deeper water, where larger waves with longer intervals between them would allow *SW* to sail more efficiently for the benefit of our expedition. We had to get away from the temptation of Shelter Point on Stewart Island and simply get on with the uncomfortable business of diligently sailing in a gale to windward. It wouldn't last forever, and what else would I rather be doing on my holiday?

Rain on a reasonably flat sea that was still heaving with an annoying swell heralded the inevitable change. I felt ready. This was it. No sanctuary required nor sought.

All that work up the driveway, all that thinking in England, all that intangible motivation built on reading about the Auckland Islands. All that had resulted after years of doing and thinking things. And now it appeared that I was living in that previously long-ago projected moment and had to do something about it. This currently entailed sitting there in *SW*'s small cockpit wearing wet-weather gear with the safety harness clipped on, waiting.

Waiting was an unlikely start, but nevertheless I convinced myself it was one. Waiting once again for the wind. Resigned to a big night of adverse weather and self-inflicted uncertainty, I tried not to feel frightened. I could stand off and on, as sailors say (sailing slowly one way and then the other), then peel off in daylight into Port Adventure elated at having sailed this far south.

I kept on mentally allowing myself the possibility of retreat, like a steam release valve in a mental pressure-cooker, but knew it wouldn't do. The only magnetic compass course that would result in any tangible progress was 180 to 170. I knew where we had to point if this trip was to be more than just a 'summer cruise to the South Island'.

17

South of the South Island

The wind arrived right on twilight. A strange lemon hue had engulfed the southern horizon; then dark, low clouds dominated the seascape until soft, almost casual, rain appeared. Then the wind came in from the southwest. No vicious line squalls like Moeraki with full-throttle slam-dunk gale force. Just a slow build over a flat sea, and within the hour *SW* was back on the wind, well balanced, with the FMF confidently handling steering duties and me suspended to windward inside, in the lee-cloth hammock where my weight needed to be, warm and reasonably comfortable all things considered.

The waves quickly built with the wind, and it promised to become a very unpleasant night's sailing. Everyone else on board agreed, so it was unanimous. By 1 a.m. we'd slogged 10 miles true south and had the measure of it. I guessed the wind to be 40 knots at the most, but without instruments couldn't accurately pick it.

With my weight to windward, on starboard, the sail plan was perfect, with the mainsheet eased enough to alleviate the worst of the gusts in the stronger patches. *SW* was ploughing on, efficiently sailing, and I was sometimes feeling like it was worth being there.

It was rough, and got rougher later in the night. From inside *SW* felt almost to be flying off the top of the close-together, steep adverse waves. The hull and rig were being stressed and flexed-out, and my interest in the jury-rigged inner fore-stay became acute. With my little torch shining its light up through the Perspex viewing dome above the starboard bunk, I could see how the mast and inner fore-stay were behaving. Or, more accurately, I could see how the mast was misbehaving without the stay that had broken; and how ineffectual the rope job I had shoddily put in its place really was. It's called 'pumping' in the industry. The mast will pump and flex forwards and backwards in its middle when beating to windward. This is not to be encouraged.

The more I peered at it through the dome with my torch, the more I worried about it. It was a bad look. The mast was pumping forwards and backwards every time *SW* dropped down into a wave trough or reared the other way. I could see how in more severe conditions the mast could simply snap in the middle and fall backwards, or wherever, if I didn't apply myself a bit more.

Getting the wet-weather gear and safety harness on while sitting inside on the bunk with no headroom and *SW* going up and down, often unpredictably, can sometimes feel like too much to physically endure. That's when anger can become a positive energy for getting things done.

It's knowing that you have to go outside and do something relevant for your own survival that makes you bother to suffer the personal physical torture of once again putting all that damp wet-weather gear on. Then you're out there, outside, half asleep, holding on tight to stop yourself from falling off. When the danger suddenly dawns, alertness prevails and you come to your senses — hopefully.

I switched on the spreader lights and instantly bathed the deck in a pale light that felt most welcome, given the horribleness of the night. With safety harness clipped on, I gripped on tight and got to the mast and dinghy on the fore-deck. In between indecent slammings and other nautical acrobatics, I managed to tighten up the temporary inner fore-stay some more.

A bit later on, peering earnestly again up through the viewing dome by torchlight, it still looked wrong to me. The mast was still flexing forwards and backwards with every wave. I hoped I hadn't made the wrong decision in carrying on, and finally sort of fell asleep just as it was getting light.

Seven-thirty in the morning on 25 January and despite an uncomfortable night having been had by all, spirits were high on board. Thirty miles made good in a true south direction in the night was great GPS news. All day it blew hard with what looked to me like a four- to five-metre swell building up. It was nothing special and expected to ease, and the sailing all night had felt productive.

All told, sailing courage in the face of foreboding conditions had made for a good start. Pleased with myself, and with *SW* sailing hard and heeled over, I boiled some water on the dangling gimballed pressure stove below me that kept swinging madly about due to what was going on outside; and heartily consumed a pot of spicy noodles. It tasted far more enjoyable than usual.

The absolutely uncomfortable motion I was experiencing could only be endured hour after hour by adopting the right mental attitude. An uninitiated landlubber on a day trip would have been shouting for his money back by then. And I totally empathized.

It was slightly strange, but I found emotional endurance in thinking about all those mundane moments I'd spent in the traffic in London, and the hours spent in the warehouse and shop in Brewery Road prepping guitar amps for overseas roadies or simply selling guitar strings and drum sticks to professional musicians and their crew.

I'd looked now and then at the pictures of *SW* and a small map of the seas around New Zealand (including the Auckland and Campbell Islands) that I'd pinned up on the wall next to my desk. I'd looked at the list of *SW* jobs to do that was pinned up next to them as well. That was in the northern hemisphere five years before. A future projected voyage provided emotional sustenance for me then, but would that daydream ever come to anything?

The walk at lunch-time down to the corner shops to get some chips, then back to the comfortable rhythm of secure but monotonous work. I'd learnt to turn the alarm off in the mornings at work if I was first in, and could put a job in the system and generate an invoice. Office work was a novelty for a while. And for that while it was all reasonably gratifying in an organized, efficient and tidy way. I enjoyed moving from being a driver to the warehouse, and then the office. I wore my ability in the office as a badge of well-justified relevance.

But the Transport Manager job had its own slightly serious staff issues to contend with. Stacey was from Cornwall and his father had worked under the sea digging out coal for the good of their country and economy. He had a staunch dislike of authority, and it seemed that I, in my new-found role as Transport Manager, was the personification of it.

The Jazz Café needed a Fender '65 Reissue guitar amp with a foot pedal ASAP. Big band, big night coming on, and for the reputation of our supply-line professionalism we had to get it there *now*. It was Friday night, 6 p.m. The working day's final bell had just gone and, in a state of anticipated relaxation, we were standing around talking about where everyone was going after work.

Agendas were different, and no one anticipated this late phone call resulting in a call to overtime action. A driver had to rise to the occasion as I prepped the amp and placed it in a flight case to put into the combo van. Someone had to go quickly. Despite the atrocious traffic that could be expected, someone had to do it. Once you got to the Jazz Café and met a grateful roadie, got the paperwork signed then got back in the van, indicated and got let out into Parkway and slowly negotiated the one-way system back to work, you'd lose an hour of your life for sure.

No one wanted to do the job. The instant incentive of 10 pounds sterling out of the 'Ready Cash' tin failed to incite any hard-up warehouse feeding-frenzy. I found myself almost reliving some Captain Bligh scenario involving longboat analogies, but pulled back at the last moment. Sacrificing my own social plans (the excuse the crew gave), I found myself sitting stoically in dense traffic with a Fender '65 Reissue amp in a flight case with a foot pedal that I knew worked in the back of the van.

Harbouring a boss's legitimate grudge, I completed the magic circle back to the warehouse without anyone waiting to commend me on my sense of duty and loyalty, and almost not knowing myself why I was trying to maintain the fragile reputation of my employer in terms of getting amplifiers and guitars down the road quickly to people doing sound-checks under pressure, and occasionally Hammond organs and other things to other parts of the country and sometimes overseas.

It's easy for one's subconscious to get preoccupied with mundane matters, most evident when you wake up at night thinking about them. Parts of previous years had been spent sometimes hearing compelling melodies from someone else's fictitious songs that I found myself listening to in a dream (often outside a venue). Realizing as I woke up that I'd made them up, I always struggled to remember them but never did, and felt disappointed that they'd gone.

Working in Brewery Road in Islington for what started feeling like a long time, just down the road from Pentonville Prison, and eating too many chips washed down with cider with my hood up on the corner of York Way, started feeling like a prison sentence in itself. But the children were growing, and I did get to go home to a boat at the end of a day that had often gone dark by the time I'd turned my motorbike off.

Holding those memories that felt like they were from another lifetime, long ago, I silently grappled with the meaning of personal motivation. Strapped up to windward on the starboard berth as

SW lifted and then dropped and then lifted and then dropped again, the only conclusion I could come to was quite simple.

I just wanted to get to the Auckland Islands and have a look. I wasn't likely to save enough money to go on a cruise ship to get there, so *SW* was it. Nothing too hard to comprehend, just a bit scary.

Slowly but successfully, *SW* worked to windward and into an ocean with a very bad reputation. The general direction we'd been aiming for since leaving Long Point just south of Cosgrove Island on the Southland coast had been a nasty group of rocks called North Trap. In the night we passed 25 miles east of them and another set of nasties further south, called (not surprisingly) South Trap.

I changed from a 1 : 200,000 scale Nugget Point to Centre Island chart (that had seen progress fixes gratifyingly well apart) to a 1 : 3,500,000 scale New Zealand and Adjacent Ocean Areas chart. It's a serious-looking sea map with the words 'Sub-Antarctic' and 'Southern Ocean' written on it. Macquarie Island and the Chathams were there as well, so it provided a very sombre overview of where we were, and where we wanted to go.

It's only 180 miles from Stewart Island to the Auckland Islands, and on this chart it didn't look too far at all. But then, neither did the little marks I pencilled on it every 12 hours. They were far too close together, much more so than before. We had a lot of serious sailing to do, that much was obvious.

The southwesterly stayed fresh in the daylight, and we sailed true south away from the South Island. There was a lot to see, but no land anywhere. Waves, with the odd bit of breaking water, albatrosses gliding low above the wetness, and a sky of clouds chased by the wind, seemingly forever moving aloof and overhead.

The sea kept splashing at *SW*, but the noise of wave-slap sounds became inconsequential. The rain squalls were becoming less frequent, and the blue sky was daring to appear now and then.

What were my friends in London doing now? Most probably asleep in their northern hemisphere night.

Why make yourself vulnerable? What's the point? This was potentially life-threatening stuff, so why bother? I was getting more tired, and knew that negativity would ride with me now as a constant, uninvited companion unless I made a conscious effort to recognize and dismiss it. I'd learnt that much about myself over the years of sailing *SW* alone.

The southwesterly wind eventually got a bit more westerly in it, then left without saying goodbye at 10 p.m. on 25 January 2007. All night, and most of the next day, *SW* made slight progress over a large, lethargic Southern Ocean swell and current that seemed at the time determined to undermine our tally of miles made good in the right direction. That sounds bearable, but it was a shocking night for me — suspended on the surface of the Southern Ocean, with no wind, rolling and dipping all the time, at every angle possible.

SW was inert and going nowhere. A sitting duck waiting to be engulfed by some low-pressure weather system circling the bottom of the globe, biding its time for a chance to pounce on a vulnerable and out-of-its-depth small sailing boat. The 5.30 marine weather forecast confirmed my negativity. A storm warning had been issued for sea area Puysegur, and we were becalmed on its southern outskirt. The barometer was of course dropping, and a sense of irrational entrapment besieged me. Irrational maybe, but tangibly true. This was bad. A gale warning is one thing, but a *storm* warning in this sea area …

While becalmed and looking at the sea and sky, especially to the west more often than was necessary, I started feeling like I had a 'funny tummy'. This was an endearing term I'd grown up with that basically wrote off the potential seriousness of any digestive disorder in its early stages while hoping for the best. But I couldn't work out why my propensity for defecation had become so pronounced. Personal hygiene had certainly been lacking, and could have resulted in a 'funny tummy', but maybe nerves had something to do with it? I was shitting myself.

It all became more uncomfortable in the night when a sudden rain squall blasted over us out of nowhere and *SW* staggered, over-powered, with way too much sail up. I clambered into my clammy, uncomfortable costume that meant exterior waterproofness and rushed out there into the wet night to sort things out. Negativity served me well as I put in a reef and changed headsails in the insipid pool of light that the spreader bulbs above provided. The final touch was getting the FMF engaged, balanced and involved in crucial sailing matters, then it was back to bed.

Once I had the sleeping bag covering me, the wind halted. The tiller smacked destructively against the stern, and the slamming of the stainless-steel gearing of the FMF was working horribly hard to create a fracture in some weak part somewhere. It's at moments like these that you have to find voluntary engagement regardless of fatigue. Involuntarily volunteering, I went outside again. The success of the expedition was made of many of these moments; a survival motivation mechanism more reptilian than human. I found it often — the sheer fundamental compulsion called survival. I've never had to eat someone to survive, but I imagine I could, if no one was looking and I was hungry enough.

'Just get up and out there and do it. There's no one else to help you,' I told myself quite often.

Outside in one's woollen undergarments, spanner in hand securing the banging bits, then back to the sleeping bag. Lying there again, rolling and pitching with no wind, and really not enjoying it. Then *slam bam* the wind back again, unseen and screaming through the black veil of no visibility to windward. The wind rushed at us like a vicious predator intent on destroying the will of all on board. That's how I was seeing it by then. Too much broken sleep. But when you understand *why* you think so, then you become more careful; or I try to.

During one unannounced rain squall my 'funny tummy' demanded an evacuation with a non-negotiable ETA. Squatting on the bucket in the companionway, hard rain driving inside and listening to the jib thunderously flapping upstairs, it was not a good look but had to be done.

It was colder now. Like a New Zealand winter, although it was summer. I'd brought my Mustang survival suit and had started wearing it. The zips took a bit of working out to start with and plenty of swear words were splurted out while I was braced inside, on all sorts of awkward angles, relearning how to seal it up. It was worth wearing now. Part life-jacket as well. Just pop over the side with the EPIRB and float about waiting for the helicopter, worst-case scenario.

I slept with the life-raft inside next to my head. A self-preservation option by your bed, what more could you want? A grab-bag full of all the other survival bits was aft of it and also waiting for its chance to become my vital friend if need be.

18

A storm in the Southern Ocean

The storm was expected to attack with a northeasterly wind sweeping in and stirring up the surface of the sea. The wind direction was certainly a sweetener; all *SW* would have to do was run downwind in a straight line to Enderby Island and Port Ross at the northern end of the Auckland Islands, only 125 miles away. But we were sailing into the open northern limits of the notorious Southern Ocean.

It was a favourable storm wind direction, so no real reason to feel apprehensive ... But what, really, should I do with a storm warning in the Southern Ocean? We were too far to retreat, and with this wind direction that was now unthinkable.

A light northeasterly filled in just before dark and got us steering 180 to 190 magnetic at about 3 knots against a leftover southwest swell. This felt unproductive, but as always you learn to live with it until it inevitably flattens out.

January 27 was a day of glorious *Swirly World* sailing. The sky progressed through all the modes of impending doom available to a meteorologist, and the barometer confidently attested to the same thing. But the wind pretended nothing was amiss and blew conveniently, and increased, from the northeast.

Many miles were hand-steered with a headsail poled out and mainsail restrained on the other side. Basic safe cruising sailing, sitting on 5 to 6 knots and pointing in the right direction. Somewhere over that horizon they were there, the Auckland Islands, only 80 miles away and quickly getting closer.

Back when we were becalmed, only the day before, and listening on the radio to what was coming, it would have been nice to have turned on a big, reliable diesel and stuck to a projected personal ETA. But our motoring progress had become a joke, and I had finally accepted that Zein had been right — the engine was poked and in need of chucking away, as he had so knowingly recommended two years previously.

I'd been listening to the SSB radio to learn about what the wind wanted us to experience. As a subject of the wind, sailors always pay grave attention to finding out what it's going to be doing, especially when lolling about in its domain. Instead of Taupo Maritime Radio telling me how bad wind things were going to be, I'd been recommended Bluff Fisherman's Radio. These were the people to liaise with re letting loved ones know that I was still alive.

More concerned with living the moments than with telling

people about them, I had failed to announce *SW*'s whereabouts since clearing away from Stewart Island. Listening to Bluff Fisherman's Radio at 7 p.m. each night for a thorough marine forecast followed by a roll call and important conversation with all sorts of mariners who were out there became compulsory. But I didn't want to contribute. Everyone I heard were big-time professional industrial fishing-boat-strength maritime locals doing the bizniz.

The SSB radio is a communal listen-in to other people talking. I didn't mind announcing *SW*'s whereabouts, but you are always asked to state your intended destination and that was my stumbling block. Details of boat, sea state, wind speed, intended destination, ETA. Everyone listening for their turn; it's like a reality TV show but in real time and, when the wind turns bad, with real consequences.

Meri from Bluff scolded me in a friendly way over the SSB airwaves when I decided to own up to being out there that night. Keith had already been in contact awaiting news of our progress, and not having heard from me she had been unable to help. The short-lived hard southerlies that had swept up the coast since our departure had disturbed Keith more than they'd bothered me.

I plucked up enough courage to state our intended destination and our size as requested, and apologized for our radio-waves absence. A 7 p.m. sked (radio schedule) was set for the coming evenings. The anticipation of communication in those isolated seas was a bit more reassuring. It was a security blanket of sorts, as is any audible company when out of sight of land.

Earlier we'd spent a day slowly following a large fishing boat a few miles ahead of us, and just seeing it now and then, between the worst of the slow-moving rain squalls, had made me feel safer.

They seemed to be fishing the side of the underwater slope on the 200-metre line that we'd been inadvertently sailing along as well. Some of the fishing boats on the radio roll call each night were cagey about giving out their position, and as I'd roughly plotted where most of them said they were, I figured I'd found one of the discreet ones.

We sailed fast towards a horizon with absolutely nothing on it. Faith in the compass course, 200 degrees magnetic (allowing for a perceived northeasterly-setting current) was all we had to steer by.

The sky was shutting down in a way I'd seen before on the eve of impending bad weather. There was nothing to do but sail on. In my own vaguely fatigued mind, it was the most necessary thing I could do. And it *had* to be done now.

When it got dark we were only 40 miles from our goal, and down to the number two jib with the FMF slewing us flat off, downwind, at 4 to 5 knots. Storm-force winds and high seas for where we were on the map was a foregone conclusion according to the Met Office, with a change to storm-force westerlies tomorrow. It was a very serious sailing situation that I really couldn't afford to disassociate myself from, even though for a few more hours I buried myself in the sleeping bag, listening to *SW* sledging down the growing seas. Sometimes we were losing control on the noisy breaking wave-tops and broaching sideways across the crest; the wind started getting more overbearing and I knew I would have to go outdoors and reduce sail again soon.

At midnight the wet deed was done, with the brand-new bright-orange storm jib hoisted and doing its job keeping the 4- to 5-knot average up but in a more controlled fashion. *SW* was then

22 miles true northeast of Enderby Island and steering 190 to 200 magnetic, aiming for the entrance to Port Ross at the northern end of the group.

Beset with a mixture of excitement and grave concern, I carefully thought about our soon-to-be-engaged approach to my long-anticipated goal. The weather forecast was truly atrocious, but the current northeasterly wind was great for progress, and with an expected change to a westerly the next day I wanted to get there as soon as possible to avoid being blown out east, away from the islands, and having to beat back. But where we were aiming for now was officially a lee shore in the Southern Ocean. The thought of running down into a gap only a mile wide at the entrance to Port Ross in relatively shallow water and in nil visibility didn't feel right.

The motion was getting more violent now, but the scale of what was happening outside was impossible to read, with constant rain and nothing to see in the now absolute blackness of a real storm at night. Despite my tired mind I completely understood that *SW* was now sailing into a potentially very serious situation all of my own making.

There were some new factors to also figure in to the navigational equation. We were now back in relatively shallow water, at 160 metres deep, and the seabed was shelving all the time. The water would soon be only 60 metres deep 5 miles out, and 37 metres deep at the entrance to Port Ross. A contrary ocean current was running against the wind, and would be stronger the closer we got to the top of the islands.

Little squiggly lines and the words 'Heavy Overfalls' are written on the chart and marked to extend up to 5 miles north of the islands. And Bristow Rock, an isolated danger, resides in perpetuity some 3 miles north as well. That didn't really worry me too much, as I knew where we were by simply gripping the GPS and holding it up outside in the night. I dreaded what would happen if I failed to clutch it tight, as it was the only one I had. It chewed through the AA batteries, but they were a small price to pay for the peace of mind it brought.

But the thought of not making the most of such a favourable, if menacing, wind was my most pressing problem. Any moment it felt like the wind might halt, then come back with the wrath of a Southern Ocean westerly gale, backing southwest and blowing us far away from where we almost were.

A little bit of daylight, even just enough to be able to identify a nearby headland or whatever, would make it a safer, more reassuring way to arrive.

Swirly World was running fast now and we would be there too soon if we carried on like this. I popped out and adjusted the FMF to bring us up onto almost a beam reach and put a bit of westing in, in case the westerly was premature in arriving. The plan was for a series of more or less broad reaches that would zigzag us downwind, slowing up our arrival time so that hopefully the sun could have a go at helping me see what *SW* had to avoid.

It was blowing hard outside by the sound of it, and now and then *SW* took a good sideways slamming, lurching and heeling way over before slowly staggering back on course as the FMF regained its composure. A few long zigs and subsequent zags killed six hours, then it was my turn to take over and sail *SW* the last 6 miles to Port Ross. I felt we were in the right place by then, true northeast of Enderby Island on the edge of the squiggly overfall lines on the chart, and ready to have a go at the final approach to what would lead to the flat-water sanctuary of Port Ross.

I closed up the main hatch with its boards locked in place (as they always were on rough days or nights whether I was inside or out), then clipped the safety harness onto the wire that ran the length of the deck. I didn't expect to see the inside of *SW* again until we were safely anchored in Sandy Bay, in the lee of Enderby Island at Port Ross, only 6 miles away.

19

Soiled-bedding soup

It was almost light, but the rain and low cloud were doing their best to keep the view from me. I disengaged the FMF and started hand-steering, getting a feel for what was going on with the wind and waves. The enormity of what I'd got *SW* involved in soon became apparent.

It was a seascape I had never seen before. The darkness had sheltered us from a grim and turbulent picture that I didn't realize would look so bad. The waves — seas, swells, call them whatever — were as high as the kauri trees behind where I live my landlubber life in Titirangi. And they were a long way apart compared with other seas I'd seen and had unsettlingly steep sides. Up on the tops of them, where we kept finding ourselves for a brief but exhilarating elevated moment, many were breaking into a cascading tumble of rushing white water.

It was obvious even to me that *SW* had already entered the forbidden zone. As far as I was concerned, there was no need for the tops of these small hills to be collapsing and rushing down faster than the wave itself, and sending a one- to two-metre wall of breaking surf-beach-type water at *SW*. It looked peculiar, and out of proportion, and it was obvious that we were in what the chart called an area of 'Heavy Overfalls'.

A Heavy Overfall of tumbling water was the appropriate description, if I had to find one myself. Of course I didn't, as some ancient mariner had already warned everyone venturing into this part of the sea, long ago, where to find them.

Slightly in awe at the scale of what I was seeing, it didn't take long to work the severity aspect out. We had to sail further into the overfalls area to get to North East Cape on Enderby Island before turning to starboard into the sanctuary of Port Ross. All the while the seabed was getting closer, according to the soundings on the chart that had been on my lap inside.

The thought of more current to contend with, and a shallower sea with a wind the speed of which I had lost the ability to estimate filled me with grave concern. This was potentially *it*. The end of us if I decided to keep running in towards a lee shore that was doing its savage best to tempt me with the vision of the flat-water sanctuary of Port Ross, tucked just behind Enderby Island.

I managed to find a wet grin in thinking that if *SW* ended up on the rocks in a few hours' time then she would get a shipwreck name, and year notice, on the next updated Auckland Islands chart. It was strewn with many others from the nineteenth and twentieth centuries. Many well-manned sailing boats had been scattered in total destruction along the coastline. At least *SW* would end up in auspicious, if antiquated, company.

Total destruction was a very real possibility as I sat there hand-steering in zero visibility, rushing downwind, aiming for a lee shore 6 miles away that I couldn't see; and listening in awe and fear to the breaking white-water wave-tops manifesting around us in random, vicious, unpredictable shapes everywhere. This was dangerous sailing, with the prospect of it getting worse the closer we got. The scale of waves and white water was enough for me to understand that a somersault could be on the cards if the seas got steeper and those malevolent, rushing bits that better belonged to a surf beach got any bigger.

My ability to transfer the GPS fix to the chart via pencil and plot a careful course had also become compromised by the wicked wind. I was doing it, but more slowly than usual. All things considered that was of no consequence in the greater scheme of things, but right there and then, it was potentially compromising the safe outcome of the journey. I'd been offered a free chart-plotter that would show up where we were on the chart on its small screen, but the Auckland Island card for it wasn't available, and seeing that Neville the neighbour had provided the paper charts I went for the cheap hand-held mobile-phone-sized GPS. I'd also been worried about getting *SW* accidentally swamped by salt water, and the possibility of losing power and then the crucially wired-in GPS no longer working. It was a prospect too severe to tolerate, no matter how compelling it would have been to watch our sailing progress on a chart on a screen. One day.

It didn't feel right to be 6 miles away and closing fast in breaking seas rushing about all over the place. This was wrong. This was not the place for a small sailing boat to be. Being on a big ship looking across or down at the breaking, rushing stuff would have been great, truly a delight to witness, but in *SW*'s circumstances it was quite something else.

Sometime in the 6 a.m. hour on 28 January 2007 I convinced the crew that we must abort the prospect of shortly arriving at the Auckland Islands. In the conditions prevailing at the time it was simply too dangerous. To be tossed into undignified floating positions was a very real possibility as far as *SW* was concerned. We were on the outskirts of a major tide race in storm-force winds with no visibility beyond our immediate circle of tumbling, rushing seas. To go west was the first impulse, to gain as much space in that direction before the wind shifted and came in from the west. Once the wind went west (blowing towards the east), we could hopefully then sail on a reach down to Port Ross.

The northeasterly had been hard out with rain for at least six hours now, and a part of me was gambling that at any moment we would, wonderfully, feel the end of it, and see a lifting of the cloud cover followed by a westerly-building change that would sail *SW* triumphantly into Port Ross with good visibility, to casually beat up to an anchorage and gloat to myself about the value of small sailing boats.

But Bristow Rock was there to leeward somewhere in the murk, and more squiggly overfalls were due to make an appearance. Plus, only 6 unseen miles away, the coast was waiting to greet us with huge swells smacking onto it. If we lost the rig through a roll or a hard sideways slam-down, then — disabled — we would have to contend with the historic cliffs and rocks waiting downwind to leeward. Down here there was no Westpac helicopter or coastguard to call to come and save us if we became dismasted and drifting downwind. The engine would be no use in these conditions. *SW* would meet the coast on the wind's and the sea's terms, and only small pieces of wreckage would be left to be found.

With my survival suit on and thinking thoughts of survival, I turned *SW* to port and the southeast, reluctantly away from where I really wanted to get to. It had to be done. To get out of here as quickly as *SW* could sail. It was a beam reach (wind side on) that was required.

The storm jib had been driving us more or less before the wind, its tiny square footage just enough to put some fast miles in without any effort on my part. But now, on a beam reach, it didn't feel that efficient. That tiny piece of sail area hoisted on the fore-stay on the bow was dragging us more sideways than forwards.

It wasn't a welcome realization, but the longer I sat there steering, the more I could feel the lack of forward, efficient sailing and, more importantly, could imagine in a macabre way *SW* ending up on North East Cape, still pretending to sail on a reach but going downwind at a terrible rate of knots. Setting the storm trysail was the answer; get a bit of sail-plan balance.

Just before I convinced myself I had to do it, a decent breaker came rushing down the face of one of the tall waves to windward of us and slammed into the side of *SW* in a frenzy of fast-rushing surf-beach white water. The broken water was running down from the top of the wave, and higher than *SW*'s deck.

Up we went, elevating fast, picked up above the sea we had just been floating in; then matter of factly slammed down and shunted sideways, with water half a metre deep over the dinghy strapped down on the fore-deck. The cockpit was full, with me up to my elbows in sea water, holding on grimly. The breaker spun *SW* round and left us facing downwind, pointing back in the direction of Enderby Island. It was almost like the sea and wind were insisting we go there.

The wave-top rushed on through to leeward, then disappeared amongst the others downwind as we quickly lifted up high again on our aquatic elevator, to be smacked by another big breaking one. *SW* felt a bit helpless in the lee of the hills, and when the white stuff came tumbling down fast with no intent to stop, you knew what was next. It was scary sailing now. These had to be the mythical overfalls extending out from the coast further than I expected.

The mainsail slides on the mast had to be removed from the track before putting the trysail on. The trysail then needed to be threaded on, and the back triangle corner sheeted in. It took longer than expected due to a lot of very dedicated holding on that had to be done, which interrupted my application all the time. I kept a very serious eye on what was pouring down the front of the waves to windward, but usually they gave me plenty of advance warning. The sea would just stand up steeper, higher, more defiantly, and I could see the current running against it. Then the whole caving-in top would collapse and rush diabolically forward, down the steep slope to engulf *SW*.

Back in the cockpit and still holding on, the smack of the dollop, a welter of white, cold salt water filling the cockpit and swamping me. It thumped heavily into the side of *SW* and onto the dinghy lashed on the deck. Over and under us the white water aerated and agitated enough to remove the rudder and keel from the sea, and bodily threw *SW* around, once again facing Enderby Island.

As sole navigator I obstinately refused to be swayed by the wind's malevolent insistence. No way. I'd made up my mind that the course was southeast, as quickly as possible please.

I got the trysail sorted, then sat wedged in the cockpit steering with the intense concentration of a person genuinely seeking to escape from perceived imminent demise. *SW* lifted, dropped, and did it all again, very rapidly, punctuated by side slams and cold-water cockpit fillings.

I scanned to windward, full of worry but totally impressed by what I was seeing coming at us and the way it did it without any consideration for our fragility. It was raw planet earth at its impartial best, exhibiting a scale of grandeur that I'd read about but only sporadically glimpsed before on other voyages. Apart from the enjoyment of the spectacle being tempered by my own personal vulnerability, it was good to be there.

SW responded well to the storm jib balanced with the trysail, and I could tell by the feel on the tiller and the wake out the back that we were sailing forward rather than drifting sideways.

I became obsessed with staying away from what was less than 6 miles to leeward, in the murk down there, totally unseen, under the boom to starboard somewhere. By midday I was worn out, and my hands were feeling very numb from the cold water that had been constantly sloshing over us. Wetness had become the least of my worries, but still it was everywhere.

What I now assumed to be a substantial current was taking us somewhere, but I wasn't sure where. The further I sailed *SW* away from the charted physical obstructions, the better.

Four hours later, the seas had taken on a different shape and size. Big monster wave faces and peaks of impressiveness collapsing in broken metres of white water, but no longer rushing fast down towards us. More just waves dissipating in a slow, self-destructive tumble.

Those four hours of tight reaching that I suspected were going to show up as a beam reach on the chart (and did) had got us away from the tide race off North East Cape and into deeper, more sailing-friendly water. When the tops of the waves started to implode where they were and gave up coming for us quite so often, I set the FMF with strict orders to carry on regardless, then took myself inside for a rest.

My bare hands had become surprisingly numb and clumsy as I fumbled with the spanner to lock in the wind-vane bolt. If we took another stray slamming wave, whacking *SW* sideways, my being inside would not make much difference. But it might to the self-steering. Those faithful mechanical parts were getting on for 30 years old, and a decent slam from white water on the stern with the trim tab engaged could fracture some vital stainless part in a sudden unannounced moment.

Waiting for that vital lapse between lunging waves from windward and above, I had picked the moment as *SW* lifted on a big, high slope as it quickly passed underneath in a rush. Hatch slid back, two hatch-boards removed, body inside ASAP, boards back in, hatch slid shut. Removed at last from that immensely volatile reality outdoors.

It was almost dark inside *SW* with the window boards on, curtains closed, the dinghy over the forward hatch window and the main hatch closed up. Only the viewing dome in the deck above the starboard berth let in the light. Below it I could, sadly, see a whole lot of water sloshing about with my cherished sleeping bag and pillow in it.

It was as if a large pot of cold, soiled-bedding soup had been prepared exclusively for me. I found no humour in the thought at the time.

On four separate occasions *SW* had been totally covered in breaking, rushing white water with the rudder ineffectual and us shunted sideways across the sea, leaving us involuntarily facing downwind. The water had found its way inside through the ventilator on the deck that, in the heat of my fixation to sail southeast, I'd forgotten to stuff with a tea towel and wrap and bind closed in a plastic bag.

It was scary sailing stuff, and I'd been distracted by the bigger basics like keeping away from physical obstacles and staying afloat. I'd had an outside fixation, and extraneous water inside had been well down on my list of immediate priorities.

My main concern was the dinghy upside down and strapped onto the fore-deck. I'd looked after it (more or less) for 20 years. It was another fine piece of boat-building craftsmanship from Michael Brien, the creator of *SW*. Built of very thin plywood and designed to fit snugly on the fore-deck, with a recess cut into its stern to sit around the mast and three inspection ports in its bottom to accommodate the inner fore-stay and provide access for two twin running-headsail deck fixtures, it's light enough to lift alone from the sea, up and over the guardrails onto the deck. It straps down and makes walking around the fore-deck difficult, but the benefits of a rigid dinghy are not to be underestimated.

It had been left neglected in backyards for years while I was overseas, and many patches of softness that meant dry rot had emerged. I did a lot of bog jobs (using epoxy filler) just to keep it functioning and floating — as long as you didn't stay out floating for too long.

Then one night it blew over from its upright perch in the

The beginning of the refit up the driveway.
Tracey Asher

New self-steering trim tab rudder and skeg prior to fibreglassing.
Tracey Asher

A tight squeeze, but we make it.
Richard Wood

Down the driveway ...
Richard Wood

... and finally off to the sea.
Richard Wood

Back to her natural element.
Richard Wood

New paint job, old sails.
Steve Raea

Beating back to Enderby Island and showing off to a nearby inflatable full of well-clad eco-tourists.
Rob Suisted

I'd been invited to dinner on *Raw Cotton*.
Carl Burling

Doing what *Swirly World*'s made for — simply sailing.
Carl Burling

A light southerly breeze filled in just when I needed it most.
Steve Raea

Starting to feel the effect of the oranges and beer.
Richard Wood

With just enough wind coming from the city to windward, sailing into the Viaduct Basin became a viable option.
Richard Wood

Chatting with John Campbell live on his TV show and trying to act normal.
Richard Wood

Looking forward to a change of diet after two months of two-minute noodles and canned tuna.
Tracey Asher

carport onto the concrete, and I found it the next morning with some of its bow and stern missing. The first practice epoxy job I did when refitting *SW* was doing the dinghy. The soft spots were all ground back, then bogged, and covered in fibreglass cloth and plenty of resin. Though a little heavier to lift out of the water, it was, and still is, worth it. I'd done years of dealing with the folding dinghy, which was lighter and less bulky to store. But it didn't have much freeboard and in any little waves it was a dangerous way to cross even the most sheltered bay.

The bulk of the hard dinghy on the deck and its associated windage had always worried me. I left the dinghy back in New Plymouth when *SW* did the Solo Tasman Race in 1994. On previous deep-water voyages I'd shied away from taking the dinghy on deck, out of fear of what seas we might encounter, and also from a lack of necessity. But an expedition to the Auckland Islands where no help, wharf or marina was to be expected demanded that I make provision for going ashore. It was that or the prospect of just staring at the land from the confines of *SW* once we (hopefully) got to anchor there.

In light of all my past efforts to preserve it, I wasn't prepared to let the dinghy be washed overboard by some malevolent breaker. But that was exactly what the waves that came aboard and swept across the deck were trying to do. There was a dense insistence and velocity in them that made me fear for the integrity of the through-deck fastenings that held the dinghy where it was.

The force of the moving water was in another league as far as I was concerned. It was totally possible that with the impact of a breaker, holes could be torn in the deck and the dinghy would be ready to fly away downwind. I made a mental note to beef up the pads under the deck where the fastenings were bolted through.

Big extra plywood sandwiches and stainless plates next time.

But the water inside was now a bigger immediate worry. Not believing in getting unnecessarily wet if I can help it, the horror of mopping up the pool and wringing out my sleeping bag and pillow put me in a bad mood.

Wedging myself up to windward, I half lay, half clung on, pretending to relax. The bad mood was amplified by the extremely irritating knowledge that we were heading away from where we had almost got to. The expected wind shift to the anticipated westerly gale made it worse. We'd have to beat back against it, or be blown away from the islands.

Around midday the wind started easing, but stayed coming out of the north. I couldn't justify lying there damp and uncomfortable, heading south of Cape Horn thousands of miles away. I eventually plucked up the resolve to go back outside, change the sail plan, and turn *SW* back around to head for Port Ross. The GPS told me we'd sailed, and been swept, almost 20 miles southeast of where we had been only four and a half hours ago.

The wind dropped dramatically, but the elevator motion of the sea was nowhere near ready to diminish. Up on deck, holding on like a little monkey that refused to let go, I got rid of the storm trysail and jib, folding and pushing the cardboard-like sails down the companionway into the dank, dark and wet cave that was by then the inside of *SW*. The double-reefed main was easy to hoist, but the halyard (rope) for the headsail started getting tangled on the folding mast-steps up the mast. The jerking up and down, extreme vertical lifting and dropping motion was something else to behold.

This violent motion was also doing strange things to the folding mast-steps. They each had a little latch system that locked them out of the way, streamlined upright against the mast. The only way to get one to fall down sideways at right-angles to the mast, and become a step, was to lift them up so they could be released to do it. They never did it of their own volition; it wasn't a design feature.

But now they did. It was like watching an invisible maniac gleefully climbing up the mast and lifting up then sticking out each mast-step; and, more perturbingly, putting the lower ones back in place on the way up. It was methodical. First the lower steps folded down, then the higher-up ones, followed by the lower ones folding up again.

It was hard to stop thinking that some unseen thing was doing it. But that was where I'd mentally got to as we turned around and headed back towards the promised Auckland Islands, somewhere west of *SW*, yet still refusing to be seen. It felt like disincarnate elemental forces were taunting and testing us.

The supernaturally malevolent intent was tangible. I'd developed a sense of physical self-preservation in many moments alone and far away from safety before. I'd got into a mind-set that an audience of sea ancestors otherwise known as sailors were gravely, and sometimes mischievously, interested in *SW*. It served me well in a way, the worrying about someone unseen (yet always thought of as more experienced than me) scrutinizing what I did on deck. They were trying to make me stumble, or whatever, and it made me try harder to do every tedious, minute action competently. I suppose it was company of sorts.

But now this felt unpleasant. Some long-dead, shipwrecked scurvy-ridden fo'castle hand grinning and drooling through broken teeth, clinging to the top of the mast while giving me the finger.

Being a member of the living I ignored him, but found it frustrating trying to untangle the headsail halyard from the folding mast-steps that refused to stop moving. On my knees, clinging to the mast with one arm, I would wiggle the rope in the vague hope that it would fly free to allow me to pull up the sail.

It was a pathetic picture out there in the Southern Ocean, surrounded by a crowd of jeering, disincarnate mariners. Very few recreational sailors had ventured into these waters and very few had come to grief, except for Gerry Clark (on a scientific expedition at the time) in *Totorore* in South Bay, Antipodes Island. It made *SW* and me even more a target of ridicule, if I let those dissolute, disaffected and dead professional sailors have their mocking way. It was a constructive mind-set for a human alone to adopt — showing the experts gathered there invisibly in the sea and clouds what we could do, and how I could live up to them.

Without going mad, I put *SW* about and we began sailing back to where we had just come from. The wind dropped right down to 10 to 15 indifferent knots, and the FMF was immediately overwhelmed by the leftover seas.

With no evil wind speed agitating the sea any more, what was left over was remarkable. Huge random hills, with no regular shape nor form, just lifting up and collapsing occasionally on top of themselves, while creating gullies devoid of wind with walls that moved in close, then almost within arm's reach lifted *SW* up their faces to a brief triumphant suspended moment on top of the water world. A vast view of a seascape totally indifferent and large and lethargic was there to be glimpsed; then down again *SW* dropped into a valley of liquid, with me looking up to windward at another salt-water hill insistently moving towards us.

It was difficult sailing. The Hauraki Gulf in a northeasterly slop was a style of sailing that had enthralled me as a teenager going to Murray's Bay for the Starling nationals in 1979. Compared with Wellington Harbour where on the odd occasion there was not much wind, we never had to deal with light winds that dished up sloppy, relatively large waves which required slightly eased sheets, and more boat speed gained by sacrificing the pointing of the bow as close to the wind as possible. A full mainsail and a more versatile helming technique was required, and although I did my best that year I finished an also-ran.

I was visited by the National Youth Coach at the time, Harold Bennett. He came down the beach in between races and sheeted in my mainsail for a look to see why I was sailing so badly. I was then the Wellington Regional Starling Champion and my lack of current competitive form had been noted in certain sailing circles. Harold took one look up at the sail filling perfectly in the light onshore breeze while I earnestly held down the boat on the beach-trolley to stop it toppling over. He announced matter of factly that for some reason unknown to him, I had a very flat-cut mainsail compared with most of the other Starlings on the beach that day. They were supposed to be one-design sails made by Hood's and all the same cut. But somehow I had a flat one. It had obviously served me well in Wellington, but on the east coast bays of Auckland, with this sloppy sea-breeze sea and non-user-friendly surf on the beach, I might as well have gone home early.

It explained why, despite my good starts and plenty of clear air, a whole fleet of others had crept up to windward of me, with more overall boat speed, and left us way down the pecking order by the time I got to the first top mark.

Now it was more sloppy sea sailing on an entirely different scale. Meticulous hand-steering was called for. I set all the sheets, travellers and pulleys in the right positions to keep the sails as full as possible, and put in some good concentrated sailing hours. It was an entirely different scale of tedious, unproductive sailing: hard on the wind in a dying northerly, with what looked like a seven- to five-metre reducing swell, unthreatening but nevertheless very uncomfortable.

All afternoon the land took longer than anticipated to arrive. I couldn't believe why I couldn't see it. A low haze prevailed, and it felt like my unwanted audience was trying to make the Auckland Islands forever invisible.

Following the comet

At 8:30 p.m. something looked like it was there — a very low something that wasn't sea; hopefully it was Enderby Island. Then, far off on the port bow I started seeing big shooting spumes of white spray ejaculating out of what had previously been just typically turbulent, but unthreatening, sea. The GPS told me it was only 3 miles away, a big shallow place with Green Island its crowning above-water glory.

The closer I steered *SW* in the light northerly wind towards the outlying shoal patch, the more impressive the spectacle of salt water shooting skyward became. It was obvious that we were being set south, quite forcibly, by the current, and if I didn't pay more attention *SW* would be too close for relative sailing comfort to the spray flying up into the air only 3 miles ahead.

The radio weather-forecasters broadcasting from Taupo were still predicting imminent doom in the shape of the next phase of our bad weather. A contrary westerly gale was due in our vicinity at any time. The sky cloud was low and again lemon-looking, and to my newcomer eyes hard to read. All I knew for certain was that being this close to potential sanctuary, we must not dither about. We must get there as soon as possible. But we were definitely being sucked south, and down onto the breaking shoal that was sending up spectacular shoots of white water into the now twilight sky.

I put *SW* about onto the other tack and settled down to some more careful hand-steering away from the maelstrom of crashing leftover northeasterly seas near Green Island, and parallel to where I keenly wanted to go. When it got dark, there was still a big sea running and a contrary tide trying to send us south, and I started getting even more emotionally involved.

With the last of the light we went about again, a lot further away from the bad-looking shoal spume but still keeping an eye on it down to leeward until the night removed it from sight. It had become a cloudy day with a low, hazy cover over the western horizon. It looked like no land could possibly be there. Then, when I'd almost given up looking for something substantial, it finally started defining itself as a dark line that became more obvious as we slowly sailed towards it.

The wind eased as it got dark and backed a bit more into the north. We were hard on the wind but had only 10 knots of it available to be used. On full main and genoa, and with a massive but passive swell, *SW* was making good about 2 to 3 tedious knots. We were tired now and ready to stop, but Taupo Maritime Radio was still prophesying doom to descend on us from the west at any moment.

It was time to find out if the engine was still going. In 1987, after seven rough days from North Cape to Pelorus Sound down the west coast of the North Island, I'd had to take the head off it and smack the exhaust valve with a hammer to get it going again.

On this trip I'd run it a couple of times for a few hours when becalmed, since leaving Jack's Bay, to charge the batteries to talk to Meri in Bluff. And since that Wellington trip all those years ago, I'd installed a sea cock where the exhaust pipe left the boat to stop sea water, when sailing in big seas, from running in from astern, flooding the exhaust pipe and slopping under the exhaust valve to constantly seize the motor.

The engine's horrible vibrations shook both *SW* and me more awake than before. *SW* started motor-sailing, a little, but not a lot, quicker towards where we needed to be.

A few disturbed broken crests and annoying wave-tops were still sloshing a lot of salt water over the deck and under the dinghy. The other trouble with the engine was that it is air-cooled and needs the fore-hatch on the front deck under the dinghy to be open, to sluice the heat away. Now that the exhaust fumes were leaking inside, the cabin quickly filled with carbon monoxide. I had got used to hand-steering in the cockpit with my head stuck out away from the thin, grey mist exiting from the open companionway.

I opened up the fore-hatch, and moved the piles of stuff on the forward bunks from under the hatch just before the first large dollop of cold water cascaded down inside. There was nothing to be done but slosh on, with as much ventilation as possible inside to stop the engine over-heating while keeping an eye on the water level under the floorboards and hoping the waves would settle down as we got nearer.

Like a concrete machine grinding away with constant, unsettling vibrations, the engine rumbled on in its slightly helpful but horribly noisy way.

Constantly in the survival suit, it was a lot colder now, and a little more warmth from the hard-rattling engine inside was good. Once again almost in a sailing trance brought on by fatigue, I wondered if carbon monoxide might be contributing to it.

I was determined to get to Port Ross before the westerly gale. A quick flash of the torch inside showed water slopping over the floor boards, and sloshing back and forth. It was more than I expected, but I knew I had almost tried to deny in my own mind the reality of water pouring down through the open fore-hatch, as it had been doing all evening.

I'd heard it in the dark. Occasionally pouring down inside. And now it was becoming a paddling pool down there. But we needed the forced boat speed to get into the sanctuary of somewhere to anchor and hide from the wind. That was the main priority. The hand-operated bilge pump in the cockpit sucked and squirted the water up its long and winding pipe from the bilge to the outside. I got the level down below the floor boards and accepted that a wet-bilged boat was what we had to be for now, until we got there.

Climbing back outside, up through the companionway to the cockpit, I noticed that the engine was dancing about alarmingly on its mounts. The nuts had worked way too loose, and it was virtually untethered. It looked like only the driveshaft going through the boat was keeping it in place. I'd noticed the vibrations below feeling more aggravating as I sat outside steering in the dark, but pretended it didn't matter as we were almost there.

154

I found the right spanner and tightened the big nuts to get it secure enough for a few more hours, then got right outside again in a hurry and focused on where we were; and where to steer to get there. I left the hand-held GPS on and shone the torch at the chart in my lap, putting my little ruler along the lines of latitude and longitude, keen to discover exactly where we were.

True east of North East Cape, 2 miles and closing. The northerly wind was still there, but now light and faltering. The sea was flattening out but was still high, judging by the night skyline as each swell rolled lethargically down from the north. Lifting us way up a benign slope and then falling away, the swells rushed underneath us down to leeward.

It was a pitch-black night, but the stars were promising to come out once the cloud cover got the message. I was getting anxious about arriving but kept it to myself; no point in alarming the rest of the crew.

Just before midnight, while again peering earnestly at the little pool of light on my lap that lit the chart of the land now only an unseen mile away, I heard the engine suddenly increase its revs from a steady concrete-mixer tone to a phenomenally high-pitched revving noise that didn't sound good at all. It was audibly obvious that the engine was working faster than ever witnessed by me, but the propeller wasn't going around. The reinforced rubber (like a piece of car tyre) that coupled the engine to the propeller driveshaft had ripped itself to pieces. The engine and prop were no longer connected. Why had it happened now? How hard did these long-gone and disconnected, unhappy, spiteful, mocking disincarnate sailors want to make this? They were trying to interfere with *SW*; by now I was convinced of this. Given the history of their past privations, it felt obvious that we were not welcome in their place in a boat this small, uninvited.

I turned the engine off and rushed outside, away from the fumes and the water sloshing around the floor boards, and into the all-consuming dark seriousness of it all. The smell of fresh seaweed and an ominous sound were waiting for me.

I'd been trying to work out what that sound was. Listening beyond the immediate noise of the engine had been difficult, but now it was obvious what I had been hearing. Dead ahead and further to starboard, yet sounding close enough to be of great concern, came the source of the repetitive deep booming sound: it was the noise of the leftover swells from our storm, arriving late and imploding on the north and eastern cliffs and rocks that surrounded Enderby Island. Driving in onto the cliffs that stretched down from Bones Bay to Gargoyle Point and North East Cape, it was the sound of the unseen lee shore that I had so feared less than 24 hours ago.

The GPS put us 1 mile true east of North East Cape and heading directly, by compass course, for it. I'd been possessed with heading west, but the tide had turned and a current was sending *SW* rapidly sideways to the north. We now needed to steer southwest instead of west.

Visually there was absolutely nothing to see. An overcast night sky shut down the possibility of the moon being any use, or company. Looking to the west there was nothing to see. But the sound was ominous. The frightening bottom-end booming sound of water on rock. The noise of instant, not too distant, destruction if I let *SW* get too close.

Identifying where the pongy seaweed smell was coming from

also didn't take long. A quick shine of the torch at the sea around *SW* revealed that we were surrounded by a floating island of thick kelp seaweed, and while the sails were still filling, we were quietly sailing nowhere. That explained what had happened to the engine: the prop had wound itself to a halt, wrapped in thick, long strands of bull kelp. The engine had insisted it keep turning, and the coupling had sacrificed itself.

In a mild panic, I pulled the sails down and pushed and prodded at stubborn bundles of the slippery stuff, one arm firmly attached to the boat or the rigging and the other straining with one of the dinghy oars, leaning over the side, trying to back *SW* out of it. After a fair bit of frantic and at times irrational effort, it eventually happened, and *SW* floated free and away from that tangled, shining, wet brown slithery trap.

The main and genoa were got back up and slowly started drawing *SW* along in a then very light northerly air, heading for the 1-mile gap between Enderby Island and Ewing Island, the unlit entrance to Port Ross.

The sound of the swells executing themselves on the unseen cliffs only a mile away was still very disconcerting. With a suddenly heightened sense of self-preservation, it was gravely obvious to me that now the engine was out of commission, the sailing would be very important. More wind would have helped. With the prospect of auxiliary engine assistance completely removed, the whole dark, heaving seascape and lack of wind took on an even more terribly threatening persona.

On a positive note, the cloud cover had started lifting and the stars came out to see how we were doing. A bit of a moon was up there for a while as well. But the most attractive celestial companion, way up there but viewable from *SW*, was a surprisingly clear McNaught comet. It was heading to the southwest, right up the gullet of Port Ross, and all we needed to do was hitch a ride.

There was another worst-case navigational scenario here, and I embraced it with a quiet sweat inside my survival suit, again without telling anyone. If the wind dropped completely, and it felt like it would, then *SW* would be pushed wherever, according to the whims of the currents running around North East Cape. This was legitimately scary. Only 18 hours ago too much wind had tried to destroy us on these cliffs and in the tide race, and now too little wind had the potential to do the same. We could be out of control due to a current and a big sea with no wind; washed onto the cliffs, and no one to save us here. No anchoring would be possible in that shocking ground-swell.

I gybed us across and got *SW* running south, parallel to Enderby Island. A mile was close enough for now. With the genoa winged out, sporting the new pole from Stark's in Lyttelton, and mainsail restrained to starboard, I was sailing for my life, and I knew it. The noise of the swells resonating on the cliffs was a soundtrack of impending doom as far as I was concerned, and I listened intently to work out if we were making any audible progress away from them. For a while I was sure I could see the white, splurting splashes of waves crashing and bursting themselves into oblivion on the cliffs, off to starboard in the dark.

Over there was the potentially hostile and unlit land that I'd come so far to see. It was discernible now, the uninviting blackness of nearby land obvious below the clear night sky's stars and the comet that filled the cold, elevated view to the west.

Despite my own negative thoughts of *SW* being becalmed, and lifted then dropped off a swell onto North East Cape with all the malevolent, disincarnate onlookers grinning and swaggering their approval at our demise, the wind stayed light from the north with enough strength to keep *SW* officially sailing at about 2 knots.

Apart from the phosphorescent flash of breakers on the Cape, not much more could be seen at sea level. All hail the GPS; conveniently trusting the satellites orbiting our earth, just up there by the passing comet, out of arm's reach in the visible universe.

I lined *SW* up when we were half a mile from both sides of the entrance at Port Ross, in between Ewing Island and Enderby. We gybed onto a beam reach on starboard and headed in to what looked like completely uninviting close-inshore darkness. The wind was now blowing lightly down the edge of the island, accompanied by a new noise that didn't make any sense at all.

I could tell by the way the sound of booming death-swells had receded that we had got south enough to have escaped ending up in Bones Bay or impaled on Gargoyle Point. The new sound was like a stream running; a stream running over a bed of rocks or pebbles. Perhaps that's why someone called it Pebble Point?

I'd never heard anything like it before on the sea. The new larger-scale chart I'd started using ('Plans in the Auckland Islands') explained it. We'd gone from fearing the squiggles on the chart meaning 'Heavy Overfalls' to now having to fear spirals drawn on the chart meaning 'Strong Eddies'. Eddies and Overfalls are to be avoided by prudent mariners, but sometimes you don't have a choice.

I was steering once again with the concentration of a very concerned participant for whom every decision made was absolutely relevant to remaining alive. *SW* was only a few miles away from a safe Southern Ocean anchorage, at 50 degrees south. Floating there silently suspended on the surface of the now almost flat sea, fighting the exiting tide in a faltering northerly wind, I was acutely aware of how tantalizingly close we were to a relative sanctuary for those in awe of the wind.

The sound of rushing surface sea water to windward near the corner of Enderby Island was disconcerting, and so was the way the wind was dropping off to nothing. Now the disincarnates with their missing teeth and drooling hungry mouths, clinging to the mast-steps on the mast, were grinning down on me with malevolent glee. With no wind in the lee of Enderby, we could be swept back out and away.

At 1 a.m. on 29 January 2007, the tide had pushed us in close to Pebble Point as it exited Port Ross, and the relatively low land to windward was beginning to shelter the water we were now travelling backwards on. Steering south with devout intent, *SW* found a bit more breeze and slowly the disturbing sound of the shallow stream running over the nearby imagined pebbles was left behind. The blackness of Ewing Island started identifying itself as something to avoid to port and leeward.

In the now clear night sky above, McNaught's comet blazed away, imperceptibly racing southwest through all that far-away space. The specialness of it all was not lost on me.

Sailing confidence re-emerged when a more consistent light breeze from the north filled in, half a mile south of Enderby Island. The torch was getting plenty of action, as I constantly flashed it on the tell-tale woollies on the headsail and the wind indicator at the top of the mast to make sure the sailing was as efficient as possible. I plugged in the 20-dollar, 500,000-candlepower spotlight and pulled its trigger quite frequently. Short bursts of intense and reassuring illumination over the surface of the water ahead was called for to avoid any more floating islands of kelp seaweed.

Creeping true west against the outgoing tide, *SW* slowly sailed into the flat, sheltered harbour of Port Ross. Three hours to travel 3 miles was a bit sad, but given the circumstances it was progress well received by me.

Now in the lee of Enderby with the light wind blowing directly off the land, the unfamiliar aroma of strange vegetation combined with what could only be animal faecal matter, wafted down from windward all over *SW*. It was an unfamiliar organic smell, that was for sure. No matter how unusual or unidentifiable, however, it was great to inhale something so aromatic after days and nights of only breathing salt sea air. The first recognition of the scent of land in your nostrils after sailing offshore is one of the pleasures associated with voyaging.

The sound of the night had changed as well. The deep, too-close-for-comfort booming sound of large leftover ocean swells sacrificing themselves on the outside of Enderby had mutated into a dull, yet still very audible, distant bottom-end-frequency resonance that almost sounded like it was coming *through* the island. Port Ross seemed to be creating a still amphitheatre where the sound of distant swell destruction, only a mile away on the other side of the island, was amplified to a bizarre degree. It was truly ominous in its low-end resonance; a most powerful and destructive tone of the sea. The whole island sounded like it was reverberating and amplifying the impact of every swell. If it hadn't been night, I might have seen it shaking.

As *SW* crept nearer to Sandy Bay, I flashed constant furtive spurts of light at whatever I thought might be in our way. A white shore-light looked like it belonged to the DOC base I'd been told was occupied at this time of the year. Then, just when I thought I'd come to terms with all the obstacles, another new noise emerged in our night sound spectrum. An animal *had* to be making it — or an orc from the *Lord of the Rings* movie. It was guttural and nonsensical, a loud, short, fierce sound that I couldn't identify from my past loud, short noise lexicon.

Eventually, as I tacked *SW* about a few times, working gradually up into Sandy Bay, it dawned on me. They were drawn on the chart, on the green land bit, in brown — but I hadn't been paying attention to the land, only the edge of it. This was the sound and scent of Hooker's sea lions living ashore on the beach. Awake and living in their own private open zoo, with personal hygiene problems by the smell of them.

They sounded quite aggressive, and I ran through a few imaginary attack scenes with the genuine concern of a very fatigued person. Of course it was unnecessary, but given the scale of the uninviting bellowing from the beach I wasn't sure what to expect.

I sailed *SW* in as close to the cliffs and kelp beds that fringed the mouth of Sandy Bay as I dared, each time gauging when to turn with the enormous help of the spotlight shining on the inevitable floating kelp on each side of the bay. A surprisingly large ground-swell could be heard through the darkness collapsing on the beach of Sandy Bay, nothing like the sound from a mile away, across the island, but audible all the same.

I finally let the anchor chain rattle its way down to the bottom to let the anchor touch what I hoped would be a sandy seabed, well away from the surf on the edge of the 4-metre line, according to the chart. The sea lions still sounded far enough away not to be too annoyed, and the ground-swell was still only that where we were, anchored out there in relatively deep water.

It was 3.15 in the morning on 29 January 2007; *SW* had officially arrived.

I wore an unseen grin and felt entitled to it. This was nothing short of brilliant. The cold, clear night; a safe anchorage for the moment with an offshore, light and fully spent, benign northeasterly wind; the stench of unusual living creatures lying on the dark beach; and the smell of the strange foliage on the low land to windward. All topped off with the macabre, distant sound of massive swells impacting only a mile away, on the other side of Enderby Island, and resonating about the bay in a foreboding way.

The sea lions barked their disapproval about something — possibly us — just over there on the dark beach, but they sounded more like shallow threats from drunken beach-bums who should have gone home when it started getting dark.

And of course *SW* was there amongst that long-anticipated and unseen scene as well. At 50 degrees south, at a place I had so often tried to visualize, but still couldn't.

Daylight three hours later sorted that problem out. There it was. A 360-degree wilderness view, with bright-orange *SW* incongruously imbedded in it.

Three hours' sleep was more than what I'd got used to in the past few days, but the excitement of being there drew me back from the total oblivion of exhausted sleeping disengagement. I woke up and keenly looked around outside. Slightly stupefied from my brief deep slumber, my sense of visual appreciation was, fortunately, still intact.

This was good. Here it was. Finally. And it looked like I had imagined it would. The low, flat scrub-like rata trees in crimson bloom, and the fragrant *Bulbinella rossii* megaherbs covering Enderby to the north. Across the sea, the whole impressive vista of high land hills to the west and southwest, the Hooker Hills and Mount Eden, Meggs Hill and Flat-Topped Hill. To the southwest down low, tucked away beneath the high Hooker Hill line, the coastline of Erebus Cove, Terror Cove, and the isolated Shoe Island deep in the heart of Port Ross were visible.

South of us, a mile and a half away, Ocean Island and to the southeast Ewing Island, the one that had worried me so much only hours ago, were also low but unmistakable. To the east-southeast, a little window of open ocean and empty horizon showed the way we had come in during the night, and explained the reason for the ground-swell noisily collapsing on the beach in Sandy Bay.

Sandy Bay. Black-and-white pictures of Sandy Bay with sea lions and seals on the beach, and supply vessels anchored with Ewing Island in the distant background. Photographs taken in the 1940s. So many times had I looked at them before.

Now *SW* was anchored in the same view, and I was looking at it.

Things had changed since then. From what I could see, the world had become more colourful. But that was about it. The rest of the detail was exactly as it had been then, and had remained so until then was now. No tower blocks and streets and wharves bustling with human activity. No signs of human development at all. They'd tried hard, once upon a time, back in 1850 to form a human settlement here, and failed.

But now in 2007 there were some humans here. I'd talked to one the evening before on the VHF radio. Every summer season, if you can call it that at 50 degrees south, DOC sets up camp and conducts research projects based in Sandy Bay on Enderby Island at the mouth of Port Ross. Their branch based in Bluff had advised me that they'd be there, but would be busy so no unnecessary assistance was to be expected. However, to ask for a fresh local weather forecast from them when *SW* was only 7 miles away and in line of sight of Sandy Bay hadn't seemed too demanding or interfering.

A loud female voice let me know we were expected, and after reading a satellite wind print-out from her machine told me that the westerly gale that had me fretting was now not likely to eventuate until tomorrow.

We'd spoken the evening before, when I could dimly see the land that looked so close yet so difficult to get to. The radio contact had been well received by all on board. During the last few crucial days, Bluff Fisherman's Radio had ceased transmitting its nightly bulletin and roll call for vessels at sea. In a slightly befuddled state, I couldn't understand why Meri Leask had deserted us. She had become reassuring to listen to, always conversing in her genuinely concerned way. Each evening I had become to rely on her, not just for the weather prediction but also for human company. Especially when, remarkably, we had regular personal conversations over all those sea miles regarding *SW*'s position, sea state, sky state and my state. All I had to say was 'And all's well on board' at the end of my self-conscious bulletin to establish that I had nothing more, at an emotional level, to divulge. I was always acutely aware of an unknown high-frequency-radio audience listening in. Them hearing where we were, and how we were, true Southern Ocean radio waves showbiz.

But it had to be done. It was the responsible thing to do. Giving out *SW*'s position in case something happened beyond our control, and people started looking ... But now Meri was gone. Not there at 7 p.m. each evening. No reason why; maybe the SSB had gone faulty?

In our serious circumstances, I almost expected the radio to give up its ghost. But there was a far more normal reason. Family issues in Australia had forced Meri to abandon her post there in Bluff and fly across the Tasman for a few days.

A very good day

None of that mattered now. *SW* had, thankfully, arrived in Sandy Bay and it was turning out to be a very good day. The light offshore northeasterly was blowing from a safe direction and the sky was surprisingly benign as far as clouds were concerned. The barometer was doing nothing drastic.

The land was refreshing to look at. It took a few minutes to readjust to looking at something other than sea and sky, but I quickly pulled myself together and rose to the view. A cluster of DOC huts where the humans lived were in one corner and the big noisy, smelly orc beasts were strewn across the rest of the sandy beach. Courtesy of daylight again, it was clear they were the ones to blame for some of the noises in the night.

The sea lions looked like big, slovenly slugs out of their

natural element, just lying there intent on an agenda of physical gratification; the warmth of sunlight at best with a bit of rooting and fighting thrown in.

This view right now was for my eyes only. I was the only human looking at it from there right then. The recent physical endurance trip was instantly dismissed, and already being mentally reviewed as definitely worth the effort.

Back to the VHF radio later in the morning, after dwelling on the view, I made contact again with Jacinda Amy. I didn't want to wake anyone up too early in case they were enjoying a DOC lie-in, but I probably waited a bit long.

Jacinda was just over there in the DOC radio hut, though I couldn't see her. We talked of inconsequential friendly survival things, then I loaded her up with my personal driveshaft problem. In this vicinity, having an engine that works was an auxiliary pleasure not to be dismissed lightly. I needed a part I didn't have on board to reattach the driveshaft and propeller to the engine. I'd worked out that all I needed was a piece of old thick tyre that I could cut up and bolt back in place. Hopefully DOC would have an old, environmentally unfriendly tyre, possibly from a shipwreck, lying around half buried in the beach that I would be welcome to.

It wasn't the case, but Jacinda said I had arrived at a most fortunate moment as a large yacht had arrived only hours before and anchored at the head of Port Ross in Laurie Harbour, and a much larger cruise ship was due in later in the day.

So while the view looked totally devoid of company for me, it was apparent that the show was about to start.

Malcolm McDougall in *Raw Cotton* shared the same voyaging ambition as me. He left Auckland in the North Island a little later than *SW*, but caught up quickly. His magnificent ketch is 60 feet (18 metres) long and superbly appointed.

Malcolm and a friend, Phil Morris, had come down the east coasts of New Zealand like us, then put into Bluff to pick up a load of keen crew members. *Raw Cotton* came down quickly with the building northeasterly, and maintained their ETA with the reliable diesel throbbing away inside during the light airs that preceded the storm. They got hammered like *SW* in the early dark hours and morning of 28 January and recorded 65 knots across the deck while running downwind. Unlike ourselves they held their course, and ran on down and into Port Ross, arriving in what had then become a benign afternoon.

I was not allowed ashore. According to DOC regulations, someone had to stay on board at all times in case the vessel dragged its anchor and ended up on the rocks, spilling fuel and other pollutants all over the place. That made sense for big fishing boats.

Jacinda kindly offered a boat-sitter in the form of Simon, a veterinary seal doctor or something, who would be available tomorrow. They'd come out in their inflatable to get me so I should stay put on board till then.

Raw Cotton was coming up to Sandy Bay later, and the Antarctic cruise ship *Orion* would soon be spoiling the view as well. Both vessels offered potential driveshaft solutions, hopefully.

Shortly after the pleasing conversation via VHF radio, masts and then a hull appeared from under the mantle of high land down the harbour, 4 miles away to the southwest. I suddenly felt compelled to dress for company. There wasn't much to change; I hadn't brought any good clothes. The warm survival suit was compulsory when outdoors, and the slightly soiled woollen long-johns and undervest never came off indoors.

Shorts and a salt water-stained black Kiwi FM-sponsored jacket was enough to cover up the woollen undergarments. And a beanie to hide my bad hairstyle and keep my head warm.

The elegant, large black steel hull came as close as they dared to *SW*, anchored as we were and hanging attached to the seabed floor with no immediate chance of moving. I watched carefully, noticing an audience of men with cameras watching *SW* as well. We shouted things I can't remember from yacht to yacht, and they went up into the lee of the cliffs to the east in Sandy Bay and anchored.

Even though it was a clear morning with Southern Ocean sunshine, the air was cold like midwinter in Auckland city. Shortly, an inflatable came racing across the water full of well-wrapped-up men. It didn't take me long to join them and enjoy the novelty of seeing *SW* from a distance as we blasted back to *Raw Cotton* and clambered up onto the deck.

And what a wonderful, stable, well-appointed deck it was. The luxury of having the space to actually walk somewhere without clinging on, or having to kneel like a continually frightened potential victim of the sea, was most refreshing. Compared with *SW*, *Raw Cotton* was a bastion of security. And compared with me, so was Malcolm McDougall: a self-made man who appeared to be semi-retired and in possession of a grand boat, and making the most of it. I was quietly confident that my driveshaft issue would not last long.

His crew gathered around my torn and ruptured vital piece of reinforced rubber that needed replacing, and like telepathic aliens focused their combined mind-powers on it. Passing it around, twisting and tugging it with grave expressions, interspersed with wry smirks, I knew it was in good hands. But they had nothing like it on board, and suggested I wait until the other, even larger, good Samaritan ship made its appearance in the bay. Slightly crestfallen but still feeling positive, there was nothing to do but agree and enjoy their company.

With the latest weather forecast printing out below in their navigation station, I carefully eyed the western high hills for any sign of a savage westerly or southwesterly wind shift. The wind was forecast to come and get us, but for the moment the time line was surprisingly vague. Sandy Bay was exposed to the whole fetch of Port Ross, and I remained acutely tuned in to the danger of a sudden, vicious wind shift. I'd seen it too often during my years in Wellington. A merciless southerly change blasting through with short notice and no compassion for unaware sailors. At 50 degrees south it was certainly a possibility.

I was full of perhaps unnecessary foreboding, and Malcolm and his crew empathized entirely with *SW*'s vulnerability. With no intention of hanging around waiting for the cruise ship to arrive, and perhaps end up with bull kelp wrapped around *SW* if a gale put us on the bricks, I made the executive decision to go and anchor where *Raw Cotton* had spent last night, up in the far corner of Laurie Harbour 5 miles away, and hopefully get some real physical and mental recovery sleep. I convinced myself that the engine in the immediate scheme of *SW* things wasn't really as important as my sleep. Our previous night's careful sailing in very light airs had been undoubtedly rewarding, and *SW* was primarily a sailing boat.

If it blew a gale the engine was a waste of time anyway, far too small with too much windage above deck from the rigging to make it helpful. I'd learnt from past experience that it wasn't worth turning it on if the wind was turned on. With sufficient breeze, *SW* could go anywhere. The engine's true value was in a flat calm. But it still worked, and most importantly I could charge the batteries to talk on the radio and show navigation lights when required.

A functioning auxiliary engine on a sailing boat certainly provides emotional reassurance. But in *SW*'s case that's about all. The emotional reassurance of being securely anchored in a reasonably sheltered spot, and sleeping like a normal human usually does, was by then the main priority.

Malcolm and co. were not prepared to let our simple problem defeat them, and kindly insisted they'd approach the cruise ship on my behalf when it arrived later on that afternoon. Leaving the pathetic small piece of ripped reinforced tyre rubber with them, I waved goodbye and pulled up the full mainsail and number one jib, bore *SW* away, and aimed up the harbour for the distant headland of Beacon Point, 4 miles southwest.

Nothing evil was brewing from the look of the sky down there; in fact, the northeasterly seemed to be freshening. We left *Raw Cotton* rolling on the ground-swell in Sandy Bay and ran gleefully away into the heart of Port Ross. This was good. We were here. We'd made it. A most satisfying sail was experienced by all as we ran flat off up towards Laurie Harbour and Erebus Cove.

Away from Enderby Island the northeasterly wind picked up, and sailing free over the flat sea there was nothing else to do but revel in the view. Others had done the same thing almost 200 years before, and the view then was virtually the same as the view now. No sign of human habitation anywhere.

While returning to England from Van Diemen's Land (Australia) in August 1806, Captain Abraham Bristow sighted land, but due to the 'lumbered state' of his ship sailed on past, heading for Cape Horn. The next year he returned in *Sarah*, again from the west, and rounded the north end of the island group he'd named 'Lord Auckland's Groupe'.

Sarah beat up against a westerly and anchored first near Ocean Island, 2 miles south of Enderby Island, then eventually got up into what he called Sarah's Bosom. He drew a distorted chart of how he saw the edge of the land and got most of Port Ross right, including the whereabouts of the isolated danger still known as Bristow Rock some 3 miles north of Enderby Island. The rest of the land he squashed into not enough space, but it still sort of resembled what it looks like today; at least, the northern part does. In 1840 Sir James Clark Ross renamed Sarah's Bosom 'Rendezvous Harbour' and it later became known as Port Ross.

Every piece of land on planet earth has now been charted, and skylines and shorelines have changed most dramatically over the years because of human occupation. The specialness of this place was its authentically unchanged nature. I was seeing what Bristow and his crew had seen. It was almost like time-travelling.

The terrible history of human suffering that this land had once witnessed made it even more compelling. Shipwrecked humans had looked longingly out from those bays before, hoping to spy the sail of a ship coming in to save them. Desperate and distraught on a daily basis, some had spent more than a year poorly clothed and underfed, looking and waiting. Waiting right there, half a mile away from us.

SW would have been noticeable to them then. Not a sailing ship, but a sail none the less. Probably a puzzlingly small sail.

The gravity of their once unsavoury circumstances was tangible to me that morning. I could almost see them waving and shouting.

The failed colony attempt called Hardwicke back in 1849 was also conspicuous by its absence. A rata forest canopy concealed the shore of Erebus Cove where once three ships had anchored in December 1849, and despatched settlers comprising medical men, clerks, a surveyor, a store-keeper, boatmen, coopers, shipwrights, carpenters, smiths, bricklayers, masons, agriculturists, labourers, 16 women and 14 children.

They cleared the large old rata trees from the low slope of Erebus Cove and made a tiny human settlement beside the cold waters, with their backs to the prevailing westerly gales in the lee of the Hooker Hills behind them; there in the Southern Ocean at 50 degrees south. They erected barracks for the single men, cottages for the married families and a house for the Lieutenant-Governor. A road was made along the waterfront, and sheep, cattle and horses joined the 'settlers' ashore to also wonder what they had got themselves into in such a remote and blatantly inhospitable place.

But it was a beautiful day today in Port Ross, and I fully understood the potential appeal of the place. They'd picked the right bay, tucked away under the high backdrop of the Hooker Hills and sheltered from the prevailing, and more or less relentless, westerly gales. I could imagine it then, a thriving little human enclave with buildings and people in the recently cleared open space.

My pick for buying real estate, from where I sat on *SW* examining Erebus Cove and the land above it, would be the slightly higher slopes behind where they built the settlement. If they'd stayed, I'm sure the Lieutenant-Governor and Assistant Commissioner would have eventually built their estates up there on Hardwicke Heights.

But they didn't stay. The weather was atrocious, worse than the north of Scotland, and growing fresh vegetables was proving difficult in the peaty, spongy bog that should have been soil. Cloudy Peak across the bay to the southwest was no doubt called that for the obvious reason. Such high land, at 400 metres straight up from Laurie Harbour, is bound to attract cloud and rain. Especially since it's the only high land for thousands of miles to the west where the wind was usually bringing the bad weather from.

Being rained on most of the days each year, and seeing those same few faces toiling their hours away each day, must have felt like torture for some. They were almost living in an experimental commune. The fiscal point of the exercise was to earn some money from the whaling trade, but the whales didn't really show much interest in being caught and the fleet of vessels that would require servicing never materialized as hoped.

Poor settlers, stuck there, more often than not in the rain, watching the gale-force gusts rip the surface off the sea in Port Ross while waiting for clients to swim or sail in so they could do their jobs as they had once done before, in the distant memory of their past lives.

By 1856 they were all gone. A failed colony soon forgotten. There were no humans to be seen, but the residue of their intense but futile endeavour was still apparent. Some buildings

175

were dismantled while others were left to slowly collapse into the rising, unattended and inevitable undergrowth. That's how the tormented survivors of the *Invercauld* shipwreck in 1864 and the *General Grant* shipwreck in 1866 finally found the area.

Desperately seeking salvation, many humans have gathered in Erebus Cove over the intervening years, all with the simple desire to survive in common.

I'd get back to them later to see how they were coping, but for now I was preoccupied with *SW*'s survival, and that meant sailing up to the head of Laurie Harbour to anchor and hopefully be tucked away from the impending inevitable gale.

Running down past Davis Island and Beacon Point in perfect moderate conditions topped off with warm sunshine, I watched as the landlocked reaches of Laurie Harbour opened up and we sledged on up to the end of the bay. The northeasterly was fresh now from behind us, and the further in we went, the more the idea of anchoring off Williamson Point started to feel less attractive. A fetch of 2 miles behind us, from where the wind was blowing, was making the intended destination surprisingly exposed and not quite what I'd hoped for.

The wind was nothing more than a local anomaly due to the high land around us, but in these latitudes I wasn't prepared to give the wind the benefit of my doubt. In my mind the northeasterly had to be the start of something evil, or so I convinced myself as I rounded *SW* up and began beating back to where we had just come from.

There were no completely sheltered nooks or crannies where we could anchor close to the shore that would suit the wind direction, so I tacked, and tacked again every time we closed on the floating beds of bull kelp on both sides of the shoreline. We slowly worked to windward and back out into Port Ross. The wind freshened more, and soon *SW* was staggering, over-powered, in the stronger gusts. A double-reefed main and number two jib soon fixed that, and even if *SW* looked slightly ridiculous with such a tiny amount of sail up, it was safe and efficient sailing.

Once we cleared Beacon Point and had Erebus Cove and Terror Cove under our lee, I could make out what looked like a substantial white apartment block floating up at Enderby Island. The cruise ship had arrived. The sky was starting to look a bit dismal and the barometer was dropping. With this wind direction the only land that would provide shelter was Enderby Island, which was a little annoying seeing that we'd just completed our paranoid lap of the harbour only to end up having to return. At least it was daylight, and I had a chance to see the numerous floating islands of kelp before we sailed into them. Being forced to go about because of their uncharted and slithery existence was a novelty. It really wasn't a place to sail or motor in the dark, unless you had to and possessed a decent spotlight.

With most of the shoreline fringed with deep water, I held on until the last moment before going about near Terror Cove, Shoe Island, Deas Head and Rose Island. It started feeling like another minor race to the sanctuary of the now well-populated Sandy Bay. But it was gratifying sailing, being in such auspicious surroundings and fully appreciating it. Mentally it was that state you enter when jet-lagged after a long-haul flight from the other side of the world, and then try to stay up even longer with a few beers thrown in for good measure. An artificial euphoria compounded by sheer physical exhaustion and chemicals.

I had no alcohol on board, and knew I was experiencing genuine fatigue brought on by an immense lack of proper uninterrupted sleep. From past experience I also knew this could become a dangerous state to be in if I didn't keep my wits about me and get my head down soon. But I was too elated at being there, and not ready to collapse yet. Besides, from the look of the large motorized inflatable boats full of paying passengers, dressed in survival suits and being launched from the mother cruise ship, *SW* had some pressing showbiz to attend to.

The *Orion* had arrived precisely on time, and was now anchored in the lee of Enderby and rolling horrendously on the ground-swell coming around the corner from the nearby open ocean. Inflatable dinghies with large diesel outboards, packed with camera-wielding and environmentally enamoured tourists, were running a circuit down to Rose Island and the channel that says 'Passage not recommended' on the chart, then back up to Sandy Bay. They were then hanging just outside the surf line on the beach and letting all on board absorb the sub-Antarctic splendour of it all, often through impressive-looking camera lenses.

It was a safe, well-organized way to view it. The process of the passengers boarding the inflatables from the low-down side door at almost water level, onto a temporary gangway, then into the boats, was a well-executed thing, especially given the rolling the *Orion* was doing.

I steered *SW* as close as I dared to go near them without becoming a navigational hazard, and had a good but discreet look at the well-wrapped-up passengers through the gap between *SW*'s upright stanchion and the windward cockpit weather-cloth. Heeled over hard on the wind, I peered at them from the anonymity of the hidden cockpit and knew *SW* was presenting a most appealing, nuggety, multi-chined look of small but sturdy seaworthiness to them.

Further into Sandy Bay, *Raw Cotton* was also found unpleasantly rolling at anchor, and after a close-quarters sail-by and conversation, *SW* ended up dangling off her stern on a long line, looking like a dinghy or, at best, a lifeboat. Malcolm had had a very productive afternoon on *SW*'s behalf. While we had sailed about Port Ross enjoying the view, he had contacted the captain of the *Orion* and had explained *SW*'s minor predicament.

The ship's engineer had got involved and a boat had promptly been despatched over to *Raw Cotton* to collect *SW*'s small shredded piece of reinforced tyre rubber for a template. The *Orion* was leaving that night, and they weren't mucking around. Just as promptly, two new rubber versions arrived on *Raw Cotton*. It was astonishing law-of-the-sea-mariner assistance stuff, and most noble as far as I was concerned.

But unfortunately, their rubber was a bit too soft. It wasn't reinforced with fabric and felt more like easily torn jelly by comparison with what had torn. We all agreed it was a wonderful and magnanimous effort from someone none of us had met, nor directly and personally communicated with. Here in Port Ross, for posterity, another — albeit minor — scenario of human compassion in assisting a slightly distressed mariner had been played out.

On board *Raw Cotton*, we all agreed that something made of hard plastic would do better. From the galley a thick, opaque plastic chopping board suddenly appeared, and found itself well fondled before being unceremoniously hacked to pieces and drilled full of holes in appropriate places. Despite the incessant rolling, it was a very good result as far as I was concerned.

It was now obvious via a new satellite-print-out weather-forecast that the westerly gale was rushing across the Southern Ocean at us, and due to arrive soon.

Malcolm wanted out of Sandy Bay for obvious exposed-anchorage potential-lee-shore reasons, and like them I was off back to where I'd just spent a few hours returning from. I promised to follow them; another run downwind up the harbour to inspect a twilight view would not be too difficult, especially since I'd just had a practise go at it. But Malcolm and his crew of merry men insisted we accompany them. It was a done deal as far as they were concerned. *SW* would be towed quick-march down Port Ross forthwith, and no bill for doing so would be presented.

It was a magnanimous and humorous offer, but I had my reservations. Five miles under tow. *SW* had never been towed before, not to my knowledge. They were all adamant it had to happen, so I assisted in attaching the tow rope and pushed off downwind as they wound up *Raw Cotton*'s anchor on their powerful electric windlass.

Then we were away. Going fast, with me clutching the tiller to counter the seemingly huge pressures on the skeg and rudder as *SW* tried to slew to one side or the other while sending up unprecedented bow waves down the sides of the hull and big, deep furrows racing out from behind. It was nothing short of scary to start with, and I feared an out-of-control slew to one side, and tripping then rolling to windward and swamping while they looked the other way, talking obliviously in their cockpit.

It took a lot of pressure on the tiller to keep *SW* tracking behind *Raw Cotton*, and I wasn't enjoying it. The stresses on the skeg and rudder if I let her track too much to one side felt awful. I imagined the new skeg just snapping off at the much-laboured-over glue-line and dangling there loose, hanging by its new bolts until we got back to Laurie Harbour.

Raw Cotton was sitting on 7½ knots, and I was noticing it. *SW* seemed to be sucked down low in the water with the velocity, and was being dragged. There was no sense of light buoyant skipping over the waves that comes from normal wind-propelled sailing.

Starting to feel genuinely tired — all the forearm work on correcting the tiller was wearing me out — I began fantasizing about going forward and cutting the line, and leaving *SW* in their wake to dawdle down in her own time. But I couldn't leave the tiller at that speed. With utmost concentration wearing thin, I did acknowledge that we were making exceedingly fine progress, and then an unexpected object arrived to boost my waning optimism.

A man called Dave stood on the back deck of *Raw Cotton* with a bottle of beer attached to the line of a fishing rod. The bottle was carefully lowered and floated, then let go in the rapidly flowing wake of *Raw Cotton* and it skipped down to *SW* on the swirling foam. It banged down the side of the hull and I managed to lean over, lift it up, unattach it and let the nylon fishing line depart back to *Raw Cotton*.

A beer with this view was too good to be true. But it was, and I started relaxing as Malcolm reduced speed to negotiate what had become the uncharted obstacle-course of floating islands of untroubled kelp that I had studiously sailed around only hours before.

At the far end of Laurie Harbour I recognized the view like

a local would, having so recently made its acquaintance. Now the wind was more from the north and easing, patchy and most patches were non-threatening. *Raw Cotton* cast us off when it was on the edge of the 7-metre line and was not interested in heading further in.

SW slowly drifted close to Williamson Point on the last of our towing momentum, and I dropped the anchor and plenty of chain over the side into 4 metres of cold salt water; suffocating the lot in a high-viscosity, good holding compound commonly called mud.

I'd been invited to dinner, and in no time at all a water-taxi arrived to take me away.

Raw Cotton represented everything I had voluntarily been missing out on recently. Warmth, comfort, company. Tonight, in this unlikely place, was the night to become reacquainted with it all. The smell of roast lamb in the oven and the heat of a large, spacious cabin down below, far removed from the cold darkness outside, was a great start.

With eight people on board, fresh water was surprisingly no issue, courtesy of the desalinator plumbed in somewhere. A hot-water shower, as if I was in a hotel, was beyond my expectations and as the night progressed so were many other things.

While salivating for the product of the appealing cooking aromas, I was led to an email machine and posted an 'all's well on board' email to people I knew who were concerned about me. Having despatched the latest bulletin on our whereabouts, dinner was ready.

Together at the round table, shoulder to shoulder with laird McDougall, we well-provided-for sailors consumed a roast dinner with gravy and all the other trimmings. Given our circumstances, anchored in that bay of many previous hungry and desperate souls, it was almost perverse. They were outside, keeping their distance, peering in with drooling mouths and very distraught countenances, exhorting their friend the hostile wind to rise to a furious strength and teach us all that we shouldn't scoff in front of them like that.

I heard and felt the first heavy gusts descending on the harbour while I was urinating over the side up on deck. It shrieked in the rigging above the human volume of frivolity downstairs, and through the pleasure of it all I wondered what that meant for *SW*.

As I looked out into the black void of absolute darkness around us, the wind was now coming in sporadic gusts, sweeping down from the steep Hooker Hills to the north. *SW* had no anchor light, as I was saving the battery and didn't expect anyone else in the bay that night.

Back at the party inside, a crew member had done due diligence on me and found some of my songs on his iPod. Karaoke was the only option left, and after fighting to the death I reluctantly obliged. There was no other way to show my appreciation for such an unexpected fine meal, hospitality, and good company.

'Forever Tuesday Morning' (an exclusively New-Zealand-only song conspicuous in the 1980s) blasted out of Malcolm's substantial sound system at 50 degrees south. I was singing for my supper. By that stage of the evening and after the previous non-stop few days I was fairly far gone, and it probably wasn't a good look.

I darted up outdoors to gauge the wind's hostility now and then, and then some time in the night it was time to go home.

Phil Morris drew the short straw and pulled on his wet-weather gear, along with me, and we left the warmth and friendship down below to get back to *SW*.

Down from *Raw Cotton* into the rubber dinghy with the outboard going. Into the absolutely black, overcast night, with only a general sense of direction, we motored cautiously along, with me at the front shining a torch to find and avoid any floating kelp. The wind was being deceptive: nothing at all, then it would come at us in sudden, unpredictable, threatening punctuation marks, short-lived gusts rushing fast.

Thankfully *SW* was still there, floating in the dark alone, hanging on her anchor chain and facing more or less north.

Back on board, it was cold by contrast to *Raw Cotton*'s innards. I could see my breath. I quickly buried myself fully clothed in the sleeping bag, and immediately lost consciousness. Two hours later I involuntarily regained consciousness, and started paying attention to what was going on outside. The westerly gale had arrived and brought with it all the social vengeance the earlier uninvited and begrudging, dead spectators had desired.

SW heeled, then slewed on large arcs of passive resistance, held on the loving leash of our precious long scope of anchor chain. The wind had shifted and was now funnelling down the valley between the Hooker Hills and Cloudy Peak. Looking at the chart with very bleary eyes, it was obvious that we were anchored in a wind factory. Add a little bit, and you'll get a lot. Add a gale, and you'll get a storm.

I clambered out on deck feeling very chilled and unwelcome. More anchor chain was let go, as much as possible, then back to bed with the lee cloth in place to stop myself falling out of bed as *SW* heeled over when attacked by another evilly violent squall. Warm and trying to feel indifferent, once again I sort of slept until it got light.

SW was still where I preferred her to be when the close-to-hand view of Laurie Harbour arrived at dawn. So was *Raw Cotton*.

The wind howled hard all that day. I had no intention of moving and neither did the anchor, which I was grateful for. We were stuck fast to the bottom, veering and yawing in a wind funnel. The wind arrived from across the Southern Ocean and rushed up over the high cliffs to the west of Auckland Island, and then constricted itself into a perfect funnel, rushing even faster down the valley between the Hooker Hills and Cloudy Peak and Mount Eden to the south.

The squalls appearing on the water to windward were relentlessly vicious in strength, and down to leeward the wind lifted the surface from the sea, creating towering minor whirlwinds of malevolent force. They didn't matter to me. I was occupied inside doing the driveshaft surgery, and making a proper meal of it.

Phil Morris had loaned me the use of a cordless drill, in case I needed one, and I found that I did. *SW*'s engine room is a difficult place to access. As said before, for years I'd contorted myself, awkwardly grasping spanners and feeling with my fingers for nuts and bolts I could never see. 'Constricted' is the right word.

The old driveshaft bolts had had a hard life from my previous, inexpert, tightening and had become even more reluctant to come undone. While the wind howled outside I lay there contorted, brandishing spanners and swear words, and undid what I had to do. *SW* heeled and tugged at the anchor, but it was nothing more than uncomfortable. With a bit of earnest drilling to get the holes just right, eventually I got the new carved-up plastic carving board bolted in place.

Things inboard looked satisfactory to me. The engine should now make the propeller go round. Only one issue remained. Was there anything still left wrapped around the propeller?

Raw Cotton had left later on in the morning, so no outdoor modesty was required. A quick skinny-dip and feel of the prop with my cold, wet fingers was all that was needed to have the auxiliary problem truly rectified. Late in the afternoon, with the squalls moderating and the blue sky sporadically showing, I found it in myself to brave the cold wind and climb over the stern and down into the freezing water. My gasping and spluttering went unheard, and my hand felt the propeller and shaft. There was no weed there. Introduced to another level of 'cold', I clambered back up into the comparatively warmish wind, towelled down and got reacquainted with the sleeping bag.

Once my body temperature had returned to normal, I turned the engine on and gave it a burst. *SW* moved forward just enough to make my recent efforts feel worth it.

That evening before the sun went down, I sat outside in the cockpit and had my usual evening meal. Satisfied that we had auxiliary power if we needed it, I chewed my ravenous way through a small pile of hot potatoes and raw garlic doused in oily, cold canned tuna. Nice. The gusts were still trying to be unpleasant, but they'd definitely punched themselves out during the day.

Dug with a knife on a bluff

Up on the steep hillside of the Hooker Hills, a rocky ledge projected out like an artificial canopy. I stared at it for a long time and imagined that if I was shipwrecked and looking for shelter, a night would surely have been spent up under there. Alone in such an auspicious and unfrequented place, I felt its history getting the better of me.

On 10 May 1864, the 888-ton sailing ship *Invercauld* with 25 crew had smacked into the northwest corner of Auckland Island. A commonly large sea was running due to an equally common hard northwesterly wind.

When it got light the next morning, 19 souls were still alive and huddled on a narrow strip of shingle at the base of the tall cliffs behind them. With no shoes, cuts on very cold feet, totally wet through and wearing inadequate clothing, their reality survivor quest began.

It didn't end well: only three alive to greet the ship that eventually arrived in Port Ross over a year later. With no wreck left worth scavenging, and cliffs to climb, they ended up with every human for itself — some allegedly eating others — with the last robust survivors making it to Erebus Cove and the remnants of the Hardwicke settlement that had been vacated more than 10 years previously.

No supermarket or corner shop. No foreseeable supply of food other than what you can forage for. And feeling cold all the time.

As it started getting dark, I imagined they were there, huddled under the over-hanging rocks up on the steep slope to our north. A better place than anywhere else to spend the cold night on that hillside. And there they were again, making their way along the rocks at low tide, along the northern shore of Laurie Harbour, heading east towards the rumour of a dead colonial village or at least the promise of a castaway depot.

Some of the *Dundonald* survivors from 1907 had done the same. By then, the New Zealand government had set up finger-posts pointing to Erebus Cove just around the corner from Laurie Harbour; and full of the thought of immediate salvation, four true survivalists had painstakingly picked their way along that foreshore. Wrecked on Disappointment Island 6 miles west of Auckland Island, the crew had made a coracle out of gnarly brush and salvaged sailcloth, and paddled across to the 'mainland'.

On a second attempt, not taking die for an answer, four men had pushed on down the big valley (the one that had accelerated the wind strength all night), found the signpost, and carried desperately on. I could see them now, slowly working along the rocky low-tide foreshore, or through the low scrub higher up the hill; all bedraggled and fired with desperate survival intent.

What would they have made of seeing *SW* anchored there? I went to sleep listening to them swearing at me from the shore.

The next day the wind had eased and veered into the north again. I took advantage of it to sail back to Enderby Island.

Raw Cotton was anchored around the corner in Erebus Cove, visiting the canopy of rata trees that covered the remains of Hardwicke, and the tiny cemetery up the slope. We waved to each other as *SW* beat past in a rapidly freshening northerly wind.

Today it was my turn to go ashore on Enderby Island, and via VHF radio we co-ordinated how best to legally take my first step ashore. DOC has worked methodically to make Enderby Island a pest-free place for indigenous birds and sea creatures to live an unmolested life. In keeping with the regulations, they offered a person to baby-sit *SW* while I came ashore to stretch my legs. They also offered to come and get me, which was an offer I couldn't refuse, especially after watching the dumping surf on the beach at Sandy Bay.

I threw the anchor over the bow and let out the chain, then waited for the inevitable dig-in down below and turn of the bow to the offshore wind to prove we really were attached to a piece of planet earth. Expecting company and the prospect of an unknown person sitting in *SW* for a few hours, I did my best to tidy up and make things look slightly inviting. There wasn't much to do; it was what it is, more a damp sail locker than anything else.

While I was pottering unnecessarily around inside, I felt *SW* lift and jerk nastily on the ground-swell. I'd brought her in too close to the shelving beach and had not put enough scope (chain length) out to compensate for the lift of each passing swell. Snubbing is the technical term for what was being experienced, and it didn't feel good. Expecting company shortly, I hastily stood on the bow and pulled up the anchor to break it free from the sand below, and let *SW* drift back a bit away from the beach. Letting go again in slightly deeper water, I watched the strong, numerous links of chain rattle out over the bow-fitting down into the sea again.

By absolute chance, my eye caught something that came as a shock. One of the welded chain links was open, torn apart by the previous snubbing, and ready to stretch a bigger gap if left with the opportunity to do so. I didn't realize that chain links had the capacity, when under pressure, to open up and become untrustworthy.

As the DOC inflatable was being pushed out by people in waders through the breaking surf on the nearby beach, I fumbled around inside *SW* looking for a shackle to compensate for what was blatantly a dangerous flaw in my ground-tackle. A thinner than preferred stainless shackle was found and inserted in the right links of chain, and I let it all out to disappear into the sea, to hopefully hold *SW* where she was.

The wind was gusting 20 to 25 knots off the beach and I figured that with a lot of chain out, she should still be there when I got back from wandering about onshore a few hours later.

Simon Childerhouse, the boat-sitter, came aboard with a good book to read, and seemed prepared to settle in for some time. I briefly explained how to pull the sails up and start the engine, if blown out of the bay, but we agreed the VHF was the key to *SW*'s salvation; a call for assistance in daylight would be sufficient. As well as that, Simon reassured me he knew how to sail.

I climbed onto the inflatable, and Jacinda hard-throttled it away for a speedy lap of Sandy Bay, like an aquatic girl-racer giving the outboard a good thrashing. I hung on like a scared cat until she throttled back to idle just out from the surf line on the beach, waiting for the right moment to make a rush for it. After a few big rollers collapsed on the sand, Jacinda booted it and all of a sudden we ran up on the beach with all hands leaping overboard and dragging the boat, as fast as possible, beyond the next incoming wave.

Firmly aground with my feet on the sand, I started staggering up the beach on my maladjusted sea legs. I'd been all set with my jandals on, ready to go ashore, but Jacinda had instructed me to wear my sea-boots as the possibility of picking up worms and other parasites from stepping in the seal and sea lion faeces on the beach was apparently very real. I didn't intend to tread on any pooh, but having landed, and judging by the inebriated way I was walking, it was a distinct possibility.

I know when I stagger sober on the land that I've got my sea legs, and I won't feel sea-sick on the sea. This was one of those moments, and it was almost comical. Definitely humour at my expense. It was a satisfactory feeling standing on the earth again, and looking out at *SW* with someone whom I'd only just met and couldn't see, inside, anchored in the bay.

All the humans on board the land were most welcoming. Three women and another man. The rest of the species lounging around on the beach looked like trouble if I ventured too close. A female scientist called Kerry, a resident vet, was finishing her doctorate from Massey University and offered to show me around the island. I couldn't resist the temptation to explore. That was what I was there for.

With her shorts and boots and a small pack strapped to her back, she marched off in front of me and I immediately followed, feeling ill-equipped but determined to keep up. Straight away, by looking at her bottom and the back of her legs in front of me, I could tell that she was fit. And fitter than me. Her legs were moving too efficiently, and I knew my determination to keep up was going to be severely compromised if we had a long way to walk.

Three hours later I knew that my initial evaluation had been correct, but I'd had a good look around.

It started with the decrepit A-frame castaway hut buried in the gnarly, wind-shaped 'Goblin Forest' close to the DOC huts. It had been built a long time ago by the look of it, and shipwreck survivors had undoubtedly huddled together in there many years ago. It had a small, low doorway, just large enough for a human to crawl in through, like a dog kennel. They'd built it in a nicely sheltered spot away from the beach, tucked down low amongst the stunted southern rata forest and bush myrtle.

Once we'd done our thoughtful staring at it, we struck out at a quick pace and walked a long, flat mile across open scrub and magnificently smelling megaherbs on a narrow wooden boardwalk. The path stopped above the northern cliffs of the island and we stood for a while, just the two of us, staring again — not at each other, but at the enormous, turbulent sea that stretched out in a 180-degree arc from the west through the north to the east.

The northerly wind was freshening and the rocky coast below

surged, alive, with swells and waves imploding then washing back into the frighteningly indifferent rough sea. It was the sound I'd heard a few nights before, the immense power of wind-driven water meeting the land. It was a sudden-death coast that needed to be avoided by a sailing boat, no matter what. If *SW* had been pushed onto there, it would have been instant doom.

The view and sound didn't seem to disturb Kerry as much as it did me, and to prove it she struck out off the wooden walkway and led me east along the cliff-tops towards the most northern part of Enderby Island. The spongy, peaty, partially boggy whatever-it-was underfoot was peculiar to step on, and I found myself sometimes bouncing along, and quietly panting, hoping my guide would slow down.

She didn't, and I started visualizing myself as a desperate castaway, stumbling frantically through the obstacle course of tussock, *Bulbinella rossii* megaherbs and peaty bog holes to get to a McDonald's outlet, or at least a place to rest and shelter, as soon as possible.

Just before turning south and heading back inland, we paused and took photos of each other in that isolated place. Out to the northeast I stared for another few minutes, catching my breath, fixating on the breakers washing ferociously over the Derry Castle Reef.

What a place to be wrecked. On 20 March 1887 at 2 a.m., the iron barque *Derry Castle* did exactly that. She was a sailing ship moving at 12 knots, nine days out from Australia and running for Cape Horn, with no idea what they were about to run into. Poor visibility and a lack of certainty as to where, exactly, they were has been the theme for most of the Auckland Island sailing-ship disasters.

The *Derry Castle* was no exception. Only 100 metres to the left would have got them past, probably unaware of what was waiting there in the black, cold night to starboard if the helmsman wasn't paying that much attention. But it didn't work out that way. Of 23 on board only eight got ashore, the other 15 perishing in the breaking waves battering the reef I was now looking at. Once in the water, survival would have been a random thing as they were washed on and sucked off those rocks. A bed of swirling bull kelp might have cushioned the slam, but the prospects from impact didn't look good. It was reported that the sailmaker clung all night to the mizzen mast, then, with daylight, leapt into the sea to try to swim to shore. The survivors already there watched him being swept out to sea.

Two tins of herrings, a pumpkin and some wheat from their cargo were washed ashore. The wheat soon went mouldy and started to sprout. Some of the bodies of those who were pounded and then flung onto the rocks, subject to the harsh lottery of the dispassionate sea, were recovered by their shipmates. The bodies were hardly recognizable, with eyes removed by equally dispassionate skua gulls. The survivors removed the clothes from the bodies, with the imperative of self-preservation foremost in their distressed minds. The warmth of a dead person's clothes. The captain, chief officer and a fo'castle hand were buried in shallow graves dug with a knife on a low bluff nearby.

The castaways found a little run-down hut, but all they found inside was a bottle of salt. Without fire, their diet consisted mainly of shellfish, as they found raw seal meat unpalatable.

Even in February, in the southern summer, at 50 degrees south the cold is not to be underestimated. The air has a winter feel to it, regardless of the wind direction. Craving heat and warmth and cooking facilities — and no doubt trauma counselling — they found that a damp revolver cartridge stuffed in someone's pocket turned into salvation. The bullet was extracted and replaced with a piece of dry cotton, then the whole thing was set fire to with a hard whack from a sharp stone. Someone knew what they were doing.

Fortunately, it didn't all end in a pathetic puff of smoke. The flash of the cartridge made the cotton smoulder, and with careful human encouragement in the form of air blown by mouth and reinforced with more thin, dry things to burn, a fire resulted. In their terribly isolated, deprived and emotionally tormented situation, it must have been a magnificent moment.

Once the fire started, it was never allowed to go out. A roster of attendants maintained the flames, and mouldy wheat salvaged from the rocks was toasted, then crushed and mixed with hot water to eat. The eight survivors lived for three months on Enderby Island, and the tobacco addicts were forced to withdraw.

Tantalizingly close, just across Port Ross at Erebus Cove, a castaway provision depot with food, clothing, and more substantial shelter was known to exist; not much more than 3 miles away. After desperate foraging an old axe head was eventually found buried in the sand, and making the most of what they found where their shipmates had drowned, they managed to build a small boat, six feet long by two and a half feet wide. Two men paddled across, presumably on a good settled day, and later someone paddled back to carefully move the remaining people back, on more than one occasion, to the comparative comfort of Erebus Cove.

Unfortunately, the castaway boat at the depot had been found to be unfit for use. The survivors then spent another month amongst the overgrown relics of the Hardwicke colony, abandoned over 30 years before. Then another form of salvation finally arrived, in the shape of a sailing boat looking for seals, the *Awarua*. The ordeal of the *Derry Castle* survivors became history.

Kerry eventually rescued me from becoming melancholy over other people's misfortune, and we struck out vigorously again, tramping south through what I was finding to be increasingly difficult terrain.

I was tired, that was all. Kerry wasn't tired at all, and was just burning a few unwanted calories judging by the pace of her gait. When she halted, I caught her up, pretending not to be out of breath. We'd trekked a short, free-form course back from the cliffs to almost the highest plateau on Enderby, at 39 metres above sea level. It was where the automatic repeater weather station lived.

Incongruous in its natural surroundings, this bastion of human technology made a refreshing change to all the indigenous flora and fauna around it. Carefully tied down with substantial guy-stays to stop it blowing away in such an exposed place, it looked fairly unimportant from the outside.

But that little, robust miniature met station had more to it than met my eye. Every day it beams out its showbiz radio signal over the SSB radio airwaves, letting all the listeners know what's up, wind-wise, at the Auckland Islands. The Campbell Island and Enderby Island repeater station shout-outs had meant a lot to me on the way down from Auckland. A robotic, matter of fact, automated voice reading out the wind speed, direction and barometer inclination and pressure.

Now I was here, and I could touch it. And I did.

An albatross colony was seated nearby watching my demonstration of admiration for the weather station. They were on their own turf there, living an unmolested life nesting in the long grass. One decided to show off, in case I came to close to its friends. It knew what it was doing, using a runway in the grass to stagger along into the prevailing wind while it flapped its rather large wings in a clumsy but relevant way. Certainly not a sprightly sparrow with helicopter-style flying abilities, but miraculously it did get off the ground, and flew away then circled around, just to show me what I, frustratingly, will never be able to do.

Fully understanding the difficulty of walking on this spongy, boggy, uneven surface, I empathized with those long-gone, barefooted and bedraggled *Derry Castle* survivors who had travelled this way before. Emotionally traumatized and physically truly deprived, they had stumbled their way over this cold place, 120 years before.

The view was the same — no sign of human life out to the south and west in Port Ross. The skyline of the land surrounding the harbour, Mount Eden, Flat-Topped Hill and the Hooker Hills, were all as unspoilt, distant and emotionally impassive as then.

My Amazon woman guide was by now almost dragging me along on a mental lead through the low scrub behind her. The pause at the weather station had sort of saved me from my own fatigue, but I was truly understanding what a lack of energy really means.

Back in the 'Goblin Forest' made of stunted rata, a yellow-eyed penguin took us by surprise. I'd always associated penguins with the sea or with ice floes, and to find one in a dim thicket of wood and shrubs, well inland from the beach, didn't seem right. It made a startled noise and then its gang mates, equally hidden in their forest headquarters, made more noise and it was all on.

One tried to block our way. The path out to the invitingly bright daylight suddenly became more important. I got ready to beat or strangle it into submission if it wouldn't let us pass, especially if its mates started circling in behind. Having come this far, and feeling tired, I wasn't prepared to tolerate losing in an inter-species 'you or me' fight situation.

Kerry pointed out that this wasn't the modern way, and eventually it moved while mocking us in a penguin dialect I wasn't familiar with.

Out of the forest and in the short grassy hillocks that bordered the beach, we found more overly self-confident species trying to block our way — massive slugs with faces that smelt bad were lying around everywhere. It was like being at Kelly Tarlton's underwater wildlife zoo without anyone having erected the fences to keep the large beasts where they belonged. That's because they belonged here, had ancestral tenure on the place, and I did not.

Once I adjusted to the novelty of being allowed to walk around in their enclosure, I pretended to appear relaxed, but it was difficult to relinquish my heightened sense of caution. They were lying everywhere, and in lots of places where I didn't expect them. Large old male seals, female seals, pup seals, Hooker sea lions, sea-bears (females), lying about indolently, for no apparent reason. Luxuriating on land. Belching, swatting flies, offering aggressive warnings and primarily just basking in the warmth of a short-lived land-based holiday before some instinct kicked in and they went back into the cold water to hunt, and eat, other less capable living things.

The young ones with their big, inquisitive eyes just check

you out in a simple, honest inter-species way. They were easy to navigate through. I took pictures of them. Young and on land, vulnerable massive slugs with appealing faces, seeing us as we were seeing them; our only real connection through our mutually interested eyes. The adult males and females required a prudent course plotted to avoid any unnecessary anger. We did so, then came back to Sandy Bay in sight of *SW* and the DOC huts.

It had been three hours of walking and stumbling, and if I had known what lay before me I probably wouldn't have signed up. But with hindsight, it had definitely been worth it.

From the sand of Sandy Bay I could see that the northerly wind was now blowing quite hard. It was a sheltered, flat-water, reasonably safe place to be anchored for now, but what was the latest forecast anticipating?

Pretending to walk in a normal way while worn out, I made it back to the buildings and found Jacinda doing her laundry Auckland Islands-style. An old-fashioned 1970s wringer set up outside was being very usefully employed, squeezing all the unwanted fluid from the garments.

Inside the main mess room, the aroma of freshly baking food surrounded by the warmth of a well-heated space felt more than welcoming. It's wonderful how we humans adapt to the cold, and cope with a constant low temperature if we have to and after a prolonged time get used to it. But when the difference presents itself by way of a solid-fuel hot-burning stove in a small building, the contrast can become overwhelming.

Inside and overwhelmed, I had to take my jersey off, and like the sea lions on the beach outside the window, I found myself luxuriating. Fighting the desire for sleep that new warmth brings, I talked to Jacinda.

She has a New Zealand Cross award but doesn't talk about it. Kerry told me on our tramp around Enderby about Jacinda Amy's reputation. I could tell by my first impressions and the way she had handled her inflatable that she was a woman of the outdoors. In 1992 she'd been stationed as a research officer on Campbell Island, 130-something miles southeast of the Auckland Islands. Most people are not known for gravitating to that kind of isolated space.

Keeping themselves occupied, she and her fellow DOC workers took to the very cold sea in wetsuits with snorkels and went swimming about the surface for something to do. Mike Fraser, the team leader and underwater cameraman, swam about looking for a good place to hopefully film any whales, if they happened to turn up. Jacinda and three others snorkelled about as well until a great white shark attacked Mike and tore half his arm off. He fought back: 'The fact my arm came off may have satisfied him a bit.'

With the natural impulse to save themselves pumping through their still-intact veins, the others kicked to shore. But not Jacinda. She swam out further, stayed in the water, got hold of Mike and towed him 30 metres back to shore. Via helicopter rides and a lot of medical help along the way, Mike Fraser lived. Jacinda got the New Zealand Cross award in 1999 for her bravery.

Not only that, but she'd also sailed with the legendary Gerry Clark in *Totorore*, the 28-foot twin-keel Alan Wright Nova design in which he had circumnavigated the world at high latitudes.

Not only that, but she had also been a field support co-ordinator at Scott Base in Antarctica, worked for DOC for years in kakapo and takahe programmes, and spent a few seasons killing rats as well.

Not only that, but more: she was now standing beside me, pouring hot, molten chocolate icing all over freshly baked fudge cake.

Inside the hut I was feeling hot now and, having discarded some layers, was ready to go to sleep. Outside, *SW* floated all too obviously in the view through the side window of the hut, in a strong offshore wind. I felt one of those total disengagement moments coming on. A couple of days and nights safe ashore here would be wonderful. Let *SW* swing and veer alone to whatever nasty winds wanted to blow through the bay. She'd lurched and bobbed to all sorts of errant gusts for seven years, floating neglected in Little Shoal Bay. What was so wrong with being alone here now for a while?

Through the haze of reassuring conversation, aromas and overwhelming warmth, the answer was obvious. There was Simon, whom I didn't really know, obligingly waiting on *SW* for me to return and relieve him of his stoically long stay at anchor, on watch, on *SW*.

Jacinda seemed to notice me sliding into a state of dissolute enjoyment, and sensitively reminded me of my pressing, serious agenda. The northerly wind was now blowing hard off the beach and DOC had an obligation to get me back to *SW* before it got dark. They weren't allowed to gad about in their inflatables at night.

I pulled myself together and got ready to go. We shared the same frame of mind, there that day in Sandy Bay. Talking of who had suffered here before us in that beautiful natural view. The seriousness of their past endurance brought an authentic gravity to the beach and sea view. I spoilt it in my own mind by thinking I was about to blurt out 'Let me stay!' and offer to scuttle *SW* and get a chopper back. But Jacinda had pointed out earlier how expensive helicopter rides this far south were.

It took me a while, but I did find the courage to actually blurt out that I had items of grave interest to me that I wished to purchase from the natives, if it was at all possible. Part of pulling myself together earlier on had included the realization that this place with humans and its own limited resources was my last chance for potential foraging for anything that I might end up desperately needing on the voyage back to New Zealand.

I went to the long-drop toilet up behind their huts as a matter of urgency, and noticed a tent strung up amongst the trees. I'd been told that was where Jacinda slept. The girls' dormitory should have been sufficient, but Jacinda preferred life out in the cold with the wildlife by herself. Good on her.

On the way back from the long-drop, I found the DOC supply of citrus fruit, just sitting there unattended, uncovered, and very inviting. A big pile of oranges. I'd eaten all my oranges on the way from Port Chalmers to Port Ross, and had started missing them. Some past-life scurvy-ridden impulse beset me, and I found my arm with a hand on it reaching out to take one. I can't remember what happened next.

It was obvious that I had to splurt out my needs ASAP or my last opportunity for vital resources could be lost. I simply had to own up for my own good, and announce that my expedition to and from the Auckland Islands was slightly under-provisioned. My spicy two-minute noodle supply was more than adequate, and possibly contributed to overall buoyancy. There was plenty of oily canned tuna wedged in everywhere and lots of weightless, dry cracker biscuits. And still enough garlic to keep loved ones away from my mouth.

But more fresh water to fill my growing collection of empty two-litre bottles was imperative. Depending on the wind direction, and my own sense of sailing resolve, I knew I might be away from a convenient tap for quite some time.

On 30 January I wrote a Father Christmas list of things I'd like, in case our circumstances changed for the worst in the coming weeks and I had to become preoccupied with staying alive. Fresh water, petrol (to keep charging the battery to talk to concerned people), oranges ...

23

Just before another gale began

I signed the visitors' book that Gerry Clark had gifted to the Enderby base. He had written in the front, and to see his handwriting provided me with another auspicious expedition moment.

Litres of much-appreciated fresh water and a few of petrol, plus a bag of oranges and a tray of still-warm chocolate-iced fudge cake, accompanied me back to *SW*. A mild jesting over the duration of a non-stop voyage back to Auckland up the west coasts of New Zealand was entered into; I settled on 21 days. Murray Blake was more sceptical, and thought I should not expect to see Rangitoto Island in the Hauraki Gulf until March.

On the beach, we all had our wetsuit/waders on, and waited for the right withdrawing surge then charged into the cold water and jumped aboard. The outboard roared, and away we rushed out to visit *SW* and discover whether Simon was still alive on board. He emerged, having done a good 5 hours' boat-sitting for my benefit.

I pulled off the set of borrowed wetsuit/waders, gave them back, and waved goodbye. Their short-lived umbrella of company and security receded into the salty haze of the breakers on the beach, and I got out my binoculars to help wish them safely ashore again. It was an art they had certainly mastered.

It had been another big Auckland Islands day for me. But it wasn't over yet. The wind was now blowing hard, and *SW* slewed and veered on the anchor chain. I let out all the scope I had, and went back inside for a fatigued think.

Looking out of the companionway, Ocean Island and Ewing Island were there downwind, low and conspicuous, over a mile away behind us to leeward. Properly prudent sailors in these kinds of places put out multiple anchors when it starts blowing and stand anchor watches all night, making sure the boat isn't dragging its anchors downwind to potential lee-shore destruction. My intention had been to get on board and pull up the anchor, then sail off down to Erebus Cove and hide away from what was meteorologically inevitable. The northerly gale would scream all night, then back as always to the west and southwest.

Sandy Bay was no place to stay with a forecast like that. Eventually there would be a hard southwest wind driving onto the beach and making even sea lions bellow for environmentally uncomfortable reasons. I could see the worst now. All would be lost, *SW* on her side bouncing on the sand or grinding on the rocks amongst the writhing kelp, and all because I stayed ashore for the night to socialize in good company.

In my dreams, or so it now seems, I made the right decision. It was too windy by then to go anywhere else and it felt like there was no other choice but to stay put. Our doom lay downwind if the anchor chain parted or the anchor dragged. No one would come to save us. DOC weren't allowed out at night, nor should I rely on them (even though mentally I had already started to).

Just before it got dark, the wind accelerated considerably and raced in savagely over Enderby Island, blasting across the flat water of Sandy Bay. The sky was filled with fast-moving apocalyptic clouds, a mixture of lemon and bruised colours, and seemed to me full of other-worldly malevolent intent. I felt my seamanship wanting, and knew I should rouse myself to do more.

Bark instructions at an imaginary crew? 'Steam forward and release the second anchor. Take up the scope on both anchors evenly and let her settle back with enough sea room to allow for the inevitable wind shift to the west, some time in the night. Be prepared to get under way at any given moment, as soon as the officer of the watch alerts me to our impending predicament.'

Instead I took to my bed and willed the puny stainless-steel shackle I'd inserted in the ruptured chain link that morning to stay attached, until further notice. I lay there resting but not sleeping, listening to every strong gust racing out off the land and feeling an immense sense of vulnerability.

Vicious squalls blasting over a rolling ground-swell did their combined best to keep me awake. Around 1 a.m. (according to what I wrote in the log book), the wind went northwest and then eased around 4 a.m. In the lee of Butterfield Point, the most westerly extreme of Enderby Island, I felt sheltered, but dreaded the prospect of a quick southwest wind shift and rising gale so common in this place.

As soon as it got light, I assigned myself some intense labour and got out of Sandy Bay. The weak link in the chain had been bothering me all night. Just the thought of it. Determined to escape Sandy Bay and deal with the broken chain issue, I manually pulled the anchor up off the seabed and gathered all the chain on deck where I could see it.

SW fell away onto starboard with the wind coming over the right side, moving us quickly towards the kelp bed and cliffs in front of us. Gybing around gave me a bit more time to clumsily sort out the anchor chain, turning it around to get the longer, unbroken scope attached to the anchor. To get this done had become very important during the night when I had been resting and thinking, and resisting the temptation of too much thinking at the expense of pre-meditated action, all night.

The sky looked untrustworthy, and within moments of our clearing Sandy Bay, a fresh northwesterly rain squall rushed through, obliterating the view of Port Ross and where I wanted to get to. I resorted to almost nil by sail, but then plucked up enough courage to keep sailing efficiently.

We were out in a volatile window of frontal weather change, and for all its impending gale-force doom it was magnificent to behold. All greys and dull shades of wind-borne cloud, all bleak and lonely and reflecting the unhappy memories of so many long-gone people. Yet we were here. *SW* floating unassisted (apart from me) in this auspicious place, just before another gale began.

The rain set in, dropping onto us and what was left of the

castaway hut a few miles away, as it had so often done before. There was no hard, fast wind with it to start with, which was good, and in only a couple of hours of light and shifting wind we worked *SW* up past Deas Head, Shoe Island and Terror Cove and drifted into anchor just off the overgrown remnants of the colony of Hardwicke in Erebus Cove.

It was pouring with rain by then, and according to the photocopied pieces of paper Danny had given me at Port Chalmers, we were in the right place to anchor. To make sure the anchor dug into whatever would be good company, I pulled out my gigantic oars that attach to rowlocks in the cockpit and did a few backstrokes to pull us away from the floating kelp and hopefully lock us in, down below. *SW*'s engine has no reverse; it's an all-or-nothing forward-thrusting thing and no good in such a confined cove, just outside the kelp line, with little room to move.

Being in quite close, we required a fresh offshore breeze to keep us away from the floating kelp, and in no time at all the wind obliged. It came down from Hardwicke Heights over the top of the crimson-flowering rata canopy, and didn't pay much attention to *SW*. It was the start of the southwesterly gale, and if I wanted to get ashore for a look around it was obvious I had better do it soon.

There was no one to boat-sit here so I let out plenty of anchor chain and made absolutely sure *SW* wasn't going anywhere. Off came the dinghy from its up-turned life on the fore-deck; the first time since leaving Auckland. This was why I'd bothered to bring it all this way. It always made sail changes on the fore-deck more difficult, but its ship-to-shore convenience made the inconvenience worth it.

The dinghy has three holes in its bottom, one for the inner fore-stay to go through and attach to the deck via a Highfield lever. The other two are for clipping on the twin running high-cut headsails that pole out from the mast, wing and wing, for running downwind. Three inspection ports permanently attached via thin lanyards are simply screwed back in before you drop it over the side to float. It always pays to remember to put them in.

Getting the dinghy back on board is a bit of an acquired art, making sure as you lift it bodily up and out of the water and over the side lifelines that it doesn't fill with water.

With my Cobra VHF given to me by Advance Trident, and a video camera, I rowed in to the calm edge of Erebus Cove and carefully dragged the dinghy up over some gravelly stones away from the slight surge of the sea. If the unthinkable happened, and *SW* decided to drag her anchor out into the distant view, at least I'd have a chance to find somewhere to make radio contact with DOC and let them know there was a vessel adrift in the bay. The VHF works by line of sight, and is surprisingly short-ranged and easily blocked by hills and headlands. There was no communication with them from where we were anchored at Erebus Cove. Butterfield Point jutting out on the southwest tip of Enderby looked like the distant, grey, hazy problem. But I figured if I did a bit of desperate tramping I'd get in range from somewhere.

The first vestige of past human habitation was there to greet me immediately, just a few metres back from the shore next to a small stream. A collapsing, dilapidated boat shed that had seen better times. There was no boat in the shed, and it looked like the remains only dated back to the 1950s at most.

Up the well-built wooden track built for tourists, so as not to have us slip over or damage the undergrowth, I made good progress climbing steadily up and out of the slightly foreboding dark rata forest canopy that for most parts shielded the sky above from view. It had to lead somewhere important, so I happily trod along, all by myself, with the best of intentions common to all tourists. And then there it was. A little fenced human graveyard on the Auckland Islands. Human remains from over 100 years ago, gathered together in that quiet, lonely place.

It was obvious that the wind and clouds above didn't care about them, nor the trees and shrubs silently growing larger, and moving with the wind around them. But here they were anyway. A collection of bones and the memories of people who used to be alive, in a very different world, many years ago.

I just stood there and looked, not quite sure what to think, and knowing that words in this context were of no consequence anyway. The circumstances of their individual departures from this human-frequency spectrum of awareness that we collectively dwell in were all different.

Jabez Peters, mate of the *Dundonald*, died on Disappointment Island to the west of Auckland Island, and had been transported here in 1907.

John (James) Mahoney, mate of the *Invercauld*, 1864. Isobella Younger, the three-month-old child of Hardwicke settlers, 1852.

Mahoney had made it on foot to what was then left of Hardwicke, but died from malnutrition, lying alone and incapacitated in a broken-down hut with a small pile of empty mussel shells and a bottle of water beside him. He'd died here, all by himself, no doubt listening to the wind blowing the bush about as it was doing now.

Totally alone, without the ability to keep foraging, and at some stage resigned to the inevitable unless by chance a vessel arrived to save him. The circumstances of his death disturbed me the most. With no one else anywhere near, he lay there alone and listening to the wind, waiting for rescue but expecting to die, like all his shipmates had done before him. And then he finally did.

The wind was picking up again, and sporadic hard gusts were sweeping down making noises in the trees and moving the tops of the tall ones conspicuously. I said goodbye to the skeletons in front of me, and carefully walked back down DOC's slippery wooden boardwalk, making very sure I didn't slip and end up incapacitated and alone, waiting to die in a nearby peat bog.

The path led back into the dimly lit, clear and sloping ground covered by the crimson rata canopy above us. It didn't look crimson from there. All I could see was the thick-set southern rata's bent and twisted tree trunks stretching up to the dark underside of the intermeshed branches and leaves. But underneath it was relatively open ground punctuated by many tree trunks. It would have meant nothing and just been a bit of land to march determinedly back through to the water's edge, had history not bestowed upon this little overgrown place far more significance.

In the 1850s, the ambitious colony of Hardwicke that, at its most vibrant, had 300 people, existed right here, where I now stood. It had once been all cleared land with orderly rows of boxes for accommodation and work space for growing things and doing other important life-sustaining activities, supplemented by half a mile of road along the foreshore.

But now there was nothing to notice. All gone. I wandered

211

about, up and down, where they all used to be. On the higher slope there were a few bases of extra-large cut-off rata tree stumps that must have been hand-sawn back in 1849. A small hole dug near the shore had a few pieces of very thick, dark glass near it. That was about it. A tree trunk called the 'Victory Tree' with carvings on it was supposed to be somewhere, but I couldn't find it.

I was starting to feel uncomfortable. Listening to the wind whooshing and intimidating me in the overhead rata canopy, I was inspired to re-visit the foreshore to stare out at the bay and make sure *SW* had not left without me. The southwesterly wind was building quickly, and I knew I was running a mariner's gauntlet by not getting back to my vessel ASAP in case the anchor dragged and there was no way for me to save *SW* from ending up lying on her side, on the rocks, a couple of miles downwind. But it was captivating sitting there by myself with all those unseen memories for company, in that shrine to another time.

I could see the hustle and bustle of humans chopping down the original ancient rata and putting up their habitat. The hard labour of consistently trying to achieve something. The emotional tensions of so few women and men consciously seeking company in a biological way. The couples had houses, presumably for the benefit of private relations and the vital life continuum that all societies essentially rely upon.

It was all there resonating with me, as I sat on a tree stump looking through the dim view and listening to the increasingly intimidating wind in the dark canopy of the trees above.

But more than just they were there. A time-lapse camera set up for the past 200 years would have caught them all. Settlers who became disillusioned, then left. Then the constant trickle of absolutely desperate and dying specimens, fully focused on the bare essentials of survival. And here they were now. Right where I was sitting. All of them had been here, in their own self-obsessed and totally forlorn state. Stranded shipwreck survivors constantly wondering how much longer they could stay alive. Some had spent a few months here, others over a year. Just foraging for food, keeping the fire going, and looking. Staring and longing for rescue. Looking out at where *SW* was now anchored.

All the poignant emotions associated with friends passing away, physically out of one's control, had been lived out right here, in that dark, lonely and now overgrown place.

To beat a retreat back to *SW* now became overwhelmingly important, and I gave up searching for the special tree and anything else that might want to confront me and got back to the dinghy and the softly trickling stream beside it. The wind was blowing hard now, but *SW* was tucked in as close as possible to the floating kelp bed and was missing most of it.

I waited as long as I dared for some malevolent, disincarnate entity to manifest itself in the forest and tell me which shipwreck he was from. But none bothered to appear. I gave them all a good opportunity, even going to the extreme of asking out loud for their company. But no one came. No one I could see.

Before pushing the fragile orange dinghy back out onto the slightly surging sea, I gave the souls of those who had died there the chance to accompany me back to New Zealand. I spoke it out loud again, asking for an answer that never came; or did it? If any place was charged with the energy of the deceased, this was it. This was what I was here for. Being alone was the only way to hear them.

SW was their perfect survival lifeboat, one that undoubtedly could transport a few people to salvation and also alert the rest of the world only 200 miles north to their shipwreck situation. But *SW* looked vulnerable there, all alone, and anchored in that view with the hard offshore wind blowing itself out of Port Ross.

For those awaiting rescue, that view had been the only portal of salvation from where a sailing boat could come, or go. That was where so many desperate pairs of longing eyes had looked, for so many accumulated moments, and now I was looking at it as well. What would they have made of *SW*, a 5.4-metre sailing boat, being there with a recreational sailor? But *SW* was, perversely, here. I was pleased, but slightly frightened as well. We'd got here. But now we had to get back.

For those shipwrecked sea ancestors, getting back had been a real problem in the past. Most took the option of waiting to be rescued, but some didn't. After a year castaway, in January 1867 men called Brown, McNevin, Morrison and William Scott decided to sail out through that view in one of the open boats from the *General Grant* and try to reach New Zealand. They'd been there over a year, and had thoroughly lost interest in the place.

With three weeks' worth of provisions but no compass or chart, it was a big ask. All those onshore had debated the best course to steer once they sailed out of Port Ross and rounded Enderby Island. Without a compass it would be a theoretical approximation, and sadly they decided on the wrong direction. East-northeast was settled on, and they were never heard of again.

They may have sighted the Antipodes Islands, but with the prevailing Southern Ocean current-set and wind directions it would have taken them more than three weeks to get to South

America, and probably less time to be overwhelmed by a big breaking wave.

The *General Grant* survivors improvised other forms of long-distance communication. Like tying messages around albatross necks, and creating inflated floating balloons from seal bladders festooned with SOS messages. Nothing came of it. A passenger named Tier made model sailing boats, their wooden hulls engraved with SOS messages as well. They had iron keels and a zinc sail. Three were launched but were never recovered, nor responded to.

By then, the nine men and one woman were living out on Enderby Island. Tier must have astutely found the right spot, with the right wind direction, to get his SOS sailing boats away from the kelp and backwash and out sailing beyond the rocks, off into the massive, anonymous seascape before them.

Rowing out to *Swirly World*, and pausing to let random nasty gusts blast past, I eyed the narrow gap downwind to the northeast in between Enderby and Ocean Islands.

For all the castaways who had ever frequented Erebus Cove, that small view of open ocean had represented their portal of salvation. So many pairs of desperate eyes had carefully stared out in that direction, waiting and hoping, and some praying, for a vessel to appear. With the gale now fully taking control of the bay, that same gap of open ocean to the northeast was starting to look like a portal of doom to me.

I knew from past experience that the longer I stayed anchored anywhere, the more apprehensive about re-engaging in sailing, and departing the sanctuary of a secure anchorage, I would become. There was no point in going anywhere. The safest place to be was here.

In the afternoon, the wind started lifting spray from the surface of the sea. 'Willy walls' rushed out from Deas Head and a constant, ferocious, blast funnelled down through Laurie Harbour to port. I was pleased we weren't sitting it out up there at Williamson Point where we had spent our second night at anchor.

The sheer strength of the wind demanded respect, and human cunning to avoid experiencing the worst of it. Laurie Harbour and the flanking high land on either side of it was a natural wind-acceleration machine. We were tucked away, but I couldn't stop myself from continually listening to the squalls shrieking down through Erebus Cove, like disembodied shipwreck casualties who obviously didn't like us being there.

SW pulled on the anchor chain and we heeled then slewed about, from one side to the other, then returned to an upright pause before the next squall had another go at dislodging the anchor from the rocky, weedy seabed below. I didn't know what we were anchored to, but I sincerely wished it well and had no intention of saying farewell for the time being.

Expecting the worst, potentially at any moment, I pulled the dinghy back up on deck and strapped it down, set up the storm jib and tied it down on one fore-stay, and put the number two jib on the other, ready to go. The double-reefed main was equally lashed down but ready to be pulled up the mast in case we were accidentally driven out into the bay and had to quickly do some serious involuntary sailing to keep away from the rocks to leeward.

Another priority was a big mixed-up feed of canned tuna, potatoes and raw garlic. The can looked a bit chewy so I discarded that, but the rest of it was very gratifying. Again I couldn't help truly appreciating every filling mouthful consumed, as if some very hungry and envious entities were bitterly looking over my shoulder.

An afternoon sort-of-sleep topped it off, but the violently audible wind in the trees to windward did its typical best to keep me awake. It screamed, shrieked and randomly convulsed its way past us in torrid gusts, lifting spray in the bay. It wasn't a place to go for a fun sail in conditions like that. We stayed tucked in close, veering to the rumbling anchor chain moving over the rocks below and heeling to nasty stray gusts, on and on and on.

When it got dark, another bad night's sleep was had by all. A part of my brain listened for and heard every gust, and the rest of me waited to feel any change to *SW*'s slewing and veering patterns that would mean the anchor was dragging and we were drifting downwind into the jaws of the all-consuming, black windy night and potential rocky doom to leeward.

Eventually daylight on the second of February heralded more of the same wind, but thankfully we were still anchored in the same place. This time the view of Erebus Cove was lit from the east by the pale sunlight and presented the landscape in a different, more appealing way. In the early morning light I could make out more of the detail of the topography and the thick canopy of crimson-flowering southern rata trees. The place almost looked benign.

Undoubtedly beautiful days had dawned before in Port Ross and although this wasn't one of them, for an hour or two Erebus Cove looked very inviting, regardless of my personal circumstances.

In 1864 the *Invercauld*, a three-mast, square-rigged 181-foot (55-metre) sailing ship, had run into North West Cape and become a total loss overnight. Of the 19 men who made it ashore only three were eventually rescued, having spent a year waiting and foraging for food with the majority dying in the Port Ross environs.

Fifty years on from the Hardwicke days, another shipwreck had resulted in another gathering of destitute sailors in Erebus Cove. The *Dundonald* had run into instant destruction on Disappointment Island 6 miles west of Auckland Island in 1907. The survivors spent five months living there, eating mollymawk chicks pulled from burrows under the tussock-covered island six miles long by 2½ miles wide. Eventually they built a coracle out of twisted, gnarly shrub wood, covered it with salvaged canvas sailcloth, and one calm day three of them paddled across 6 miles of sea to the large piece of land they had so longingly been looking at off to the east. They'd heard that castaway provision depots existed on Auckland Island.

They took fire with them in the form of a smouldering piece of peat, and managed to generate a smoky signal fire to let their stranded brethren know they'd arrived. The going was too tough for them as they tried to tramp from the western cliffs where they'd landed down the valley in between Cloudy Peak and the Hooker Hills; and astonishingly, and to the disgust of those who had pinned their hopes of salvation on them, some days later they returned to Disappointment Island.

Two months later a repeat journey was embarked upon. It can only be assumed that the next lot tried harder, as eventually, after four days, four men staggered their way along the edge of Laurie Harbour into Erebus Cove, worn out but alive. By then a castaway depot had been built and maintained some years before on the edge of the bay, complete with an open boat equipped with oars and sails.

The inventory of what was waiting for them in the depot in that previously silent place must have been a gratifying discovery. 'Biscuit, preserved meat, dripping, tea, sugar, salt, medicine, clothing, boots, blankets, knives, fishing lines and hooks, matches, axes, saws, rifle and ammunition, cooking utensils'. Unfortunately, most of the food had been pilfered previously but there were plenty of hard biscuits available.

Having found relative paradise, they didn't linger long. Within four days they had rowed and sailed back around the top of Auckland Island and down the west coast to Disappointment Island; then returned the whole party back to Erebus Cove. That short voyage in an open boat with no engine was a feat in itself in a place so unpredictably volatile as this. A trip only to be undertaken in the best of settled conditions if possible.

The prospect of going up around the northern corners of Auckland Island and then down to Disappointment Island, only a few miles off that westerly-facing cliff line, was a big ask. I'd do it in a vessel with reliable auxiliary power, but not in *SW* — or an open rowing boat with a short mast and a sail area that couldn't beat efficiently to windward. Not unless the weather forecast was right. Not unless the life-and-death stakes were much higher.

The *Dundonald* survivors didn't have a weather forecast or a barometer that gave any indication of strong winds. They immediately took their chances to relocate their stricken cohorts; their life-and-death stakes were much higher. Who knows what the weather was like when they went round and got them? They were living on the edge, taking a chance with the wind; today, if you did it for fun it would be called foolhardy.

The group got rescued a month later, but while they were waiting they got to know Port Ross, capturing wild cattle and seals for food and industriously building a jetty and reconditioning an old flagstaff that, presumably, flew a new SOS flag as well.

As the morning progressed it was obvious that the southwesterly gale was losing interest and easing in strength. The clouds and rain squalls were not blasting overhead quite so low or quite as fast, and blue sky seemed keen on making more frequent appearances.

I began fixating on important jobs that simply had to be done before going back into the open ocean. I smeared copious amounts of Vaseline on the cockpit inspection ports, so that if swamped with waves they wouldn't let water inside. A lanyard (rope fastening) was attached to the main-deck air-vent cowling in case it came loose and got washed away, as it almost did before our arrival.

I climbed the mast to secure the folding steps to it, removing the possibility of them getting in the way of the halyards again. This was a major priority, as I didn't want a repeat episode of sinister, disincarnate elemental forms using them as play-pole foot steps from which to taunt me and interfere with my manual outdoor duties. In between gusts I clambered up beyond the spreaders and stuck a matrix of gaffer tape over the steps, holding on tight as *SW* slewed and heeled over to the odd stray gust.

The barometer kept rising, the sky kept clearing and the wind started easing, and if I wanted to depart to head north and make the most of the favourable wind direction, then soon it would be time. The weather signs of an impending sailing exit were becoming apparent.

If time had been of no consequence, then I would have happily turned right out of Port Ross, skirted the eastern bays and headlands, and set off down for a look at Carnley Harbour. Especially the site of the *Grafton* wreck (1864) and their subsequent self-built hut 'Epigwaitt' where they modified their ship's boat and then departed and sailed non-stop to Stewart Island. The site of their very successful survival episode will always be worth a look.

And the place where the German ship *Erlangen* was beached in September 1939, on the verge of World War II. They had cut down 400 tons of rata forest for firewood to supplement their restricted on-board fuel supply before escaping to South America.

But I had a life to get back to. I was only on an extended holiday, and I wasn't sure how long I had before my absence from work would render me redundant.

The VHF radio had been rendered truly redundant by the nature of the land in between *SW* and Sandy Bay, and it had been nil words by mouth since our stay at Erebus Cove. Bluff Fisherman's Radio had stayed silent on the SSB frequency, and I felt I'd been living a form of solitary confinement.

But the SSB radio was still picking up weather forecasts and repeater readings from around New Zealand, including the recently visited Enderby automatic weather station. Taupo Maritime Radio was estimating 5 metre swells for us, and decreasing southwesterly winds once we cleared the northern extremity of Auckland Island. There was no horrendous wind expected to be following in the short term, so it was really a sailing situation that we had to make the most of.

This was it then: up anchor and away. I'd become ensconced there, and the option of leaving this relatively secure and sheltered place wasn't that appealing. But it had been hanging over me, and contaminating my pleasure in being there the whole time. An underlying vulnerability that was made more acute by our audacity in getting there in the first place. Now we had to get back. Only halfway home. Plenty of miles and untrustworthy wind to cope with yet.

A part of me couldn't really be bothered. Wreck *SW* on the rocks and step off safely, call DOC, wait for an expensive taxpayer-funded helicopter to come and get me. Meet John Campbell the broadcaster at the airport, and talk him through it while acting normal. It would definitely be the physically less arduous option in the long term.

Invercauld (1864), *Grafton* (1864), *General Grant* (1866), *Derry Castle* (1887), *Dundonald* (1907), *Swirly World* (2007).

It was to think the unthinkable, but it had to be thunk. That slither of relaxation, basking in the contentment of having got here, now disappeared in the realization of the enormity of having to escape from here and sail back to New Zealand 180 miles north.

I pulled up the anchor, not without difficulty as it was more than secure staying where it was. *SW* drifted quietly back away from the shore, and downwind into the harbour. I got the double-reefed main and number one jib up and flapping, then sheeted the sails in, reaching across towards the mouth of Laurie Harbour. Clear of the shelter of Erebus Cove, the wind was still slamming hard down the vortex of the harbour. I set the Faithful Mechanical Friend and replaced the number one jib with the smaller number two. I'd been over-optimistic about the sail plan.

Reaching back in close to Sealers Creek, I turned the VHF on and got an immediate response from Jacinda on Enderby. The forecast was indeed conducive for a good ride north, and *Raw Cotton* had departed in the morning to achieve exactly that. She'd assumed from my involuntary silence that *SW* had done the same at some stage in the last 12 hours without saying goodbye.

Finding out that *Raw Cotton* had already done a runner made me feel slightly more pensive, as if I'd already left our own run too late. It was time to get a move on, so I let *SW* bear away to rush flat off for the gap of open sea between Enderby and Ocean Islands.

As I looked back against the wind and white-capped, short waves growing larger as we got further away, Erebus Cove quickly receded into the bigger picture of the overall hillside above it. I couldn't see anyone waving from anywhere there, even though I looked very hard. Some of them would probably already have written off our chances of making it back safely, but the mental buoyancy of optimism is a wonderful thing. In my own mind I was taking the keen ones back with me. I'd offered them a free ride but wasn't sure how many had decided to come along. I didn't have time to count just then as *SW* sledged fast down Port Ross towards the open water.

I'd drafted a telegram-style message for Karyn, and Jacinda kindly offered to use the satellite phone and hopefully get an instant reply.

Leaving today. Prepared to complete circumnavigation — ETA Auckland twenty-third Feb. Or proceed to Bluff depending on home and work situation. What do you think?

Work commitments had been a slightly open-ended affair when I left on Boxing Day. We'd just finished up as breakfast DJs at Kiwi FM, and were moving into the drive-time afternoon slot in the new year — but how far into the new year had not been finalized. I'd burned up all my holiday pay by now, and the rest of the time I stayed at sea would be unpaid leave. How long the fiscal side of my life could sustain unpaid leave I wasn't sure, but figured Karyn would have a handle on it.

She signalled 'All's well on board', and words to the effect of forget the dosh for now.

Plan B had always involved the reassuring possibility of peeling off into Oban on Stewart Island, or Bluff at the bottom of the South Island, if after visiting the Auckland Islands I didn't feel confident enough to keep going up the west coasts of New Zealand, around the top of the North Island, then back down to Auckland. I'd find a mooring for *SW* in Bluff, then go back an easy way, probably by sky, and return the following summer for stage two.

I'd visualized *SW* hanging forlornly from a mooring for a year, growing a beard of weeds somewhere in Bluff harbour, so often that I'd almost thought myself into it. But with enough food and water on board, and the will to keep sailing combined with a green light from home, anything was now possible.

Jacinda had the last word: a warning that we wouldn't be alone out there that night. It took me a while to work out why, until she explained that the squid-fishing season had just begun, and many massive, foreign fishing ships should be expected floating where I was heading.

By her tone I could tell they were the enemy, and I later learnt they were regarded as partially responsible for the declining sea lion population that they counted in Sandy Bay. Many mothers out hunting for food for the pups on the beach never came home, and were ending up as by-catch on the ships, caught up in the industrial-scale nets that they dragged behind them. The pups were left to starve to death on the beach.

From over a mile away I thought I could see multiple waves from the DOC staff by their huts in Sandy Bay, and Murray who had wagered a bet with me that it would take us more than three weeks to get back to Auckland non-stop. He wasn't prepared to accept that we could be there before March. I couldn't convincingly argue back, as the answer would be decided by the wind, and who knew what it wanted to do with us?

I steered *SW* well clear of the tide race off Enderby and headed out east further than was probably required, to make sure the wind-shadow of the low headland would have little effect, and not forgetting the sheer menace the outside of the island had represented the last time I passed this way. Charged with the usual nervousness that denotes a significant sailing departure, I concentrated on keeping *SW* sailing efficiently, and under control.

When running downwind in fresh conditions, I always spend almost as much time quickly glancing behind the boat at what's coming to get us, as looking where we're going. The surface of the sea is like litmus paper is to a change in acidity or alkalinity: a sure give-away of what the wind is doing. I learnt that years ago in the gusty northwesterlies on Wellington Harbour — a sense of sailing self-preservation based on actually looking, and eyeing the evil dark patches on the water that meant a hard gust was coming for you and about to strike. Then suitably compensating with pressure on the helm and enough resolve to hold the boat planing on course, sometimes surfing, hard-pressed, and often on the verge of capsizing. It's one of the thrills of sailing.

SW was all sealed up so that no salt water could get inside this time; hatch-boards in, safety harness clipped on, just a little boat and me, alone again naturally.

I was prepared for the worst just north of Enderby, a little gun-shy after the pasting we'd had trying to get there. It was a pleasant surprise to find the wind drastically easing the further away from the land we got. Not unlike Wellington, it was obvious that the topography of high land combined with deep valleys was truly a natural wind-acceleration factory.

In order to maintain any semblance of progress in what was quite a sloppy, short, confused sea, more sail area was required. I shook out a reef (as the initiated say) and went for a bigger headsail. Still cautious that once clear of the influence of the receding land the southwesterly might be stronger, I sat severely concentrating on sailing as efficiently as possible at 4 knots, steering to the north-northwest.

Unlike the *General Grant* sailors who had headed out without a compass and been convinced that a course northeast would find them the New Zealand coast, I knew that — given the east-setting current and prevailing wind — the best course anyone could steer to get there was where we were going. The more northwest we could get, the more secure from a navigational perspective I would feel.

24

Sea area Puysegur

It was almost dark when I waved goodbye to the Auckland Islands. By then we'd escaped the errant influence of the land and the wind was blowing moderately and consistently from the southwest.

Looking back over my shoulder there wasn't much left to see. Just a dark, low-lying mass shrouded in cloud and looking foreboding. Despite the seriousness of it all, it was thrilling witnessing that slowly receding, severe view.

I could have stayed in my sleeping bag for a quiet night in Erebus Cove and with the dying wind would probably have slept quite well, but it was too late now to turn back. No real sleep until Auckland. Well, not quite, but certainly no sleep tonight as we sailed away and got the wind blowing clear. The leftover

5-metre ground-swell predicted by Taupo Maritime Radio started making its presence felt. It was far higher than 5 metres where we were then, in less than 90 metres of water on a relatively shallow seabed plateau.

The ocean swells circling the world at 50 degrees south arrive here after having moved along in depths of 3000-plus metres. Some 20 to 30 miles west of the Auckland Islands they meet the shelving seabed, an underwater mountain-side, then get constricted by the relatively shallow sea depth and the swells then grow steeper and higher.

It was great to witness the massive, far-apart hills of lethargically moving salt water. Impermanent valleys, slopes and hill-tops, each offering a different way of seeing and not seeing what's around you. In the valley there's nothing much to see except the sight of salt water, and then comes the constant and rapid elevation up to the top as the swell moves on through your water-space. On the top a short glimpse of far-distant, similar watery hill-tops, all relentlessly slowly surging to the northeast.

Occasionally a big crest would topple like a breaker on a beach, but there was no force in it and *SW* just lifted to the white water, slammed buoyantly and defiantly sideways, and then off we went again. The hill-tops were so far apart and high that it was almost ludicrous from an around-the-buoys racing perspective. Water hills like this in the Hauraki Gulf would trigger a tsunami alert. But they were normal here, and quite something to behold — the scale of what the wind and water combined are capable of.

On board it was constant movement, lifting and dropping a long way, bracing yourself to lock in with the motion of the boat, and revelling in the other-worldliness of it all. Rain squalls continued to drift down from windward to obliterate the horizon and force me to put a bit more pressure on the tiller to keep *SW* on course and accelerating north.

That feel of the wind being turned into forward momentum is the essence of many a human's sailing fixation. I'd have to go to Sailing Anonymous to be cured of that one.

The first of the enemy fleet arrived out of a rain squall, on our port bow, while there was still plenty of light.

As the hazy rain drifted away northeast, a big ship was clearly there and slowly motoring to the east on what looked like a potential collision course. Someone would have to cross someone's bows, and by the slow, almost stationary movement of the ship, it was hard to work out which side I should turn to.

There was plenty of time, it must have been at least a mile away but visible all the same. On our very determined course north-northwest I wasn't prepared to wait for it to pass, so we stood on. As a sailing boat we had right of way anyway, or so I told myself as we got closer.

Closer up I could see they had huge cables stretching out almost horizontally behind the ship, exactly where I had decided to go. They were motoring forward and the distance had been deceiving. But how far back did the cables and associated nets go? How close were they to the surface, and how far back did they extend?

It didn't look good. I made my decision to gybe and run down northeast to clear their bow and sail ahead of them. The wind was fresh enough and we were sailing as fast as possible — fully in control of our own momentum, but not theirs. To pass in front of them and not become tangled in some rusty cables and nets suddenly became my supreme goal in life.

I called them up on channel 16, the VHF distress channel that every ship worth its weight in squid should monitor, but no one replied. I tried the SSB radio distress frequencies, but again no one answered. It was all up to me to avoid a collision.

SW did manage to pass in front of their bow; they didn't slow down, and I doubt if they even noticed us. We were close enough not to see anyone on the bridge or on deck.

SW's sails slightly flapped in the distant wind-shadow of the now personified evil beast to windward. The sight of the large cables, taut and straining out over the back of the ship like a trip-wire for the mast of a small sailing boat, was chilling to behold.

While I was thinking that that was that, in a very relieved way, another duplicate ship emerged from the haze of the next passing rain squall, and I went back on red alert. The further we tracked north the more ships appeared, all motoring on an easterly course, and in our way. Jacinda had been right: we weren't going to be alone out here tonight. This was worse than the Hauraki Gulf for traffic. And dangerous, indifferent traffic at that.

They were obviously working the 60-odd miles of shallow seabed plateau that stretched north of the Auckland Islands, and were a severe inconvenience to me. All night yet another one, well lit up, would appear from over the horizon and I'd do my best to decide whether to head in front or behind them. It was a serious matter of self-preservation.

We never got as close to being squashed as on our first encounter, and by the time the sky grew light with another day there were no more ships to be seen. That was because by dawn on 3 February, *SW* had sailed 70 miles and into deeper water.

The Southern Ocean current had helped us, and all the desperately interested disincarnate passengers on board had willed it so. That's what I imagined as I lay there uncomfortably wedged in the under-sized port quarter-berth, trying to move slightly and alleviate the soreness of my compressed body. Blessed or possessed by disincarnate company? I had little else to think about, so the supernatural kept me amused for a while.

I'd found that beautiful point of balance between wind pressure, sail plan and rudder-to-wind-vane pressure some time in the night, and left the FMF to look after the necessity of more or less steering the compass course. Having clambered up and out through the hatch to stare at passing squid ships on a regular basis, I knew where they were and had increasingly found the allure of the sleeping bag inside hard to resist. The wind was veering to the northwest and we hardened up onto a tight reach, then I lay down inside to pass another day listening to the water slapping and physically bumping the thin plywood sides of *SW* while we tracked north at 4 knots.

The wind kept easing and hauling northwest, but *SW* kept sailing and I kept uncomfortably turning my squashed body into hopeful positions of relaxation, but found none that lasted long.

By 6 p.m. on 4 February we lay almost becalmed on a big, lazy, leftover but diminishing swell, wallowing with a view of something that looked like land only 35 miles to the north.

At first I convinced myself it was The Snares, a group of little islands I'd been aiming for, but at some stage realized I was being too optimistic given the veering wind direction. I pulled myself together, and with encouragement from the GPS experienced the minor epiphany that what I could see was actually the South West Cape end of Stewart Island. By comparison to where we'd come from, the view made me feel like we were just rounding North Head into the Waitemata Harbour and revelling in the sense of security a place like that represents after an offshore voyage.

But we were closer to Stewart Island than I would have liked. It was nice to be this far north already after only 48 hours of sailing, but my preferred track was way more northwest and ideally I'd expected not to have even seen the bottom of the South Island.

In these waters most gales and storms, of which there are many, blast in from the west and southwest, tracking east or northeast, and the whole set of ocean currents heads in the same direction. But so far the wind hadn't let us get out left of New Zealand. The more westing we could claw, the better.

The wind came back from the southwest, and once again, with a possibly unwarranted sense of navigational concern, I pulled the sheets in and we headed off to the west-northwest for the night. There was just enough breeze to keep the FMF functioning and *SW* sailing with me paying no attention at all, just lying there inside, all squished up into the port coffin quarter-berth, sort of sleeping.

By 10 a.m. the next morning we'd scavenged 30 miles to the northwest. Our view of South West Cape on Stewart Island had changed angles, but it was still the same distance away. The daylight made the wind turn into a westerly and it stayed that way all day. I was suspicious of it, and felt in some way that we were being sucked into the vortex of Foveaux Strait, even though it was 40 miles to leeward.

It could be said justifiably that I was overly cautious and paranoid about getting too close to anything that looked like land in this vicinity. There was nowhere safe to stop on the west coast of Stewart Island. As the day progressed I got to see more of it, but happily it seemed to be receding ever so slowly into the distance. With full sail area up and hand-steering with deliberate intent to get as far west as we could, we sailed hard on the wind as efficiently as possible, close-hauled into the light westerly wind.

The next morning Solander Island became something to look at, 25 miles away, sticking up like the isolated tall rock that it is. The wind kept veering more northwest and I conscientiously hand-steered *SW* as close to it as I could without luffing and stalling the sails, and slowing our very slow progress even more.

Sometimes I fell asleep, but always the shaking noise of flapping sails as *SW* pointed into the eye of the wind woke me up in a state of mild panic.

Meri Leask at Bluff Fishermen's Radio had come back on the airwaves, and every evening in the 7 p.m. hour I dutifully called in and explained our snail's pace progress, and position. In her wonderfully buoyant and engaging tones, she always fully informed me and everyone else who was listening what the wind was expected to do. It became an obsession from my fragile perspective to get away from that southwest corner of the South Island.

On the way to the Auckland Islands the weather forecast for sea area Puysegur, where we now were, had usually been nasty. Gale-force most times, and from the west, northwest or southwest. The repeater station at Puysegur Point had often registered over 30 knots of wind speed, and represented to me a truly dangerous sea area for a sailing boat to be in. Gale warning, storm warning, this was the corner of New Zealand that took the initial brunt of the low-pressure systems circling the world in those high southern latitudes.

But for now it was suspiciously still. We were virtually becalmed, 25 miles southwest of Puysegur Point. It didn't feel right, but I did appreciate the meteorological irony of it.

At lunchtime on 7 February a light southeasterly filled in, and set *SW* sailing flat off to the northwest. It was unexpected, but most welcome; almost too good to be true. For the first time on our voyage, I found the audacity to haul up *SW*'s new black gennaker headsail and revel in its huge lightweight-fabric pulling power.

By 8 p.m. that evening we'd sailed 25 miles and then been left becalmed only 15 miles true west of Cape Providence, just north of Chalky Inlet. The white cliffs that resembled chalk could easily be seen from that distance, and so too the high mountain line inland that stretched off into the hazy distant north. Even that distance away, I felt we were too close for comfort. A motorboat with plenty of reliable horsepower would have made my feelings of vulnerability redundant. But wallowing here, going nowhere, with such a magnificent nearby view, in a tiny sailing boat that relied on the wind for salvation, I started lacking maritime confidence.

We had to get away from this foreboding coast as soon as possible. We were committed now to a northerly course up the west coasts of New Zealand; and from now on, the less I could see of the land, the better. If our circumstances had been different — plenty of time and a powerful auxiliary engine — then it would have been great to linger and look through the remote sounds of Fiordland. But for now that coast represented trouble and travelling time lost.

The weather forecast of 30 knot northwesterlies compounded my desire to get away from the land, and as a moderate northerly wind developed I happily set the FMF and went to bed strapped up in the lee cloth on starboard, heading away from the South Island.

It was a night of the usual stuff, resting but not really sleeping. Feeling the harder gusts as they got stronger and more overbearing, hearing them calling me to come up on deck and reduce sail to keep *SW* sailing well, not staggering or stalling or losing momentum. The unstrapping of the lee-cloth ropes, the bright white LED-lamp light switched on, and the bracing of oneself in that small, damp space as it jerked over and off the building waves. Pulling on the wet-weather smock and safety harness, then going outside. It constituted the true moment-by-moment tedium of what kept *SW* sailing where I wanted to go.

The defining success or failure of our projected voyage relied on this simple physical attention to uncomfortable detail. How many disgruntled times I did it, I can't remember. But I do remember that for a lot of the time I didn't like doing it, but did it like an automaton all the same. Some reptilian survivalist part of the brain was overriding the uncomfortable nature of it all and forcing me to just get on with it. A bit like normal life really — having children and having to fiscally and emotionally provide for them. Almost a biological joke that you don't get to laugh at until you get to look back at it, a few years down the track.

The sky had shut down again and the barometer kept dropping; the northwesterly freshened, forcing us west which didn't feel like a very productive direction. Meri was expecting a southwesterly gale in the morning, and who was I to doubt her, so we went about in light rain onto the starboard tack, and sailed west to await its arrival.

Sixty miles true west of Dagg Sound, we had enough sea room not to be intimidated by the coming wind in the night. But the wind didn't come in the night. Instead, the northwesterly slowly blew itself out.

Inside, while the wind had remained the night had been quite nice. But when it finally left, the sporadic banging of the self-steering gear as its stainless-steel arm smacked into the stainless-steel upright restraining pins (they stopped it overreacting) became a bad sound to hear. I'd heard it so many weary times before, whenever the wind fell away and our forward progress had become negligible.

It was a dangerous sound, as the metal slamming on metal could shear the arm off and then the FMF would be useless. And with so many solo sailing miles still ahead of us and my heavy dependence on the FMF well established, it was not a breakage worth contemplating.

Once repeated a few times, this noise was one that always managed to automatically draw me out of the sleeping bag, no matter how fatigued, to head out into the small cockpit to hand-steer, or completely give up and lash the tiller to one side with little or no sail area up and go back to bed, leaving *SW* to do inane circles waiting for a decently manageable breeze.

Some time in the early hours of 9 February I did exactly that, giving up the short-term prospect of sailing for the time being.

We were safely more than 60 miles away from the Fiordland coast, so who cared if we drifted about going nowhere for a few hours? Rolling about but enjoying the consolation prize of being able to lie in the comparatively comfortable starboard quarter-berth, securely strapped in by the lee cloth, I slept while waiting for the impending gale. A gale that would blow us north where we wanted to go.

Captain Cook had taken advantage of a similar wind shift more than 200 years ago on one of his voyages up this coast. You could tell by the straight-line track his vessel took and what he had written in his log book. But he was braver than me, in that he travelled as close as he dared to the long land stretching north beside him. Unlike him at the time, I knew exactly where all the salient corners and dangers were and had no intention of going anywhere near them.

Dozing, snoring or whatever I was doing, at some stage the new sound of water trickling past *SW*'s hull became audible and a part of me registered that the wind had returned. Outside it was just getting light; 5 a.m. Tasman Sea time. *SW* was shuffling slowly forward, hove to. A quick glance at the compass in the cockpit confirmed that the wind was coming from the predicted southwest. It freshened quickly, and content with only the number one jib up and poled out for pulling power, we bore away on a compass course of zero degrees, happily heading north. Dressed for doom in the survival suit which by now smelt well and truly of me, I sat myself in the cockpit, hand on the tiller, and settled in for some seriously productive sailing.

By 8 p.m. another sailing day had gone by and I'd had enough of sitting there like a stiff, inanimate mannequin, only moving my forearm like a battery-powered autopilot. We'd made good

55 miles and were now 100 miles true west of Milford Sound, according to the GPS, and that suited me fine.

All day the wind had increased, blowing us where I wanted to go and building a steep, occasionally breaking sea behind us. It was great sailing and a gratifying example of what I'd come for. But my application to steering duties was flagged-out by then, and all I wanted to do was go inside and hide. I re-engaged the assistance of the FMF, went inside, and got the last of my supply of sprouting potatoes cut up and boiling on the madly swinging gimballed stove.

Back outside with nothing to do but enjoy the view, I had a good look at the turbulent seascape rolling up from behind. There was no one else there looking but me; or was there? A day earlier I'd heard Meri Leask and a fisherman discussing Andrew McAuley, an Australian solo kayaker who had left Tasmania almost a month before attempting to set a record for crossing the Tasman Sea. He had paddled well, and was by then somewhere in the same sea area as *SW*. He was expected to reach Milford Sound the next day and complete his phenomenal feat of physical endurance. His loved ones and Carol Hirschfeld from the current affairs TV show *Campbell Live* were all ready and waiting for him.

I'd spoken to him months before on the breakfast radio show at Kiwi FM prior to his first, aborted attempt, and asked him if he was scared. He confirmed that he was, but he wasn't prepared to let fear put him off. Now here he was, somewhere slightly nearby, and putting up with the same sea state and cold wind and water that I was.

As I stood there clutching *SW*'s Perspex dodger, braced to the roll and lurch of a small sailing boat rushing as fast as it could downwind, I couldn't help but feel afraid for Andrew. It was getting dark and the wind was bitterly cold for the summer season. The sporadically breaking waves were the main concern. They were nothing but uncomfortable for *SW* and me, as we rushed directly before them, sometimes surfing north. But to paddle at water level, waves side on to where he wanted to get to, looked like a horrendous undertaking.

I wasn't burning calories like Andrew, nor getting as obviously wet. Every breaking crest would have required a careful rounding-up to take them bow on, or else he would have been instantly rolled. The scale of the white water collapsing down the front of the occasional waves was full of paramount danger. This was no place for a kayak. Unless you had a support boat to retire to on a night like this, but he didn't.

In awe of his endurance and consistent application, I went below and scoffed a big pile of hot potatoes and cold tuna and garlic, then closed up the hatch-boards to seal myself inside and went to bed. Rolling and slewing, but heading more or less where I wanted us to go, I listened to the sound of *SW* racing through the cold salt water millimetres away from my dry cocoon inside, and drifted off into an exhausted but satisfying short sleep.

In the morning I expectantly held the GPS up to the sky outside to get a fix on our position. Sure enough, another 50 miles north had been made good.

My black toilet bucket lashed upright in a corner of the cockpit outside was two-thirds full of sea water, testimony to the presence of the breaking crests I'd heard occasionally boarding *SW* and flooding the cockpit during the night. The wind was easing a bit, and as always I felt the simple satisfaction of having weathered a gale, short-lived though it was.

Now within range of New Zealand AM radio, the morning news was bad. Overnight a mayday call had been received from a satellite phone, and a search and rescue mission had been activated in the sea area just south and east of our current position. Initially, some concerned people on shore had thought the call had come from *SW*, but since we had no satellite phone those in the know had immediately discounted us.

McAuley was in trouble. The north-setting current further offshore where we were was serving us well, but the closer one got to Fiordland a south-setting current existed and had been pushing relentlessly against the contrary gale overnight. That subtle saline underwater force would have pushed the waves up to a more steep, exaggerated and breaking degree than any a fatigued kayaker would have willingly invited. But that's what he got, and some time in that wild, remorseless night he'd been overwhelmed by a breaker and ended up in the water, clinging on to his swamped kayak. Somehow he'd turned on his satellite phone and sent a distress message, then clung on as long as he could.

Hoping for his best but expecting the worst, *SW* was by then 80 miles northwest of the search area and too far downwind of his terrible personal drama to be of any use. The wind was easing, but it was still out of the southwest and we ran on to the north in a decreasing sea with a rising barometer.

I pulled up more sail area, and ended up with the full mainsail and genoa poled out, wing and wing, sledging safely north over the surface of what I now felt was a far more dangerous and indifferent sea.

25

Deep-sea sleeping

Another day and night of downwind sailing later, after the Meri Leask Bluff Fisherman's Radio roll call I heard *Raw Cotton* talking to Enderby Island. They were then anchored in Dusky Sound and were, characteristically, having a great time. I took my chances and had a go on the 4417 SSB frequency, and surprisingly got through to Jacinda hundreds of miles south. I reasserted my intention to win the bet and get back to Auckland city before March.

The next morning, as we ghosted north with the dying south-westerly 180 miles true west of Westport, the news came through that Andrew McAuley's kayak had been found swamped and without him. An Air Force Orion, a helicopter and numerous fishing boats had been looking and had got a result. The kayak was found at 44.17 degrees south, 166.52 east, 60 miles from where we had been on the night of the ninth.

The western coasts of New Zealand curve eastwards as you travel north, and if you were to sail a straight line from Fiordland to the top of the North Island you would at some stage end up 200 miles west of the land. And there we were, 200 miles west of the Karamea River and listening to the bad news, well beyond the sight of land. *SW* was making great progress and riding the convenient conveyer-belt of the north-setting current.

The twelfth day of February was the last day of searching for Andrew McAuley. With no life-raft or anything else to cling to, it was obvious he was gone. Why had he not turned on his EPIRB? The emergency position-indicating radio beacon that sends a signal to a satellite and lets everyone concerned know where one is within minutes. It was probably stored somewhere too inaccessible for a fatigued man to reach, but no one will ever know.

SW sailed on. A light southwesterly wind over a slight, benign swell made progress north a bit slower than before.

With the knowledge of recent death by probable drowning in the waters we were frequenting, I became more cautious than normal. Every hand-hold while moving about the deck to change sails became a little more important than before. But ours was an easy way to travel over the sea. I just let the wind create progress and adjusted the sail area to get in balance with the wind in a harmonious way.

Progress in a sailing boat doesn't require burning as many calories in comparison with kayak paddling. In my case, I would often just lie inside, listening to the sound of watery progress going by outside and confident that the FMF would keep us heading in the right direction as long as the wind didn't shift. It was an almost meditative state, fully immersed in forward progress that cost nothing and feeling constantly fulfilled at some primate/reptilian level. Just lying there on top of that mass of saline fluid called sea, moving towards where I wanted us to be and only the wind taking responsibility, with the odd correction from me.

Somehow we'd officially travelled from the South Pacific Ocean into the Southern Ocean, and now we were in the Tasman Sea. And our new sea area, after Puysegur and Milford, was called Grey. Grey stretches from Jackson Head to Kahurangi Point almost at the top of the South Island.

My new focus as the marine weather forecasts were announced each morning and evening became sea area Grey. *SW* was probably a little too far west by then to qualify as being in that sea area, but anything Grey was going to get we were probably going to get first.

For a day a light southeasterly filled in, all good sailing on a broad reach on a compass course of 000 and 020 magnetic, depending on which wind angle brought the most progress as defined by the sound of the water moving past the hull outside.

I'd run out of compelling reading by then, and was making do with the radio. With us never really that far away from the coast of New Zealand, local radio signals were usually available. All the way up the west coasts of the South and North Islands I kept telling Meri Leask where *SW* was, along with the sea state, sky state and condition of the crew. 'All's well on board' was the sign-off each night.

Although too far offshore for the line-of-sight VHF frequency radio to hear other people talking, I didn't feel hard-done-by, as normal AM New Zealand radio did beam in, most conspicuously during the daylight hours. Almost a little too much so. A lot of news of terrestrial consequence happened in New Zealand while *SW* sailed around New Zealand. Talk-back radio always sucked me in, and usually had the loudest AM signals. That and the omnipresent National Radio doing its South Pacific version of the BBC.

In sea area Castlepoint I'd found out via the radio that Graham Burton had killed someone on a quad bike up a fire break near Wainuiomata. Everyone had an opinion on what to do about him. In sea area Portland, as we beat to windward into that first southerly gale, Saddam Hussein was hanged. In sea area Grey, a bus full of tourists had rolled in the central North Island and arms had been amputated.

And Andrew McAuley, the Australian kayaker, had become missing presumed drowned when I had been in sea area Milford.

Opinions from all perspectives had made up a good many hours of my listening time through all the sea areas that surround New Zealand, apart from south of Stewart Island where we went out of range. In my isolation pod I found the company of humans talking about current affairs surprisingly reassuring. The company of inconsequential, yet somehow essential, verbal dialogue. I was alone and relatively vulnerable compared with the people I was listening to. That explained it. At night the Australian radio stations slammed in and overwhelmed most of the available New Zealand frequencies. Listening to Australians talking about what really annoyed them, and hearing their news read in that accent, was equally reassuring.

It had become a pattern of life lying inside *SW* sliding up the west side of New Zealand listening in the day and the dark to people I couldn't see talking. It was sublime sailing-boat progress, and hundreds of miles went by under the keel and me until we were theoretically at the top of the North Island. Of course I couldn't see any land, and hadn't since 10 days before, off Fiordland. But according to the GPS I was in for a visual treat soon.

Running flat off, double-reefed mainsail restrained to one side and poled-out number one jib to the other, *SW* was getting along nicely at 5 knots, thank you. A bit of exaggerated rolling now and then, but otherwise fine.

How quickly the sea areas changed, from Grey to Stephens, to Raglan, to Kaipara. And then it was 16 February and I held great expectations of seeing land again.

Another front was coming through, and the southwest following sea behind *SW* had been building all day. The wind had everything to do with it, and it was great to witness that seascape slowly building as the wind increased with its seemingly volatile agenda. The wave slopes behind *SW* kept growing taller, but not menacing, and I revelled in the sleigh ride, *SW* self-steering and running flat off to the top corner of the North Island of New Zealand.

The last time I'd seen Cape Maria van Diemen was in 1990, sailing *SW* back from Wellington after a late '80s hibernation on the hard at Evan's Bay Yacht and Motor Boat Club. Sailing back to Auckland with no GPS, I'd been relying on the RDF (radio direction finder) and wasn't having much luck. Going by dead reckoning since New Plymouth, a few days and nights had gone by sailing and drifting in benign conditions. The RDF beacon had broken down at Cape Reinga, but I didn't know that at the time.

In low cloud and then occasional rain, I had, surprisingly, sighted high, rugged land to the north and discovered I was looking at the Three Kings Islands — I had overshot the top of the North Island.

But this time I knew exactly where we were, and we weren't there yet.

I found myself far more navigationally concerned than usual. Once we got within the 200-metre seabed line, 30 miles southwest of the top of the North Island, I expected fishing-boat company and I wasn't let down.

Paranoid about getting too close to Pandora Bank, just southwest of Cape Maria van Diemen, I clipped on the safety-harness line and ventured forward to gybe the jib pole and boom while rushing, slewing and rolling, in the general direction of where we wanted to go. It was a precise and very careful moment when I unclipped the little pole and pulled the jib across the foredeck to flap in the lee of the fully pressed mainsail. Getting the bird-like nose clip to lock onto the mast and take the load of the flapping sail I was wrestling with was, at the time, a very important moment. It personified the simple difficulty of a voyage like this. Physical toil and short-term emotional trauma. How much can you cope with?

It was a successful gybe and *SW* pulled more to the north as we ran northeast, and I felt more comfortable according to the compass.

After days and nights without needing to keep a proper watch, I had become far more concerned about running into, or being run into. Now here I was bothering to execute a gybe — and lo and behold, as I looked off across what had for two weeks been just a seascape of similar waves and sky, there was a fishing boat, rolling badly, with big metal arms out stabilizing and doing whatever it was doing, on a large inhospitable sea. Pleased it wasn't me, I wondered if anyone on board was keeping watch as they were slowly motoring across our intended path.

With the proximity of company I felt more secure, but also more determined to get round the top of New Zealand without any complications. A front was meteorologically predicted to arrive in our sea area at approximately the same time as we got to the top, and we had no other option than to put up with it. It was the worst forecast we'd had since sighting Fiordland.

At 8.15 p.m., just before it got dark and with what looked like a possibly bad night ahead, I sighted Cape Maria van Diemen. It came into view as a more grey than usual lump on the horizon, emerging from the low cloud to provide a gratifying glimpse of New Zealand.

The seas grew steep and closer together as we closed on the coast, and the odd breaking crest put me back into a heightened sense of self-preservation awareness. No point in stressing out the rig, or my mental wellbeing, so I opted for the simple poled-out number one jib and FMF to sail northeast until we got into the lee of the land, and the predicted wind shift.

SW passed Cape Maria van Diemen 10 miles to the northwest at 11 p.m. on 16 February, running fast before the fresh to almost gale-force southwesterly. Big, steep waves were being noisy outside as they collapsed, with me inside sort of listening but not feeling threatened; just being there floating on top of that turbulent wind- and tide-influenced array of waves. The closer we got, the more interest I took. Finally, it felt only right to pay attention properly and I went outside, determined to hand-steer *SW* around the top of the North Island of New Zealand.

The importance of holding on to something to help you stay on board has always been vital to getting about on *Swirly World*. There had been plenty of outrageous but unrecorded moments of *SW* leaping and falling off bizarre wave formations, like being in a lift that's gone berserk, climbing two floors up and then hurtling back down to do it again immediately. *SW* always recovered from the fall into a valley of salt water, and always rose back up onto a crest again to view the rows of salt-water hills to windward, and leeward, and everywhere else.

Around 1 a.m. the wind suddenly backed to the southeast and the veiled night sky cleared. The stars came out from the cloud cover they'd been hiding in, and the wind blew cold but consistently at 15 knots off the land.

With it came the intoxicating aroma of the damp bush and scrub to windward. After a few days away from the land, the smell of it all becomes far more potent than normal. It's a primal pleasure to experience that first whiff.

The sea flattened out, leaving a low ground-swell rolling northeast that induced a strange feeling of unsettled sailing as each passing swell urged *SW* to accelerate beyond the wind-driven boat-speed. I got the mainsail back up and sheeted in the number one jib, getting *SW* sailing hard on the wind to come in close as possible to the land east of Cape Reinga.

When it got light, it was there alright. The top of the North

Island 5 miles away, two weeks out from the Auckland Islands.

A big high was moving onto New Zealand and the prospect for progress down the east coast to Auckland city didn't look good. But I didn't care; as far as I was concerned we'd got over the worst of it. The southeast headwind would make for a slow trip down the east coast, at least for the next 24 hours. So I just lay inside, suspended in the lee cloth and feeling *SW* slowly sailing true east and away, clear of North Cape, back into the South Pacific Ocean.

It was a novelty looking back at North Cape as we headed east. I knew from past experience that the rest of the coast south of North Cape was fairly low-lying.

Going about onto port tack at midday, 15 miles away from New Zealand, I instantly knew I had picked up an offshore lift. The compass course promised the Cavalli Islands well south of Cape Karikari.

I got the FMF set up and sailing us on a slightly eased port tack, against a sloppy sea but with enough wind to keep us moving forward at 4 knots. I gently wedged myself into the port coffin windward berth and lay there, uncomfortable but elated by how high we were pointing down the east coast of Northland, and by how smoothly *SW* was sailing with me just lying there, a true passenger. The only thing that changed was the angle of the sun shining itself on the sea around us. The further west the sun went, the less I could glimpse the distant headland of Cape Karikari.

When it got dark there was little of the North Island yet to be seen, and in a relatively flat sea it felt we had reached a sanctuary of sorts by being there off Great Exhibition Bay and heading southeast for the Cavalli Islands 25 miles away.

We'd sailed through the western edges of sea areas Grey, Stephens, Raglan and Kaipara in the past two weeks. Now we were on the verge of being becalmed in sea area Brett, but I wasn't complaining. The tiller was, however, as it bumped and banged in the light southeasterly with the FMF no longer able to cope with the lack of wind. I sat slumped for a few hours, hand-steering, then gave up and let *SW* just drift, 15 miles true east of Cape Karikari.

We were within VHF range now, thanks to the repeater stations down the east coast. I left it on, listening to the odd short, isolated conversation on channel 16 for a change; and fitfully dozed in between frequent looks upstairs to make sure *SW* was not about to be run over by anyone else who was out there that night.

Surprisingly, just after midnight Taupo Maritime Radio came in loud and clear with an emergency bulletin. An EPIRB had been turned on a few miles north of Mangonui Harbour. A fishing boat on the rocks. All 'shipping' within 25 miles had to report in for potentially serious high-seas duty.

On the verge of almost-sleeping again, I found it in myself to re-engage. I called Taupo Maritime Radio and explained my position and availability. I was only 10 miles away but too slow to provide any assistance, so my offer was declined. The fishing-boat crew ended up OK, but the boat was a write-off from what I remember.

That night the big cruise liner *QE2* was expected to come up the coast and pass us at some point early in the morning. On the VHF I heard its captain speaking in well-modulated tones from their bridge to one passing sight-seeing vessel just off Cape Brett, but was uncertain as to what time to expect them to possibly run me over. I developed a keen navigational bent on drawing as close to the land as possible.

Despite my best intentions to stay alert and awake, I found

myself drawn to the lure of the sleeping bag and the attraction of disengaged, glorious oblivion full of well-overdue sleep. Some time in the two-hour window of self-indulgence that followed while we were virtually becalmed, the huge cruise ship passed us, no doubt all lit up; hopefully it didn't have to change course to avoid us.

When it got light, *SW* was close in to Stephenson Island at the mouth of Whangaroa Harbour. Again, the smell of the land was compelling. All damp-bush aroma, overwhelmingly earthy and drifting out on the offshore early-morning air. After all that smell of nothing but salt water, it was another great nostril sensation.

Sea area Brett was about to become Colville, and for the time being it was a relatively benign pair of sea areas to be lingering in. These were Northland late-summer settled conditions with a big high sitting over the Tasman Sea and New Zealand.

I was in no real rush now, but as always it still seemed worthwhile to work what was left of the wind as efficiently as possible and sail south as best we could. I turned the engine back on to help the wind, then discovered that some grub-screws which were crucial to keeping the driveshaft attached to the propeller had become loose, and ineffectual.

Again the engine was useless. It would take a few hours and need a good set of Allen keys and the other spanners to take off pieces before I could access the grub-screws. That meant plenty of difficult horizontal positioning, lying inside holding tools and stretching awkwardly to undo, then tighten up, what had become undone. It was the last thing I could be bothered doing after having dismantled it all so recently in Laurie Harbour.

In the night the wind came lightly from the shore and off *SW* went again, heeled slightly over on starboard and gurgling the water out of the way. Heading for the clear sea east of Cape Brett and the Bay of Islands, *SW* was slowly reaching south into relatively well-frequented waters. The wind was patchy and could hardly be called helpful, but it was enough to get *SW* to the Poor Knights Islands before it removed itself completely.

The television show *Campbell Live* had started paying attention to *SW* after the loss of Andrew McAuley in his kayak. Now John Campbell was determined to come and have a look for himself to see how small *SW* was.

I was then in mobile phone range, and sources reliably informed me that Karyn would also be accompanying him. A visit from a helicopter wasn't something I was used to, so spirits ran high as I readied *SW* for airborne company.

It's quite a long way from Auckland to the Poor Knights Islands (70-odd miles), but in less than an hour a little high-flying speck in the distance looked like company to me. Sure enough, it got closer, up high, then descended until it hovered like an alien giant insect just to the side and above *SW*. The down-draught from the rotor blades blew strong gusts across the water towards *SW* and threatened to knock us flat if they came too close. Fortunately the pilot knew about sailboat susceptibility to his presence, and kept his polite distance.

I saw Karyn and Carol Hirschfeld and John Campbell waving at me through the window. I stood on deck grinning for a bit while the FMF held *SW*'s course, on the verge of being over-powered by the helicopter down-draught. The noise from the blades and engine was deafening that close up, and the unnatural, gale-force wind speed beneath it was most disconcerting. Storm sails would have made me more comfortable, as then we could almost have shaken hands, but there wasn't time to change the sail configuration.

Then they were gone. Spiralling up high above and moving off fast, like a UFO, back to Auckland. A cameraman on board had got what he wanted and *SW* was going to be on the news that night. And that was that. A brief encounter, then left alone wallowing off Sugarloaf Rock.

On the phone they wanted an accurate ETA. Subject to the wind we were getting, it could take another four days to make it to the city of Auckland. The prognosis for a favourable breeze wasn't good. No one knew for sure. That's the randomness of sailing boats. It's finally up to the wind in the end.

After John and Karyn and Carol and the cameraman and the pilot left, the light wind followed their lead and did the same. With a large, benign high moving onto the North Island there wasn't much I could do about it except take the opportunity to have a go at fixing the driveshaft issue. Totally becalmed 8 miles magnetic north of the Hen and Chicken Islands, I went inside and spent the afternoon contorted into the ridiculously small space called the engine room, and sweated and swore and skinned my knuckles trying mostly unsuccessfully to grip an Allen key with a pair of vice-grips and tighten what was too loose.

As it got dark I managed to emerge from that constricted tomb and have a look around. We were still becalmed, rolling on a glassy, low ground-swell more or less where we had been 6 hours earlier. The sun was dropping down behind the Whangarei Heads and the promise of a still night (apart from the rolling) looked evident.

Now that I'd fixed the engine, we should be able to dawdle a few miles slowly south under mechanical power alone. I turned the engine on and gave it a rev up, then leaned over the back to view the wake that indicated we were moving. There was no wake to see. No matter how hard I revved the engine up, nothing came out the back. I hadn't fixed the problem at all. The grub-screws had slipped again, straight away. Six hours wasted. The only thing to do was to go to bed and try again in the morning.

All night, nothing. No wind; just tedious, uncontrollable, incessant rolling. Wedged in the starboard berth with the lee cloth up and being thrown slightly to this side then the other. Constantly bracing to stop from involuntarily rolling to this side then the other. Some time in that ponderous, drawn-out night I had an epiphany regarding the driveshaft issue.

Back in Laurie Harbour when I'd inserted the new make-do plastic chopping board as a coupling substitute, I'd made sure I tightened up the alternator drive belt good and proper. At some stage in the previous sweaty, frustrated afternoon it had crossed my mind that the alternator belt had felt quite tight. Perhaps too tight. It was providing more resistance to the driveshaft turning than it needed to, and perhaps was contributing to stopping the grub-screws from locking onto the stainless quarter-inch shaft when initially loaded up.

The next morning did eventually arrive, and with it I found a new vigour to tackle the problem. It had been a bad night rolling uncomfortably, and I had also mentally rolled uncomfortably when now and again I had let myself think about being run down by a passing vessel. When confronted with a ship not keeping a proper lookout you need to be able to put your vessel somewhere out of their way, quickly. Being without any ability to move quickly, I felt slightly anxious.

A pair of 3-metre oars plus rowlocks in the cockpit serve *SW* well in calm conditions; by standing facing forwards in the cockpit good steady progress can be made. But without the wind to sail us out of harm's way, and no engine for a quick burst of salvation away from the bows of an ocean liner or deep-sea fishing boat, the thought of just floating there relatively unmanoeuvrable wasn't good.

The next morning we were still floating there and still hadn't been run over, becalmed 7½ miles away from Coppermine Island in the Hen and Chickens group. Full of renewed ambition to tackle the driveshaft issue again, I providentially came upon a fresh set of Allen keys stowed somewhere I had not looked before. It was like a gift from someone who cared, and I went about a repeat performance of dismantling the relevant nuts and bolts to get to the grub-screws. The fresh Allen key was sharp of edges and had, thankfully, yet to be rounded into well-used, worn curves, like the one I used yesterday.

I convinced myself before I started that I could get more bite with this one. And I did; I could feel it as I lay there contorted, sweating again and willing all my physical power into my forearms, wrists and fingers, clutching the vice-grips which were clutching the thin Allen key that was biting into the grub-screw that locked the driveshaft onto the bit that connected to the engine.

I'd done it before to no avail, and now I did it with more-desperate intent. It was a flawed system with no traditional keyway to take the loading, but that was what it was. I made sure the alternator belt was more on the slack side, not tight, and turned the thing on.

With low revs at first, no fast burst to nullify the hours of previous application, it worked. A wake formed behind *SW* and I jubilantly stood in the cockpit, leaning on the Perspex dodger and heading slowly towards Little Barrier Island.

Less than an hour later that afternoon, a light northeasterly wind arrived with enough presence to let us broad-reach with the big black gennaker up, hand-steering 150 to 170 magnetic down towards Auckland, once again under wind power alone.

26

Oranges and beer

It was great light-air sailing. Before it got dark the wind freshened a bit and *SW* started getting over-powered as we raced along with the gennaker making the most of it. I'd ease the sheet a bit and let it flap now and then, but usually tried bearing away. The rig felt hard-pressed and with it fully loaded up, I was paranoid that we'd pop a shroud and then be turned into a Search and Rescue victim or forced to slowly motorboat it into Leigh.

Worse still, John Campbell might have turned up in a helicopter to watch.

So the gennaker came down just before it got dark and I let the ample genoa and mainsail work harmoniously with the FMF to sail us efficiently into the Hauraki Gulf. All night the northeasterly wind stayed my welcome and constant companion, 12 to 15 knots of relatively warm air blowing us where I wanted to go. A big 3.5-metre incoming tide helped as well, and we sailed slowly along with Little Barrier 13 miles away beside us, its dark, high mass a silhouette in a night of surrounding stars.

That evening, once it got dark a new noise started up in the cockpit. Initially startled, I soon recognized the tone. A loud live creature had joined us on board. Actually, more than one. It was the unmistakeable sound of crickets.

I'd seen no plague of crickets roaming over the sea while becalmed for 24 hours, but perhaps they'd flown aboard the night before and had been too exhausted to make a noise. We'd only got within 7½ miles of Coppermine Island, so they must have done some hard flying to find us. One could only surmise that there was a plague of crickets on Coppermine Island and some intrepid members of their society just wanted to find somewhere else to colonize. Unfortunately for them, after repetitive warnings about the proximity and volume of their discourse, I decided to set them free and hurled them up and out to ride the northeast breeze downwind to the Bream Bay coastline where they wouldn't annoy me any more.

I lay inside that night as *SW* self-steered into the Gulf at 3 to 4 knots and felt slightly guilty about the crickets. I wondered off and on whether I should have kept them in a box to let them go once back on land, so that one day they could return to Coppermine Island and brag about the colony they would have established if only they'd survived. It was something to think about other than talk-back radio.

As long as we sailed on, the lure of the sleeping bag remained irresistible, but out of a desire for self-preservation I set the egg-timer alarm at 30- to 40-minute intervals, and crawled out to look about at the dark nothingness for any sign of lights that might have meant danger.

Then as it got light again, the wind snuck away to leave *SW* wallowing about and once more going nowhere. Low mist hid the coast of Waiheke to the south and the Coromandel Peninsula southeast. Only the faint, distant shape of Tiritiri Matangi Island was visible, looking like a short, dark pencil line on the horizon. It was the end of the Whangaparaoa Peninsula and evidence that despite my lack of interest we had done some productive sailing miles in the night.

But there was nothing happening now, just a glassy grey sea under a dull grey sky; by comparison with all the other miles recently sailed, it was gratifyingly benign. I went and lay down again for the last time, but found it hard to disengage completely.

A low vibrational buzz travelling through the vast medium of salt water surrounding us became audible as I lay there inside. I knew it well. It was the underwater sound transmitted from the engine and propeller of another vessel somewhere, usually near, through the water beneath us and audibly into the boat. Always a great warning sign that motorboats are about if you're not paying proper attention on deck. I quickly did just that and saw a yacht heading directly for us, although some way off.

Surprised to have such a collision course becoming apparent, I opened the sea cocks that would let the engine water-cooling system work and got out my Very pistol flare-gun ready to fight to the death if the approaching vessel was full of Hauraki Gulf pirates. The Gulf is notorious for cut-throat contraband-smuggling demons from the *Pirates of the Caribbean* movie, and I was on red alert. To be bumped into now would be comical.

It turned out to be a yacht with a man and woman on board who were heading back to the Bay of Plenty after completing a circuit of the South Pacific over the last six months. They were well-experienced offshore sailors and we had a good early-morning chat drifting a few metres apart and going round in circles, until they motored off again, aiming direct for Cape Colville.

When they left, a light air filled in from the south, and it was enough to get *SW* tight-reaching at one-sixty to one-seventy towards the city called Auckland. The wind came once again pungently reinforced by the scent of the land.

Sailing at 3 to 4 knots in the final right direction, another obstacle loomed up from over the horizon. A grey top-heavy-looking warship — the same one I'd seen off the eastern edge of Banks Peninsula and to whom I'd been asked to give an account of myself. It was HMNZS *Kahu*. I happily volunteered another account of myself as it raced past, looking far more composed than when I had last seen it off Banks Peninsula, rolling so unpleasantly.

Rangitoto Island emerged through the low grey haze, and then I was informed by cell-phone that another visitor was about to arrive. John Campbell had sent out a water-taxi to get my video camera tapes for an item they were making for his TV show. I obliged but demanded a price, and when the boat rushed up alongside, a bag of oranges and a box of beer were handed over as well.

But John had a counter-demand. He wanted me to try to arrive at the Viaduct in the Waitemata Harbour in time to be broadcast live in his show. Not being keen on deadlines nor convinced I could meet one, obligingly I said I'd try to do my best and would update them in case their imposed ETA was unrealistic.

The wind wasn't up to much, so I gently got the engine going and *SW* began motor-sailing against the strong outgoing tide. I sat there in the cockpit poking my head out the side past the Perspex dodger, making sure I didn't pass out from the exhaust fumes pouring out of the companionway. Chewing oranges, slurping beer and breathing fresh air compensated adequately for the fact that we were only doing 2 to 3 knots over the ground below.

Just off Rangitoto's black-and-white beacon a light southerly wind shift finally kicked in and it was hard on the wind for *SW*. With enough wind to once again be able to forget about an engine and since we were on the start of the incoming tide, progress felt guaranteed.

Soon friends on boats arrived. Steve Raea on *Alnilam* led the way in his 34-footer. Gawaine and Barb and Craig on *Enshala* came alongside with a bottle of cider tied to a long stick that they dangled across to me. Then *Ethel* with Tom Leary, Steve Parsons, Karyn and most of Kiwi FM sitting on the coach-roof came motoring into view around North Head.

It was immediately clear to me that I was about to commence a very intense though short period of immensely conspicuous sailing.

Sailing up towards the Harbour Bridge on port, a light southerly was coming off the large buildings to windward and was one of the more welcoming sailing angles I'd had the pleasure of using over my years of sailing up the Waitemata Harbour.

Then we were almost there but not quite.

With the arrival of the consistent southerly wind, our

scheduled time of projected arrival had become less ridiculous, and in fact surprisingly achievable. I focused heavily on sailing *SW* most efficiently up the harbour while trying not to get too drunk. Casually shouted conversation across to *Ethel* and friends punctuated the sailing, and I tried to make sure I wasn't slurring my words.

Somewhere through the relaxed frivolity of it all, I knew I had to be going in through the little gap of a space they call the entrance to the Viaduct Harbour. Once in the Viaduct I would have to reach then beat then reach again into where I was expected. Somewhere in my orange- and beer-clouded mind I realized I had a very concise piece of steering to do. Would I sail in or pull down the sails and putter in under the auxiliary?

Once again the wind was everything. In the shadow of the tall city it came at us in sporadic gusts, firm and welcomed, bringing good progress if handled efficiently. What I feared were the numerous lulls between them. No wind equals no control for a sailing boat, and just like that night at the Auckland Islands I now felt uneasy about a lack of wind.

But to turn the engine on didn't feel right. I asked my disincarnate passengers what they thought, but all I got was inaudible derision. This close to Auckland city it was only now down to *SW* and myself, a simple matter of keeping up sailing appearances.

I opted to sail in and risk the potential embarrassment of becoming becalmed and having to push off from the bows of superyachts, hopefully without scratching them. The wind was light and blowing directly out of the mouth of the Viaduct. There was enough to bother with in having to beat to windward into that small gap without an added audience. I paid close attention to every nuisance of the wind, and *SW* behaved appropriately. On the wharf beside and above us, as we earnestly tacked and tacked again at the mouth of the Viaduct, some friends stood and taunted me about trying to sail in.

The option to give up and tie up to a smelly, low-tide pole somewhere before *SW* smacked into a superyacht was always there, and I tried to keep that default position at the back of my mind while methodically sailing around the bend to where we had to go.

In through the gap and bearing away to starboard we reached up in the superbly flat water with just enough wind to keep *SW* functional as a sailing boat. I was worried that the beat to windward would be without enough wind to get *SW* up to windward then around onto starboard while being able to stay in control and glide us into where the television cameras were waiting. But the wind obliged when I most wanted it to, providing just enough for me to act like I knew what I was doing.

In such a confined space, with an audience waiting on the dock, I did my best to get the round-up right. Veering round to starboard with a little bit too much momentum and no foot-brake, but ready to act as a human fender if need be. At the last moment I felt need did be and rushed forward, stretching out my legs to take the load of the vessel-versus-pontoon impact.

Then we were there, Auckland Islands to Auckland city, 19 days non-stop, arriving 21 February 2007. I'd won the bet.

Over the past few hours I'd consumed many oranges and bottles of beer. Faced with a camera and audience I couldn't see, I did my best to act normal.

When the cameras and audience and friends had gone away, I pushed *Swirly World* around to where *Ethel* was moored and tied *SW* back up alongside. Exactly where we had been on Boxing Day 2006, 58 days before.

Auckland to Auckland via the Auckland Islands. Three thousand miles under the keel. Apart from the broken inner fore-stay and port forward stanchion, *SW* was in remarkably good shape.

By then I wasn't, but my friend Dave had stayed to drive me home so I continued revelling in the simple, secure feeling of being on land and no longer on personal survival guard. Handing over the control of my survival to Dave driving the Jag out west, I relaxed and enjoyed the novelty of being in the passenger seat and not paying proper attention.

After all the excitement and attention I started feeling unwell, but managed to tell Dave to pull over in the nick of time so I could expel all the oranges, beer, cider and champagne inside me into a gutter that I hadn't had a good look at before. Having become used to punctuating life with expulsion-by-mouth episodes on my voyage, I managed to register that as always that I felt momentarily better afterwards.

And then there I was, back up that driveway from where I once thought *SW* would never escape.

And with children and a woman who still remembered me. *And* a bed with plenty of leg room inside a house surrounded by trees that smelt as terrestrial as they could possibly smell.

27

The chart in the cockpit with me

Once again I let *SW* grow a beard on the waterline and around the bow as more weeks and months of boating inactivity went by. Short trips to Waiheke or around the inner harbour was about it.

July school holidays 2009 came with a family invite to Tauranga and the Mount Maunganui foreshore for a week. I was up for a quick sailing trip, but failed to secure the interest of more crew. I opted for getting *SW* to Tauranga and back in the two-week holiday window we had.

There's more than 150 miles between Auckland and Tauranga by sea, so I hoped for a favourable wind to straight-line it to Channel Island on the tip of the Coromandel Peninsula, then hang a right down the eastern side of the ranges. I didn't have to wait too long. Listening to the VHF radio relaying the automatic wind readings as I sat in *SW*, Channel Island impressed with 60-something knots from the west being recorded.

It was getting dark, and *SW* jerked up and down uncomfortably to the pull of the mooring chain as the short westerly waves moved past underneath into Little Shoal Bay. I got the double-reefed mainsail and number two jib up, and picked the right moment as the jib flapped then filled to throw off the mooring that was attached to the dinghy, bouncing and banging alongside. Rushing back to the cockpit to put pressure on the tiller and pull in the sheets, I got *SW* actually sailing, instead of staggering sideways, downwind, onto the other boats moored nearby. It's always an adrenalin-fuelled moment trying to escape Little Shoal Bay in a fresh west or southwesterly wind.

With the night coming on, I knew the westerly wind blasting away at Channel Island would ease. It usually works that way. The dark time often provides a slight pause in the severity of it all.

SW rushed under the Harbour Bridge on the start of the outgoing tide, and all the bright, well-lit windows of the high-rise buildings in the Auckland CBD appeared as indifferent to us as I was to them. Out into the darkness beyond Devonport *SW* once again sailed, 23 years after we'd first done it together.

It took 37 hours to get to Tauranga. The wind stayed with us all night, but not in a nasty way.

It got light once we got round the corner of Cape Colville and we'd sledged inside Channel Island with only 20 knots of wind to shout about. The rest of the day got used up working the offshore wind down through the Hole in the Wall, past Mercury Island and

Castle Island, Shoe Island, the Alderman Islands, Slipper Island, and then, as the sun went away, Mayor Island.

It was relatively close inshore sailing, and the slightly distant view of the coast was another reason I was sailing past there. A few miles offshore always makes me feel safe, just in case the wind drops and a sailing boat loses control and starts drifting on a malevolent current. From 5 miles offshore the wind coming out over the land to the sea where we were was fairly consistent. Any closer inshore, and there was the possibility of being becalmed in the wind-shadow of some high piece of land.

But once again the wind decided not to bother blowing any more, and since we were quite a few miles away from Tauranga it looked like I was in for a long, dull night. And it was. As it got dark, I wished for but could not see Mount Maunganui sticking up on the horizon. I certainly expected it there visually, but it wasn't. Time versus distance.

The equation was not resulting in an agreeable answer at all. I went below and started the new Lifan air-cooled 6.5-hp petrol engine. The original old 1974 Honda 7-hp engine had finally stopped running completely. I took it out with the help of Steve Parsons, a highly skilled sailing friend. Twice before on calm days I'd managed to get the engine under my arm, over the side and into the dinghy by myself, but my confidence was failing.

I'd already unbolted the engine and exhaust and associated hoses a few days before. Steve held the dinghy firm against the hull, and I straddled *SW* and the dinghy, balancing myself to take the weight when I had the engine awkwardly under my arm.

A westerly wind had kicked up a surprisingly short and steep (for a dinghy) wavelet scene, making the dinghy bang up and down. I picked my moment and lifted the engine up over the transom then down into the dinghy. Bent over and holding on, while trying to control a soft landing, I lost control and dropped the engine on its edge onto the thin plywood bottom of the dinghy.

It went straight through a bit, cutting a concise L-shaped breach in the dinghy's watertight integrity. Salt water spouted in numerous little fountains like a scene from a movie. We were going down. The dinghy was quickly filling up, and the extra weight of the engine wouldn't make our prospects for floating any better.

In a moment of crisis-induced survival-strength focus, I picked the engine up again and put it back in *SW*'s cockpit. Steve rowed, and with my foot on the water fountain and my hand on the bailer we got back to shore without swamping.

One coincidental Little Shoal Bay day, while driving away on the road I'd seen a van in front of me with signage that said 'Mobile Small Engine Man'. I'd written down the mobile number, then lost it, then found it again and called it.

He was on to it, full of engine knowledge, so I insisted that he should try to get my old one going again. I drove out up State Highway 1 and found his lifestyle block and workshop with only livestock guarding it. I left the engine there. A week later he invited me back to explain the bad news.

It was terminal. He'd got the seized-on head off, but what was obvious was the blown head-gasket that had been blown prior to heading around New Zealand. That hot blast I'd felt when I put my hand near the exhaust outlet wasn't from the exhaust connection. It was the hole of the blown head-gasket. All those unbelievably slow motoring miles sitting or standing there in the closing moments of hopefully getting somewhere soon, now all made sense. The way *SW*'s interior always became part of the exhaust pipe. It had not been good.

The new engine took a year to install. It was a different shape, and to make it line up with the driveshaft I needed new engine mounts to be built, and major modifications to the exhaust and water-cooling system to make it all line up and work. No big deal to a go-kart enthusiast, but that's why I'd been putting the job off for years.

Utilizing plywood epoxy sandwiches to serve as engine beds, combined with expensive copper exhaust-pipe welding, we'd finally done the job. And now, with the sun going down and no sign of Mount Maunganui on the twilight horizon, I engaged the assistance of my newest mechanical friend.

We were motoring in a flat calm at 3 knots, to conserve fuel with a long way to go. This sort of progress never brings out the best in me. But as we got closer, the black mass of Mount Maunganui became obvious against the lights of the town. I kept steering for the black hole in the well-lit horizon line ahead, alternating between using my foot or lower leg to steer while standing up, or sitting down on the high edge of the cockpit and holding the tiller extension.

All sorts of well-charted navigational lights came into view, and I diligently kept account of what they meant to a tired amateur navigator like me. Listening to the breaking surge of the sea on the rocks at the base of Mount Maunganui right beside *SW* at around 2 a.m. local time, I felt that the proximity of imminent danger sounded louder than I liked.

All that long-distance puttering was of no consequence

compared with this. *SW* could smack into a rock now within seconds of inattention, and all would be lost. The bright leading lights became disorientating and I made an error of navigational judgement. The chart in the cockpit with me was another old one, and the enormously bright leading lights on the shore were not marked on it. I assumed they were both stuck to poles in the sea and all *SW* had to do was get up close to them, then turn to port (left) and head on up the equally confusingly well-lit channel into the sheltered harbour.

The more I stood there staring at the rapidly growing-larger illuminated triangles, the more uncomfortable I felt. Suddenly it dawned on me that what I could see, courtesy of the short bursts of spotlight beam shone ahead, was actually sand at the base of one of the lights. They were attached to the land, devoid of water and rapidly approaching through no fault of their own. I made the decision to hang a left ASAP while waiting pensively for *SW* to go aground.

We kept floating and I found the channel, but further up the harbour managed to overshoot the marina (this also wasn't on my old chart), and as the keel bumped onto the seabed only waist-deep below, I once again felt most uncomfortable. The tide was now coming in and *SW* bounced about a little bit before I managed to change direction and prod her off with an oar to motor back to what had obviously, with hindsight, been the red and green gap between breakwaters that I'd misread.

I tied *SW* to the refuelling pontoon just inside the reclaimed wall and clambered down below to once again disengage, 37 hours after leaving Little Shoal Bay.

Tauranga was great, and then we had to go home. The others once again drew the long straw and were using a motor car to get back to Auckland.

I knew my return voyage wasn't going to be as swift as theirs, and resigned myself happily to a few days and nights sailing alone. But the wind had other plans. Something was coming from the sub-tropical northwest and there were projections of bad weather on TV. But it was hard to put a time line on when it might arrive.

I had a time line for sure. I had to get back to work on Monday. So *SW* set out motoring on the outgoing tide past the Mount, and up out north with not a breath of wind to help us on our way. We motored all day with the constant vibration of the air-cooled engine thrusting us forward slowly. No more exhaust-pipe fumes in the interior, and every sea mile of progress gratefully received by me. The only thing that happened quickly was the change in the weather forecasts.

As we puttered very slowly back up past the Katikati Entrance and Waihi Beach, then focused attention on the headland that meant Whangamata, I counted the flotilla of small recreational fishing boats out there anchored and fishing. Judging by the numbers (over 30), this really was the Bay of Plenty. At times I had to alter course through a lack of attention to avoid running into one. They all seemed oblivious to the weather forecast, but with their engines and nearby sanctuaries, they probably didn't feel the need to be as concerned as I was.

I became very concerned as we gradually motored over the silver, oily-looking surface of the sea all around us as the morning became late afternoon. It was then confirmed that a storm from the north was rapidly tracking down to the top of the North Island. Sea area Brett was in for 50-knot easterlies and it was apparent that *SW* would soon have the pleasure of their company as well.

The barometer was dropping. Especially when I tapped it. The sky and clouds that hung so low were imbued with malevolent colour tones that looked like the harbingers of doom I'd met before. It was a bad twilight sky, and instinctively I wanted to be tucked away somewhere safe beyond the realm of having to care. But I had to care.

It was almost dark, and with the subtle change of light came the start of the prophesied wind. For a moment I favoured peeling off into Whangamata, but apart from the flashing light at the entrance to beckon us in, it looked like there wasn't much space to negotiate in the narrow river mouth. Underestimating myself, I concluded that in the dark I could definitely get it wrong going in, and it would be truly dark by the time we got there.

Gale-force easterlies going southeast and blowing straight into the river mouth with *SW* at anchor for a few days while I went back to work was what was expected. This was before the marina was built. If I'd been there keeping an eye on the sea state, then fine. I'd have the ambience of Whangamata to look forward to enjoying. But leaving *SW* at anchor in the river was an uncomfortable thought. And once the heavy rain kicked in, who knew what might come floating down the flooded river to get tangled up in the anchor chain?

Slipper Island light flashed every 15 seconds up to the north of us, and I sheeted in the sails to round *SW* up a bit more. Just to the right of Slipper Island was the place to go, and I sat seriously hand-steering, trying to work out which coming bay down to leeward on this coast would be the best to seek sanctuary in.

They were now forecasting 50-knot easterlies for Cape Colville at dawn the next morning. It was dawn the next morning when I expected *SW* to be at Cape Colville. To stop somewhere overnight and let the worst go through felt like a fairly sane thought. But where?

On a tight reach making good time, I thought about Tairua Harbour only 3 miles north of Slipper Island, sporting its own light on Royal Billy Point. But it was a lee shore now with a river-bar entrance, and despite the lure of exploring the well-heeled Pauanui enclave to port once inside the harbour, it didn't feel right to run in.

The more I pondered, with a grave sense of self-preservation, the less confident I felt. Flashing somewhere in the back of my mind the garish neon-lit words 'Don't get caught out' would not go away.

There was no one else out around us now, no navigation lights of other vessels, and the truly dark, heavily clouded night shut down all possibility of moon- or star-light. But like a new and important friend, the Slipper Island light winked reassuringly for a few hours at me and I made sure that *SW* reached slowly past to windward of it. It was obvious that Mercury Bay or Mercury Island were my only two real options.

With the quickly freshening easterly wind reaching us along, side on, *SW* could easily get to Old Man Rock light and go through the Hole in the Wall passage in the sheltered lee of Ohinau Island, and then beat up into Huruhi Harbour at Great Mercury Island. Sailing-wise it made sense. About 20 miles away, we should have it covered off by 2 a.m. and be safely anchored with the storm blowing through the rigging off the land over flat sea.

The prospect spurred me on to diligently sail *SW* faster, and get there sooner. But the more I sat and steered, the more I worried about getting back to work on Monday. When the storm blew through, as they so predictably do, an adverse hard southwesterly wind was more than likely to follow.

Tomorrow was Saturday, and getting under way on Sunday against a southwesterly on the nose to sail 40-something miles from Cape Colville, zigzagging making it even more miles on the wind back to Auckland, just didn't seem right. To abandon *SW* somewhere safe, find a land ride back to Auckland and return when the wind was right, hopefully on a weekend to complete the return voyage, was a plan that started making more sense.

Unless I was prepared to leave *SW* unattended at anchor at Great Mercury Island and find my own way back to the North Island, that option was out of the question. I thought about it. All the chain out. Rowing ashore in the hard easterly gusts. Tramping across the land to meet Sir Michael Fay (the owner of the island), or probably his housekeeper; shocking him or her in the early morning storm.

I decided I'd wait until at least 9 a.m. to sound him out about using his helicopter to get me back to the mainland ASAP. But *SW* at anchor for how long? Until I got back it would be too insecure with too many elemental variables.

Mercury Bay was the one. At the head of it is Buffalo Bay and the township of Whitianga. There's a tight river mouth with plenty of current depending on the state of the tide and recent rainfall. On board was one of the original charts I'd found on *SW* back in 1985. It was all brown and stained, and dated back to the early 1960s. Mercury Bay. The land and rocks were still in the same places, but the night-clad lighting show had changed. My 2007 Nautical Almanac had the current light list, so that was no drama. I knew what to expect.

All that was required was to sail until the downwind lights of Whitianga in Buffalo Bay showed up, then bear away and run down to the river mouth corner beside the beach. I'd been told there was a marina there that I'd never seen but was a reality. The last time I'd been in by boat had been with Steve Raea and that was pre-marina 1992. The flow of tide had impressed me.

Once past Slipper Island and pulling up to windward of the Big and Little King Rocks I went to bed, leaving the FMF to keep us moving under full main and jib, sailing us north as quickly as possible.

The weather forecast at 7 p.m. was another truly appalling one. The storm (not gale) was expected to engulf us within the next 12 hours. The east coast of the Coromandel was definitely not the place to be. This was a wicked doomsday scenario, a sailing boat lee-shore where anyone out on the sea should realistically only expect the worst.

By midnight the wind had forced me on more than one occasion to get out of bed and reef the mainsail. *SW* was sailing well, and the sea had yet to build into anything debilitating. A short, close sea-set was side on but with enough wind to not let it bother us, it was good efficient sailing — a small boat balanced, with no hand on the helm, sailing at 4 to 5 knots on the right compass course. Regardless of having to shortly avoid impending doom, I enjoyed the realization that *SW* was sailing for my self-preservation, and it was good sailing at that.

Caught out in the school holidays, who would have thought it?

28

Birds on board

The lights of Whitianga eventually appeared downwind in Buffalo Bay at the end of Mercury Bay, and *SW* bore away to run down towards the well-lit, beckoning lee shore where the map promised I'd find a drainpipe of a river entrance to deal with. The wind was coming harder now, but with it blowing from behind us I found the courage to carry more than enough sail area, keeping *SW* running fast without an involuntary gybe.

I took responsibility for the involuntary gybe that occurred shortly thereafter, using the excuse that I had been momentarily disorientated by shining the little torch at the chart on my lap and steering by the pressure of the tiller on my calf, looking intently and alternately at the real version and then the paper version of what was waiting for us up ahead.

The rapidly increasing wind velocity was welcome, as all I now really wanted to do was get there as soon as possible. This wasn't the Auckland Islands, with all that the wind did to the sea and delivered up then. But running downwind into Buffalo Bay, watching the light on the point flashing every few seconds, it felt just as dangerous. *SW* had to be in the right place, and it was up to me to do that.

South Sunk Rock then Motueka Island followed by Moturoa Island became my immediate concerns, and I was fretting that I might have cut the corner too tight into Mercury Bay.

Sailing by the glow of the GPS in one hand and holding the blunt pencil and chart in the other, I felt mildly certain that *SW* was not about to run into anything. In the dark of dark I could still make out the closest high pinnacles of rock nearby, but flashing strobe lights further down the bay put the fear of the unknown in me. My chart was too old to have them drawn on it, but they were there alright.

Motukorure Island in the middle of Mercury Bay was now sprouting flashing lights. So too was Cook Bluff to the south. That was how I interpreted what I saw as *SW* raced down in no uncertain terms towards the sanctuary of Whitianga.

The high bluff ahead and slightly to port with the flashing light on it was all that was required for me to know where to go.

Until the last moment, when the wind-shadow of the point became evident, *SW* sailed well, surfing down with a fresh following wind that was now verging on gale force. Rushing downwind in the dark without an updated chart and looking forward to finding somewhere to stop for the night.

In the wind-shadow of the high hill at the mouth of the river I pulled the sails down, got the engine going and paid close attention to steering *SW*. It was immediately clear that a lot of water was rushing out of the Whitianga Harbour and we were in its way. The channel markers lined up in front of my spotlight torch beam said it all. The water was going out fast, and the markers were leaning over with the pressure of it all.

To make headway against such insistent fluid opposition, I went for maxi-blast engine power. In the lee of the high bluff, sailing was out of the question. The wind went from nothing to too much in randomly wicked gusts, coming in all directions from over the headland beside us.

The pressure of the current on the tiller resulted in all sorts of unnecessary deviations which I tried to overcome, and extremely slowly we moved up the constricted mouth of the Whitianga Harbour. Heavy gusts swept down from the high land while I concentrated on steering as far up against the current as possible; keeping a lookout with genuine interest for the lights of the breakwater entrance to the marina.

It slowly became obvious, and once well upstream and on red alert against the power of the savage current, I let *SW* side-shuffle across to what looked like the mouth of the marina. In we popped, out of the fast-flowing stuff, and at 2 a.m. tied up to the end of a jetty finger. Standing on the floating pontoon, I got a good gauge of what was going on around us. The wind was now blowing in very fierce and random gusts from over the high land east of the marina.

The water was flat inside the breakwater, and the lack of a fast-flowing current was bliss. Outside the wall in the open mouth of the constricted river the water was moving scarily fast. Even though it was almost dead-low tide, the flow was impressive.

My years on the Thames River in England, motoring against the flood waters that so often beset us each winter, had been good steerage training. The slightest angle of over-steering can put you too far off course, too quickly. I'd learnt that feel steering against flood waters, and now here in Whitianga I had put that past water experience to good use.

With *SW* strapped in tight to the floating pontoon I went to bed, happy to hear the noise of the gusts rushing at and over *SW* but knowing they were of no concern to us any more tonight.

When it got light I woke up and walked down the pontoon, finding my way into town. The wind was blasting its anticipated 50 knots now and the heavy rain showed no sign of going away. Buffalo Bay beach was alive with waves foaming themselves into destructive self-oblivion, and I was pleased *SW* wasn't there with them. I wanted out.

Resigned to paying whatever price the marina chose to exact, I circled about, dry in the rain in my wet-weather gear, waiting for the first signs of life in the marina office. It was more expensive than expected, but I willingly subjected myself to their fiscal upper hand. Having sussed the bus timetable back to Auckland, I briskly plodded back to *SW* to get my things together and make a run for the nearby bus, soon to depart.

A foolish last-moment lack of concentration saw me lock the padlock on the main hatch before removing my vital keys to the rest of my universe from inside. On a 15-minute countdown before the last bus left Whitianga for the weekend, I went back to the marina office and threw myself on the mercy of the duty officer.

He was expecting lots more boats to come scuttling in to escape the storm, and happily thought nothing of explaining how to use the bolt-cutters that he gleefully introduced me to. As he said, they cut through padlocks like butter and I instantly knew I was back in the running for the bus. The only snag was that *SW* would now have to remain unlocked, so I grabbed the bag of important electronic gear (EPIRB, GPS, VHF), and arranged the padlock to look at a glance like it was there for a purpose, then rushed off to return the bolt-cutters and jog as fast as I could to the bus stop.

In torrential rain I was welcomed aboard the backpacker bus, and partially disrobed in front of my newly acquainted and equally confined bus mates. For this leg of the journey the vehicle was called a minibus. The driver blasted the hot-air heater full on, and through the misted-up windows we sometimes saw the wiggly roads and valleys that he was racing us through. The occasional accidental rub against the thigh of an attractive Nordic backpacker sitting next to me when the driver threw us around a windy corner was nice, but didn't compensate for the lack of air and general feeling of nausea that was permeating my being.

A part of me felt like I'd chickened out and should have kept going. It was, after all, a rare but completely favourable wind direction. Once past Great Mercury Island it would have freed up into a broad reach, then once round Cape Colville a flat-off run to Whangaparaoa Peninsula and Auckland. *SW* had been in the bad stuff before, so I should have stuck at it. A lack of nerve, or sensible caution?

I had to admit I'd been afraid of that 10-mile stretch they call Colville Channel. I figured I would have been there by dawn and hopefully got round the end of Coromandel Peninsula before the tide started departing the Hauraki Gulf. But if we were late, and Cape Colville set up a wind-against-tide party to welcome us there, then we could have been rolled, somersaulted, thrown from wave-top to wave-top, or whatever.

The feeder minibus dropped us in Ngatea. We passengers all spread out and claimed a doorway or veranda out of the rain and wind, and waited for the next, hopefully bigger, bus. I bought a paper that had the 10 July storm picture taken from a satellite and dramatically coloured in dangerous-looking colours. The storm was front-page news.

The next bus was indeed bigger, and then we were deposited at the Sky City tower terminal in downtown Auckland. Waiting for the next bus home, I pulled out the VHF hand-held radio and had a listen to the automatic repeater readings coming from the various locations around the Gulf.

In the suitably dispassionate, automated tone that never clouds such practical information with personality, Channel Island in the Colville Channel said 'Nine zero' — 90 knots. Tiritiri at the end of Whangaparaoa Peninsula was on five zero. Fifty knots.

I'd long since agreed with myself that the Channel Island wind-reader machine overstated the velocity. It's potentially a wind-sheer issue, given the steepness of the 79-metre-high island. But even allowing for that, the wind was probably peaking at 70 knots or thereabouts. I was glad *SW* wasn't there, and felt slightly vindicated in having given in to the desire to seek shelter.

It was a couple of months before *SW* escaped from Whitianga and Buffalo Bay.

I drove back after a week when I realized I couldn't afford to keep paying indefinitely to stay in the marina. The harbour master found a less expensive swing mooring for *SW* out in the stream, and so some more weeks went by. I watched the weather charts for a weekend window, but the prospect of beating to windward up the Hauraki Gulf remained unpleasantly such.

Then an unusual midwinter easterly air flow came upon the upper North Island of New Zealand, and it was obvious some sailing had to be done. An early morning start by car got me and Steve Parsons into Whitianga equally early enough to catch the departing tide, and off we went.

Five hours to windward beating out of Buffalo and Mercury Bays got us to the Hole in the Wall where we bore away, just missing Needle Rock, and broad-reached confidently north towards Colville Channel. It was only 19 hours all up from there to Devonport and the Waitemata. Steve took over hand-steering, and made a far better job of it than the FMF. I dropped him off just before it got light at Devonport, on the end of a long, slippery low-tide wharf.

All night the easterly had stayed moderate and kept pushing *SW* into the Hauraki Gulf. The ease of sailing downwind for the majority of the miles had made the wait worthwhile.

Another couple of years have gone by now. *SW* keeps growing the obligatory mooring beard and I get round sometimes to shaving it off. When the prop and shaft become a barnacle-and-mussel farm and the engine hardly creates enough thrust to move the hull through the water, you know you should have cleaned the bottom some time before.

Leaning against the piles in Putiki Bay at Waiheke, *SW* quietly took the ground as the tide went out, gradually revealing the undergrowth that usually lived under the water. All sorts of dangling weeds became evident. No wonder the overnight sail down from Auckland had taken so long. They all came off with little persuasion, and by that evening we were floating again, becalmed and at anchor in dense fog, back in deep water.

I was in no hurry to go back to Auckland, and the fog and lack of wind was a good excuse not to. Lying with my feet up inside, I stared vacantly out of the open companionway at the dense white nothingness beyond the port stern stanchion.

Thinking nothing in particular, I suddenly found my view more interesting. A pair of small birds I didn't recognize landed on the aft weather-cloth and had a good look around. Perhaps disorientated by the fog, or simply inquisitive and checking out the new orange boat floating in their bay, they looked inside in no uncertain way. With tiny little eyes and twitching their heads from side to side on high alert, they seemed to know they had the better of me if I chose to become aggressive.

One of them started squawking loudly, and it sounded like the little bird was shouting at me. I stayed still and heard it out. They didn't seem to want to go away. The loud one opened its mouth wide, and for its size had a lot to say. I wasn't sure quite what it was saying, but the other one which kept quiet and listened probably did. It kept looking at me alertly. I returned its stare. I quietly let out some long, low-vocal-frequency noises from my throat and mouth and both birds paid grave attention to me. To their credit they didn't fly away. They just sat there and listened. and then when I stopped the loud one started up again.

We exchanged noises for a few minutes more, then the loud

one did a shit on the deck and they both flew off. They came back later, sat and looked intently at me, and we repeated our inter-species banter. Then they were gone, this time for good, heading for somewhere I couldn't see as they disappeared into the dense white fog.

I envied them their instant, accurate mobility. Were there any long-gone humans inside them? Friends or interested parties reincarnated into birds? Probably not, but it was a thought that kept me occupied for a while after their departure. The way they scrutinized me, and the way the loud one had shouted, it seemed like it could have been someone telling me off or exhorting me to sail to somewhere new.

The fog lifted in the afternoon, and a very light northerly wind filled in. *SW* quietly drifted out of Putiki Bay. I wasn't surprised; been here and done that before. Twenty years before and more. Same boat, same place, same person.

I never knew where I would sail *SW* successfully to when I was doing the same thing here, back then. And I never know now where *SW* will one day have got to, and hopefully come back from. The strange pleasure of solo endurance sailing; the mild thrill of uncertainty. That's what makes the sailing more stimulating.

The usually gratifying results generated by one day convincing yourself that you will go and try to sail somewhere, for no apparent reason other than wanting to do it.

It's a great way to spend some time if you can organize your time, and be bothered to do it.

Glossary of sailing terms

200-metre line (100 fathoms)
The edge of the continental shelf where the seabed shelves to deep ocean depths of 2000 metres or more.

Abeam
Side on.

Aft
At the back of the boat.

Bear away
Turn the bow (front) of the boat away from the oncoming wind.

Bearing
A compass-derived line of position, used when navigating.

Beat
To sail against the wind, sometimes called close-hauled.

Board (as in beating and tacking)
Sailing hard on the wind on one tack (either port or starboard — left or right).

Fetch
The distance between your boat and the nearest land or perceived obstacle.

Flat off the wind
Sailing with the wind coming directly from behind the boat. Otherwise known as running downwind.

Flogging sail
A sail not sheeted in, and left for the wind to shake and harass it in a most audibly annoying way.

Freeboard
The space between the waterline and the deck of the boat.

Gallows (boom)

In *SW*'s case, the spray dodger acts as a boom gallows. The boom can be lashed down onto the spray dodger devoid of sail when running downwind under headsail alone.

Gybe

Tacking downwind. Can be most hazardous if not executed well.

Hard chine

Refers to the angle of the hull. A hard chine hull can be made up of multiple horizontal sections, as in vogue with current Volvo Ocean Race yachts.

Knot (as in speed)

Equivalent to approximately 1.2 miles per hour (on land).

Lee cloth

The hammock-like cloth that can be hooked beside a bunk to stop oneself falling out when the boat is heeled over hard. A very relaxing place to sleep.

Lee shore

Land downwind, and where a boat with no propulsion may end up when it's windy.

Leeward

The side away from where the wind is coming.

Mile (nautical)

Equivalent to 1.8 km (all miles in the book are nautical miles, not land miles).

P Class

7-foot (2.13-metre) centreboard sailing yacht. Originally used for training young people how to sail, now usurped by the Optimist dinghy.

Pintle

Pin or bolt on which a rudder turns. Intimately associated with the integrity of the steering.

Port

Left side of the boat.

Reach (beam reach, tight reach, broad reach)

Sailing side-on to the wind at various angles. Beam reach — at right angles to the wind; tight reach — almost pointing up towards the wind, like being close-hauled but not quite; broad reach — almost flat off the wind, but not quite.

Reef

An area of the mainsail which can be taken in or folded down, reducing the area exposed to the wind to find a harmony of sail versus wind. Also a rocky outcrop to be avoided.

Rhumb line

Direct straight-line course, used to plot a boat's course on a chart.

Sail plan

The amount of sail one presents to the wind (lots when there isn't much wind; a little when there's too much wind).

Sails

The important bits. Each sail is suited to a particular wind velocity, more or less. Pick the right sails to suit the relevant wind strength. Full mainsail can be reefed to reduce the sail area. Genoa — for light airs; No. 1 — 20 to 25 knots; No. 2 — 25 to 35 knots; storm jib — 35 knots or over; storm trysail (to replace mainsail) — 35 knots, depending on where you want to go; gennaker — for light airs, downwind and reaching sailing; spinnaker — downwind sailing.

Sheets and halyards

Sheets are the ropes that control the sails. Halyards are the ropes that pull the sails up the mast to set.

Sked (radio sked)

A pre-arranged (scheduled) radio link-up between two parties.

Skeg

The short protuberance under the hull that supports the rudder on SW.

SSB (single side-band radio)

Long-distance marine radio that allows you to speak, and be heard, over hundreds of miles, if you feel so inclined.

Stand on (as in right of way)

To hold one's course. Most commonly associated with having right of way, but some people stand on when it may have been prudent to stop …

Starboard

Right side of the boat.

Tack

To sail through the eye of the wind. To change the side from which the wind is blowing onto you from starboard or port.

Traveller

Helps control the mainsail by adjusting how far inboard the boom can be sheeted.

Trim

To adjust the sails in relation to the angle of the wind. Crucial to efficient sailing progress. Also refers to the loading of a vessel, how it sits in the water (is it trim, bow down, stern up?).

Trim tab

On *SW*, the self-steering trim tab is attached to the aft edge of the rudder. It is also attached to a small gearing unit connected to the wind vane. The pressure of the wind on the vane affects the trim tab and *SW* sails herself relative to the wind direction.

Weather-board

SW has two weather-boards in the hatchway. These block the outside world away from the inside, and, combined with the sliding horizontal hatch on top, make *SW*'s insides more or less impervious to water.

Windage

The more one has sticking up above the water, the more windage is created. It can compromise forward momentum in severe conditions.

Windward

Look to where the wind is blowing from; anything closer to the wind than you is to windward of you.